The New Documentary in Action

The New Documentary in Action:
A Casebook in Film Making

Alan Rosenthal

University of California Press
Berkeley, Los Angeles, London

University of California Press
Berkeley and Los Angeles, California
University of California Press, Ltd.
London, England
Copyright © 1971, by The Regents of the University of California
First Paperback Edition, 1972
ISBN: 0-520-02254-8
Library of Congress Catalog Card Number: 78-139776
Designed by Steve Reoutt
Printed in the United States of America

For my Father
and in memory of my Mother

Contents

I am extremely grateful to the following for their courtesy in allowing me to reproduce various illustrative materials relating to the films discussed in this book: Allan King and Aquarius Films Ltd. for budget and notes on *A Married Couple*; Arthur Barron for his preparatory notes on *The Berkeley Rebels*; Peter Watkins and the BBC for the script extract from *The War Game*; George Stoney and the Louisiana State Mental Health Association for the extract from the outline proposal for *A Cry for Help*; and Antony Jay and International Computers Ltd. for the script extract from *The Future Came Yesterday*.

I am, of course, deeply indebted to all the film makers appearing in these pages for giving so much of their time, energy, and help in this venture. I am further indebted to Dr. Jules Heller, Dean of the Faculty of Fine Arts, York University, Toronto, for his support in general, and in particular for his assistance in helping to fund the necessary research.

Finally, my thanks to Norman Swallow, who gave so much good advice at the beginning, and to Ernest Callenbach, who bolstered me with his enthusiasm, and gave unflagging editorial help at every stage of the preparation.

The aim of this book is to explore the working methods and production problems of first-rank documentary film makers. Its purpose is to provide an insight into the day-to-day pressures on film makers' lives in an attempt to understand the variety of conditions that both help and hinder the creation of the good short film. What interests me essentially is *why* films turn out as they do—and why one route is followed in preference to another. Was it inevitable and determined from the start that *Salesman* would concentrate on Paul? Was it chance or strategy that determined the subjective finale of *What Harvest for the Reaper?* Was it deliberate bias or force of circumstances that made the film maker show only one side of the argument in *Hard Times in the Country?* These are some of the questions that intrigue me.

The emphasis, then, is on practical problems, and as such the book is addressed to the film maker in general, but more particularly to the aspiring film maker, the person whose fingers itch at the sight of an Arri, whose desk drawer contains a dozen film scripts, and who knows only a celluloid religion. If the book succeeds in its objective, it should offer the novice film maker a hard core introduction to the complexities, tensions, and rewards of the documentary profession.

The book will also be enlightening to movie enthusiasts generally, to those intrigued by the thorny paths that a film must follow before it comes into being. As for the critically inclined, they will discover that history, theory, and aesthetics have a way of creeping in unasked, even in the midst of the most practically oriented interview.

In trying to bring this elusive business of film making down to earth, I have opted for the principle of the case study rather than a general discussion of film-making methods. The technique of individual film analysis is, of course, not new. Lillian Ross used it to great advantage in her classic report on the making of *The Red Badge of Courage*. Lindsay Anderson has written about the trials of Thorold Dickinson's *The Secret People* and Jean Cocteau's *Diary of a Film* provides a revealing account of the author at work on *La Belle et La Bête*.

However, such case histories have so far been devoted only to features, to the neglect of the documentary. The problems of documentary, however, are in their own way as complex and diverse as those of features and equally worthy of study, particularly since the rise of television and the concomitant spread in influence of the social and political short. This book, then, is a beginning attempt to fill that case study gap by following a number of films from inception to final print and examining the decisions made by the production teams along the way.

In selecting the individual films I have sought for a range of work which seems to best illustrate the variety in style and practice of documentary filming today, both in England and the United States. In so doing I have tried to cover the different genres of films most likely to involve the incipient film maker, from direct cinema* to reconstructions, and from television journalism and social analysis to the sponsored documentary. I have also attempted to ensure that the films selected are among the best of their kind, and that the film makers interviewed are among the leading experts in their own particular fields.

Beyond exemplifying types of films, my selection has also been made on the basis of the need to illustrate certain specific problems such as editing and writing, or research and team cooperation. As a result (and to prevent repetition) some of the interviews deliberately concentrate on one or two phases of production and do not embrace the total making of the film. Thus, the discussion of *What Harvest for the Reaper?* revolves around gaining the cooperation of one's "enemies" when making the investigational film, while Burnley's comments on *The Dream Divided* are largely concerned with his choice of a certain structure or framework for the film.

Because the interaction of the various members of the film team is of crucial practical importance as well as of theoretical interest in any discussion of film as a "cooperative art," I have included a number of double interviews. I have also included three interviews on *A Married Couple* to illustrate the evolution of what I consider to be one of the most important films of the decade.

Although the book is organized by convenient categories, these must not be taken too rigidly. *Cathy Come Home* is, for example, placed under the heading of "Reconstructions" but the questions

---

* The terms *direct cinema* and *cinéma vérité* are used interchangeably in this book in accordance with general practice.

raised also relate to the whole matter of film as an agent of soci. change, a topic which is mainly discussed under "Television Journalism." Similarly the discussion of *High School* is not limited to direct-cinema methods, but applies to other techniques as well.

In the interviews I have tried to isolate the film maker's original idea and follow the translation of this idea into filmic reality. This has brought certain revelations, including a much greater awareness of the infinite number of modifying factors and pressures exerted on the artist and an awareness of the constant battle to maintain both an artistic and professional integrity.

The film maker is not unique in this battle or in his struggles. All artists work under constraints, whether formal, economic, organizational, or human; and an understanding of these constraints helps our understanding of the artist. It therefore becomes very pertinent to grasp a few of the limitations confronting the film maker, from the nature of his society to the feeling of his environment.

The acceptance of a film may be subject to the overall mood of artistic and intellectual freedom current at the time. Moreover, unreliable human elements affect the film. The choice of *A* instead of *B* as cameraman may be disastrous, while the inexperienced camera assistant may fog the unrepeatable take.

The system will also start to cook the film maker. Is his work subject to network pressures? Can distribution outlets be found outside the usual and rather constricted channels? Does the director have to meet an air date? Is his shooting time limited? Is he really in total control or are sponsors continually breathing down his neck with suggestions? Are the producer's marvelous ideas being quashed for lack of finance, and is he finally forced to agree with George Stoney that the name of the game is money?

These factors and others impinge on the evolution and development of the film. Slowly, that beautifully straight and simple original idea gets pulled into a curve, an arch, or even an unrecognizable squiggle, till the words, "If only I could have done it the way I wanted," become the saddest a film maker can utter.

In reality, it is doubtful whether there ever was any straight creative line. Too many factors are at work pushing, pulling, prodding, suggesting; and it is the artist's immediate and often gut response to these factors which determine the final shape of the film. And this, in essence, is what this whole book is about. It's about new paths in film making; it's about changing forms; it's about experimentation in Britain, Canada, and the United States. But more than anything else

3

it is a study of the decision-making process of the film maker under stress, where chance and pressure can make a film as well as ruin it.

In order to understand the present conditions that shape the evolution of documentary, one has also to be aware of the traditions of the past. In retrospect it is easy to see that the early 1950s mark a watershed in the development of documentary in England and the United States. And it is possibly the luck of history that just when it seemed as if documentary would be assigned to the grave, television appeared —to transform concepts, opportunities, and styles in the short nonfiction film.

The history of documentary films on the two sides of the Atlantic presents divergent paths prior to 1950. In England documentary had for years been linked to the didactic approach established by John Grierson. According to Grierson the purpose of documentary was to instruct and educate—to develop a social awareness of the contemporary scene and to formulate and condition public opinion.

These concepts were for more than fifteen years brilliantly carried out by film makers such as Harry Watt, Basil Wright, Arthur Elton, and Stuart Legg working under the actual or spiritual leadership of Grierson, within government-financed agencies such as the Empire Marketing Board, the General Post Office, the Ministry of Information, and the Crown Film Unit. This period, 1930–1945, saw the emergence of the greatest of the British documentaries, such as *Night Mail, Target for Tonight,* and *Listen to Britain.*

If the war years signaled the peak of British documentary, the years 1945–1950 mirrored a sad decline. The reasons for the deterioration are various: the reemergence of British feature films and the loss of various documentary directors to the feature industry; perhaps a growing distrust for the paternalistic lecturing of the documentaries and a preference for entertainment rather than sermonizing; the failure of documentaries to gain theatrical distribution; and the decline in the enlightened sponsorship that had given birth to the movement.

Early English documentary film making is characterized by two things: a sense of group purpose working towards a common aim and a long period of sustained sponsorship by the government and its agencies. Early American documentary represents the complete antithesis. In place of the group purpose and long-term sponsorship, one sees the individual film maker struggling with his solitary concept as best he could.

Pre-World War II American documentary was created by isolated film makers, like Pare Lorentz, Paul Strand, Ralph Steiner, Willard Van Dyke, and Leo Hurwitz, attempting to bring films to the screen in the face of public and governmental apathy. Admittedly, films like *The Plough that Broke the Plains* and *The River* were indirectly financed by government sponsorship, but this sponsorship was limited to an extremely brief period and then cut off completely when Congress killed the United States Film Service in the late 1930s.

The early war years saw a brief liaison between the documentarists and the government. For a while massive amounts of money were poured into factual and propaganda messages for service and home consumption, such as the "Why We Fight" series. The honeymoon lasted till 1945, when most of the American governmental agencies having anything to do with film were either abolished or returned to very limited and specialized instructional film making.

After the war the American documentarists faced a situation similar to, if not worse than, that of their English counterparts. A few outstanding documentaries were made such as Robert Flaherty's *Louisiana Story* and Sidney Meyer's *The Quiet One*, but these were mainly the result of industrial and private sponsorship rather than the product of enlightened governmental backing.

Ultimately the total transformation of the scene for the nonfiction film maker came through the establishment of the postwar BBC television service in England in 1947 and of a network television service in the United States in 1948. Strangely enough, it is clear that the relevance of these two developments to documentary was not at first noticed. Thus the 1951 edition of *Documentary Film* by Paul Rotha scarcely mentions the subject.

Yet it is television which, without any doubt, gave life to the expiring documentary film. As the medium has grown in hours broadcast, in revenues, and in a spotty sophistication, it has provided the film maker with the three essentials of his existence: a demand for his films, an audience for his message, and the money needed to go out and shoot. But like the Devil in *Faust*, television has also imposed certain conditions. A full discussion of these conditions is beyond the scope of this book, but references to these limitations arise in many of the following interviews and in particular in the discussions with Peter Watkins and Arthur Barron.

In early television one of the most significant events was clearly the first broadcast of Edward R. Murrow's and Fred W. Friendly's "See It Now" in February 1951. "See It Now" appeared continuously on the CBS network from 1951 to 1958. In 1959 it was succeeded by "CBS Reports," which appeared for the most part under the executive hand of Fred Friendly. Possibly because of its controversial nature, "See It Now" had few rivals on the commercial networks. In 1960, however, NBC began its "White Paper" series produced by Irving Gitlin, assisted by Al Wasserman, while in the same year ABC started its documentary series "Close Up."

In England the most significant early current affairs documentary magazine program to use film was "Special Enquiry." This was a weekly series run by the BBC from 1952 to 1957, with Norman Swallow as senior producer. Though the series ended in 1957, "Searchlight," produced by Tim Hewat between 1958 and 1960, continued in the same tradition of hard investigation on film.

I entered film in 1960, when current affairs television was becoming increasingly dynamic in both England and America. The weekly and daily documentary magazine programs "Panorama" and "Tonight" were capturing larger and larger British audiences, while the quiz scandals in the United States were acting as a direct incentive to the networks to improve their shoddy image with more public service broadcasting. However, in this climate of increased documentary activity the golden words of the broadcaster's creed were still neutrality, objectivity, and impersonality.

As for the short educational or sponsored film it still seemed well set in the deepest of conservative grooves, with a style compounded of authoritarian reenactments and voice-over filmed reports. There were, of course, exceptions like Lindsay Anderson's sponsored *Every Day Except Christmas*, a film about the workings of London's Covent Garden market.

To the observant person it was also clear that other films from the British Free Cinema group to which Anderson belonged, films like *Momma Don't Allow* and *Nice Time*, were getting closer to the social realities of life in the England of the fifties than most of the British features then in production. Similarly in Canada the vérité style approach of Wolf Koenig and Terry Filgate in films like *Days Before Christmas* and *The Backbreaking Leaf* did much to revitalize the documentary techniques of the Canadian Film Board.

In the last decade and a half the film revolution has come and gone, leaving a few corpses and bringing on new faces. All kinds of private cinema have come to the fore, while a more tolerant society has even allowed the film maker to show intimate sexual relationships on public screens.

One of the more interesting aspects of recent changes has been the slight move away from the cool objective statement to a more committed personal point of view in film. Joseph Strick's *The Savage Eye* is much more than the record of a divorced woman's loneliness in Los Angeles in the mid-fifties. If the film means anything at all it stands for a diary of hell and increased alienation in the twentieth century. Peter Watkins' *The War Game* is another vision of hell after an atomic bomb has dropped on England and is light years removed in style and conviction from *Why We Fight* or *Victory at Sea*.

I suspect that the chaos in Vietnam, American campus unrest, the increasingly divided nature of American society and the rise of racism and "Paki-bashing" in England have all brought in their wake a tiredness and distrust for the neutral, balanced statement. This has both negative and positive connotations. Complacency has been replaced by involvement and action, which is fine, but I am not so sure about the glorification of the Panthers in a film like Leonard Henny's *Black Power*. Nor am I happy with the naive emotional reasoning of a film like Robert Kramer's *Ice*, about civil war in the United States, which substitutes dogmatic assertion in place of hard political argument. Yet in spite of a personal unease with these films, which arises out of a suspicion of emotional as opposed to rational political appeals, it is obvious that in a free society such directors must be allowed to go on publicizing and showing such films without any hindrance.

What is clearly of a positive nature is the effect of this mood on the networks. In 1963 National Educational Television (NET) and Westinghouse television refused to broadcast Douglas Leiterman's *One More River* because of its "extremism" and negative point of view. Yet in 1970, NET's series "Black Journal," one of the most dynamic and deliberately one-sided statements of black militancy ever seen on television, was given an Emmy award.

The second drastic change to take place in the 1950s and 1960s is the artistic challenge to the film maker posed by the development of lightweight film equipment, and as a consequence the influences exerted by direct-cinema pioneers like Drew Associates in America; Filgate, Koenig, and Kroitor in Canada; and Jean Rouch and Chris Marker in France. This combination of technical breakthrough and exploration of forms by such a group of gifted film makers has radically altered structure and approach in the documentary.*

* Much of early direct-cinema work and approach seems to have been foreshadowed by the efforts of the British Free Cinema directors such as Lindsay Anderson, Karel Reisz, and Tony Richardson. Their problem was that they arrived on the scene *before* the advent of lighter cameras and the crystal synchronization revolution of the sixties, so that some of their most outstanding ideas suffered from technical limitations imposed by cumbersome equipment.

The prescripted documentary still exists, but mainly in the world of the industrial or educational film. Elsewhere this approach has gradually been supplanted by a tendency to work in looser and bolder forms. Today the director is far more likely to work from a rough outline than a written text, or, as Wiseman reveals about *High School*, with no outline at all, merely a sense that the random shots will eventually blend into a meaningful film. Adaptability is thus of the essence, and the film maker becomes akin to the bareback rider who must be able to adjust to every swing of the beast.

Fundamental working relationships have also been modified, particularly in regard to the director's dependency on his cameraman and editor. As Allan King points out in the discussion of *A Married Couple*, when the director has to rely on the undirected spontaneous work of the cameraman, there has to be an extremely sophisticated understanding between the two or the film concept can be ruined.

The editing room, too, has assumed a position of uniformly greater importance and has become the place where, more often than not, the film is really composed and structured. This is not to disparage or dispute the place of creative editing in the films of, say, Lorentz or Jennings, or to forget the brilliant rhythmic sequences of *Night Mail*. It is merely to be aware of the strikingly different problems in working from fully scripted, controlled footage and in trying to create order out of material caught on the fly. This means in practice that the editor's task has increased both in difficulty and creative potential, and that the conscientious director has to direct the editing even more closely than he did in the past.

Sometimes the changed relationships are given formal recognition. *Salesman* is listed as a film by the Maysles *and* editor Charlotte Zwerin. Richard Leiterman was given an associate director's credit in addition to a cameraman's credit on *A Married Couple*. Even if the teamwork is not formally recognized, one continually finds director-editor teams such as the Maysles and Zwerin, or Mort Silverstein and Larry Solomon, staying together for picture after picture. In view of all this one could almost say that the best documentaries are characterized by a multiple authorship, as opposed to the lone *auteur* theory in commercial features.*

Subject matter and approach have also been caught up in the rad-

* Even where continuing director/cameraman or director/editor relationships do exist in features, they do not seem to me to exhibit the same quality of multiple authorship as is necessitated by a team working on a vérité film where a cameraman's decisions, for example, have to be far more spontaneous and unguided than his counterpart in features.

icalization resulting from the new techniques. Quite clearly, the barriers are down between the film maker and his subject, while the pendulum swings towards a concern for people rather than things.

This does not just mean the growth of the biography or VIP film or the film dealing with social issues. What one detects, instead, is a movement towards the acknowledgment of the primacy and importance of feeling. Now, equipped with its new, inconspicuous, prying eyes, documentary is able to explore private as well as public emotions. Filmed T-Groups and psycho-dramas bare the problems of sex, loneliness, divorce, and alienation, while *Salesman* reveals the essential disintegration of a human spirit far better than any play of Arthur Miller.

How has the short film reacted to the changed climate on both sides of the Atlantic? There are two relevant matters to consider when assessing the English position: the nature and influence of the legacy left by the original BBC broadcasting monopoly, and the absence of sponsorship and its implied control of programming in commercial independent television. The combination of these two facts has undoubtably allowed a greater freedom of experiment in England than in the commercially controlled American network system. The freedom from sponsorship is easily appreciated. The subtle effect of the BBC's earlier television monopoly on independent commercial programming is a little harder to grasp.

British broadcasting traditions derive from Lord Reith's years of control of BBC radio and the establishment by him of the tenets of public service, responsibility, experiment, and freedom. When independent television was sanctioned in England in 1954 it had to contend with a public conditioned by BBC standards. This has meant, in practice, that the shape and direction of documentary and public affairs programming has followed the broad, open BBC tradition rather than the more limited paths of the American networks.

In England the last ten years have been characterized by television experiment in all aspects of the political, social, and art documentary. Two offshoots of this freedom have been the growth of the highly committed personal film, as seen in the work of Peter Watkins in *The War Game*, and the highly stylized experiments of BBC directors like Ken Russell in *Delius* and Jonathan Miller in *The Symposium*. Not all the efforts have been either popular or critical successes. Dennis Mitchell's *Chicago* was considered too violent for many people, while Russell's film on the life of Strauss provoked a chorus of hostile press reactions.

Besides the expansion of the personal and stylized documentary, there have also been a number of interesting British experiments in form. These have ranged from historic reconstructions such as *Culloden* and drama documentaries such as Jack Gold's *Ninety Days* and Sandford's *Cathy Come Home*, to experiments in biography (*The Dream Divided*) and fantasies about automobiles (*Crisis on Wheels*, produced by Stuart Hood). In 1969 and 1970 the BBC also conducted a series of experiments with films shot entirely from a helicopter. These were released under the title of "Bird's-Eye View," and had Edward Mirzoeff as executive producer for the series.

Although there have been some excellent examples of the postscripted documentary such as Jack Gold's and Alan Whicker's *Death in the Morning*, the main movement of the decade has been towards the noncommentary documentary. This has been due to the influence of directors and producers like Richard Cawston, Dennis Mitchell, Jeremy Isaacs, and Norman Swallow, to name only a few, with one of the best examples being provided by Cawston's own portrait of Billy Graham, *I'm Going to Ask You to Get up out of Your Seat.*

However, not everything on the British scene is totally rosy; there are severe handicaps to working or attempting to work in England. As Peter Watkins shows in his remarks on *The War Game*, officialdom can be twice as officious as that of the United States. It is extremely difficult for the beginning film maker to get a union card. Finance is a problem even within the BBC and independent television (ITV), and Britain has far fewer foundations willing to assist the film maker.

The main problem, though, is the almost total impossibility of finding or creating work outside the BBC and independent television channels except in sponsored or educational film, which have severely restricted markets in England. By way of contrast the American can still find a small place as a film maker in more than 500 local stations. He can work within university film units and, as has been proved by Leacock, Pennebaker, and others, he can sometimes achieve a viable existence outside the system, though with some difficulty.

While the English television film makers have been willing to try every style and method, the cornerstone of the American network tradition has clearly been the news documentary. Highly influenced by the drive and devotion of producers such as Edward R. Murrow, Fred Friendly, Irving Gitlin, and Al Wasserman, series like CBS's "See It Now" and NBC's "White Paper" have amply demonstrated what can be done with courageous and often dynamic reporting. *Biography of a Bookie Joint* and *Sit In* are excellent examples of the best of social and investigatory reporting, and show what the commercial networks can do when the spirit is willing and the producer-director is given some leeway.

The love affair with news documentary has, however, been played according to the strictest of rules, with few side flirtations at other film attractions. The news and reportorial bias has led to a deep suspicion of any kind of experiment in either form or style. Thus Arthur Barron's attempt to use a variety of film and dramatic techniques in *The Berkeley Rebels* led to a severe reprimand from the top executives of CBS.

The commercial networks have also been highly antagonistic to subjective films. Luckily there have been some exceptions, notably ABC's encouragement of the films of Drew Associates such as *Yanqui No* and *The Children Were Watching*, the latter being a highly personal, impressionistic portrait of a white and a black family in New Orleans, both of which support racial integration.

The advent and growth of NET has done a little to modify the situation. It has not been afraid of experiment, and in the dual role of program originator and film outlet it has been responsible for revivifying the cultural and art documentary and providing a platform for the more way-out and hip film maker. Yet in spite of the work of NET, the challenging ideas in form, technique, and subject matter are mostly coming from without rather than from within the networks. So if one wants to sense the tempo and tensions of American life outside the political and racial arena or wants to come to grips with a personal vision, one has to turn to the work of the individual film maker outside the system.

The most interesting and successful of these film makers, outside of the exponents of the underground film movement like Jonas Mekas and Stan Brakhage, are still the old names of vérité or direct cinema, plus a few new men like Allan King and Fred Wiseman. The guiding rules for these film makers are nonpreconception, the need for rapport with the subject, and observation without interference. The key questions for them, as for others, still remain how to obtain vision and insight: how to obtain an aspect of the truth, if not the sum total of the eternal verities.

Direct cinema is clearly a technique, and the discussions of it as a philosophic battle cry in the early sixties have merely served to obscure the issue. Originally the technique provided a greater capacity for exploring the private individual under tension as in *Susan Starr* and *On the Pole*, or the inner world of the celebrity as in *Jane, Showman*, and *Will the Real Norman Mailer Please Stand Up?* Lately one begun to see the beginnings of a break away from the VIP and ography formulae to a renewed interest in the events of the everyday environment, such as the police convention in Leacock's *Chiefs* or the Maysles' study of Bible hustlers in *Salesman*.

Among the new practitioners of direct cinema, the most interesting may prove to be Fred Wiseman. All Wiseman's films are complex studies in power relationships and, though focused on specific situations such as that of a hospital or a high school, reveal a great deal about the main institutions of American society. The truths that Wiseman reveals are not always pleasant, and he has thus had to spend a considerable time in court fighting against censorship and for freedom of distribution.

What strikes one about Wiseman's films technically is his ability to get away with a very loose structure. This contrasts very greatly with many of the early direct cinema films, which were built on extremely conventional dramatic tenets or on structures clearly limited in space and time. Thus, *On the Pole* bases its dramatic thrust on Eddie Sachs' final performance in the Indianapolis 500, and *The Chair* has all the elements of conventional suspense, with the audience awaiting the verdict on Paul Crump's appeal against his death sentence. In a similar fashion the limits of *Don't Look Back* were conveniently defined by the beginning and end of Bob Dylan's English tour.

The more recent efforts of Allan King, the Maysles, and Wiseman have been outside these predetermined structures. The resulting shared problem has been to find a meaningful backbone on which to hang the flesh of their films. The editing room has in consequence again assumed prime importance.

Had not a certain amount of luck intervened in the filming of *Warrendale* and *Salesman* it is conceivable that the lack of defined structure at the time of shooting could have been disastrous. In *Warrendale* it is the death of a Negro cook that provides the needed peg. In *Salesman* it is the disintegration of Paul that provides the required focus.

Whereas *Warrendale* was a remarkably intense portrait of life in a center for disturbed children, *A Married Couple* traces several months of a marriage in crisis. In this latter film Allan King deliberately destroys the chronological order of his material to create artificial situational and emotional links. This use of nonscripted, unstaged material to arrive at a hybrid "fiction documentary" form is perhaps the central problem of film making today, and it is one reason for considering *A Married Couple* as one of the most important pioneer films of the last decade.

King himself recognizes that the next step may well be for the film maker to act as a catalyst in bringing people together in various situations which are left to develop and be filmed. In the past few years some of the possibilities inherent in this approach have been explored by Jean Rouch in *Chronique d'un Eté* and by John Cassavetes in *Shadows* and *Faces*, but not in quite the pure form envisaged by King.

Whatever the dreams of the film maker, at some point he has to face the brutal external realities of the film business. In England, as stated earlier, the fact is that one cannot really exist outside the BBC and independent television system, and it is extremely difficult for even the most highly talented individual to break in. Once one is a member of the system, and in spite of incidents like the banning of *The War Game*, the film maker is allowed a relatively high degree of freedom.

The main problem of the American commercial networks is that they are primarily business structures, geared to profits and the stock report. So too, one might argue, are publishing and record companies. The difference is that the air waves supposedly belong to the public, and the concept of service to the higher needs of the community has, at least theoretically, always been acknowledged by the networks.

Lip service is in fact paid to the concept of public information by an abundance of current affairs and news hours, but too often the quality of the programs leaves much to be desired. There are supposedly a few Federal Communications Commission (FCC) rules of conduct, but these are laughably vague and unenforced when compared to the severity of the governmental strictures laid down for British independent television. Nor has there been a paternalistic BBC tradition to mold public taste.

In a situation where the business manager often provides the guiding hand and possibly the ultimate authority, it is not surprising to find that the commercial networks are basically unhappy in their whole relationship to film and documentary. Shows like *I Love Lucy* and *The Beverly Hillbillies* entertain, pacify, and keep the balance sheet in the black. Documentary has the double deficiency of being a severe financial risk and of disturbing the sponsor if there is any hint of controversy. So at best documentary is tolerated, at worst, feared, and certainly never loved.

This attitude and background affects documentary in various ways. One generally looks in vain to the networks for the film of human revelation, for the subjective essay, or for the unusual treatment. The

13

h gain easiest approval are those which are the most in-
the biographic paean of praise, the compilation war film,
scriptive surface film. The analytic or critical film is treated
re harshly, although the track record is improving. The
public may acclaim a probing report like *Harvest of Shame*; but the
mood in the executive suite is likely to be neutral, if not hostile, to
this needless stirring up of a hornet's nest.

When the networks explore controversy, it has for the most part
to be by means of a cool presentation of ideas. Grooviness is out and
Olympian detachment in. *The Berkeley Rebels* was therefore doctored not merely because of its techniques but because, according to
Barron, more "balance" was required. One wonders how many more
network films have suffered a similar fate. But even though it was
severely emasculated, *The Berkeley Rebels* at least appeared on the
air. This is more than can be said for Bill Jersey's *A Time for Burning* or Douglas Leiterman's *From Harlem to Sugar Hill*.

Behind the alteration or rejection of films like *The Berkeley Rebels*
and *A Time for Burning* seems to lie the belief that somewhere there
is a marvelous "objectivity" or "neutrality" to which documentary
should aspire. This is to deal in the realm of myth. Once raw film
material is put into any kind of structure it takes on overtones of
meanings and ramifications that cannot possibly be classified as objective. The structure imposed by the director is very much *his*
attempt to give meaning to the material; it is obviously not the only
one-and-inevitable interpretation which could be made of the subject.

People who agreed with Peter Watkins' views in *The War Game*
thought the film fair and "objective." The papers and politicians
who disagreed with his picture of the consequences of atomic warfare
attacked Watkins for "not being objective." Quite plainly this whole
search for objectivity in documentary would appear to be the pursuit
of a false trail. Any worthwhile documentary is bound to be propaganda in the sense that it expresses a film maker's specific point of
view. And this is the way I believe it should be. To aim for a certain
neutrality appears to be theoretically feasible, but in practice it has
tended to result in sterile films which merely propagate the most
widely held and noncontroversial views.

Meanwhile, related to the whole subject of objectivity is the
equally vexing question of "equal time." Here the field is strewn with
misapprehensions. FCC rules merely require that a station's *overall*
programming be balanced. This most clearly does not mean that each
individual program must be balanced or must have a pro and con

14

format.* I would therefore argue that even if Jack Willis had not asked food manufacturers to express their views in *Hard Times in the Country*,** and had merely set out to present a series of accusations against the American food industry, he would nevertheless have been fully justified in his approach.

Hesitation in regard to the advisability of broadcasting certain material because of lack of objectivity or for other reasons is not, however, confined to the commercial networks. The fairly liberal NET turned down Wiseman's *Titicut Follies*, possibly because of the legal complications in which it was embroiled. They also originally looked askance at William Greaves's *Still a Brother*, a highly provocative portrait of the black middle class in America. *Warrendale* was commissioned by the CBC who then refused to show it (because of the children's profanity), while BBC Director General Sir Hugh Greene declined to let the British television public see *The War Game*.

Yet there is an illusion of freedom, sustained by the proliferation of noncontroversial films on controversial subjects. Sex, drugs, youth, alienation, the universities, and pollution have all had their day but normally after the event. The prisoner is pardoned with a graceless gesture after he has already broken free.

And what of the subjects that are never touched because of political, legal, and personal pressures? No one has yet provided a deep analysis of the British aristocracy, nor has the FBI been touched on American television. Admittedly both CBS and NET have done documentaries on the plight of the migrant worker, but it stretches the imagination to think of the commercial networks ever doing an analysis of the food industry comparable to NET's *Hard Times in the Country*. Too many sponsors would be lost. Nor can one see them doing a dissection of the banking system comparable to Mort Silverstein's explosive *Banks and the Poor*, which was run by NET in November 1970.†

---

* Edward R. Murrow's 1954 attack on Senator McCarthy in "See It Now" was entirely accusational. McCarthy was given equal time in a *later* program to reply.

** As Willis points out in his interview, most of the food manufacturers ultimately declined to appear and say anything in their own defense.

† *The Selling of the Pentagon* (CBS, 1971) was broadcast after I had already written these rather pessimistic few paragraphs. I wish I could say that I think CBS's excellent report will herald in a new era of penetrating and courageous network documentary. Frankly, I doubt it.

For the film of human revelation and personal documentary one therefore looks beyond the networks to the individual American film maker, whose financial problems are severe. Films of the nature of *Hospital, Monterey Pop*, and *A Married Couple* can cost anything from $50,000 to $200,000. Even if a network showing can be arranged, the return is miniscule. To combat this situation a number of film cooperatives have been set up in recent years for the sole purpose of distributing nonfiction films. They have not, however, been very successful in making the distribution of the feature length documentary a paying proposition. University showings offer a certain amount of exposure, but the financial returns are minimal.

One alternative, explored by King, Pennebaker, and the Maysles, has been for the directors themselves to assume responsibility for distribution of their films through independent cinemas and art houses. This is haphazard but has possibilities. But even with the growth of art houses, it is still an uphill fight. Discussing the situation in *Newsweek*, Don Pennebaker had this to say of independent distribution: "It's like selling some rare kind of tropical fruit. The theatre owners are receptive to films about surfing and pop singers, but if you've got one that doesn't look like a sure thing they're not interested. [Documentary film makers] survive in the face of the system, not because of it."

It has already become trite to talk of the film age, the age of McLuhan, the age of mass media shaping and influencing our lives. Television proliferates. In America the three-television house is joining the two-car family. In Israel, Japan, and the Far East *The Forsyte Saga* is watched with as much rapt attention as in London or Toronto.

My own interest in filming has always inclined towards the analytical documentary and the film for social change. But after ten years of filming I am still uncertain as to the influence exerted by these calls to action. The paradox is that, while the crusading examination film has never been better done, we have seemingly reached the point of saturation and apathy. Gas bombings in Yemen, atrocities in Vietnam, the rape of Czechoslovakia no longer stun or shock. The first thing a producer learns is that he will get more sympathy and action for his ten-minute film about the condition of one blind child than for his masterpiece on racism in the South that took a year out of his life to make.

Occasionally, a film like *Cathy Come Home* manages to penetrate the haze of public indifference and draw hundreds of volunteers to actual involvement in a social campaign. As a result of *What Harvest for the Reaper?* there have been a few minor changes in state laws regarding migrant workers. And Jeremy Isaacs' piece on drunken drivers for "This Week" clearly helped the adoption of new breathalyser laws in England. But these are isolated examples of concrete action following specific films and not typical of the general case.

Is one to assume, therefore, that the crusading film accomplishes little except salving one's own conscience and influencing a small section of the open-minded who have bothered to watch such a program at off-peak hours?

This conclusion strikes me as unduly pessimistic. Though it is difficult to correlate specific films to specific responses, it seems to me that the overall pressure of television in the postwar era has been enormous, even if the impact of any one single program has been small. Television has without the slightest doubt diminished regionalism, racism, warmongering, and jingoism generally. Series like the BBC's "Cause for Concern" and the Canadian Film Board's "Challenge for Change" have been vital in spreading a climate of social understanding, while the news broadcasts of Huntley and Brinkley and of Walter Cronkite have tended to put the world and domestic scene into a calm, balanced perspective.

What of the future? Will the network system and "showman" controlled movie theatres still dominate to prevent the dissemination of everything except the film with the approved seal of taste? The UHF television stations planned by some American universities may be one way around the impasse. The growth of cartridge systems, such as CBS's Electronic Video Recording or RCA's Holographic System which allow film to be recorded on the equivalent of a five-inch tape reel, will also have an effect. Film makers may then be able to have their films transferred to cassettes, to be rented or sold for playback through ordinary television sets using an auxiliary cassette player. Cable television will exert its influence, and ultimately the concept of the "wired city" may break all conventional distribution patterns.

We are now at a stage where films can be designed and created by computers. But computers are cold, scientific, rational machines; they can produce films of patterns and colors, but never a *Man of Aran*. Living documentary takes its force from emotion, sensitivity, and concern.

It is the human being, then, and human impulse which are still central to the future of documentary. Fifty years on from Flaherty's *Nanook*, the key words are still belief, passion, empathy, and integrity —while the dominant image on the screen is not the moon or the stars, but man himself.

Direct Cinema

1

A Married Couple

Allan King

A Married Couple *(1969) has been variously called a comedy, a psychological study, and a bitter commentary on contemporary life. Allan King, who directed and produced the film, chooses to call it an "actuality drama."*

A Married Couple, *shot in the summer of 1968, covers ten weeks in the life of Billy and Antoinette Edwards. At the time of the filming Billy was forty-two, and his American wife was thirty. Most of the film takes place at the Edwards' home and provides a remarkable insight into the intimate relationship of a rather extroverted, flamboyant, and funny couple. It also provides a grueling look at the tensions of two people who are extremely fond of each other, and yet still capable of tearing each other apart.*

Prior to A Married Couple *one would have said that King's best film was* Warrendale. *Yet by comparison,* A Married Couple *seems to be far more innovative in showing future possibilities in direct cinema. What one sees is neither documentary nor fiction drama, but a curious blend of the two formed by creating fictitious emotional links in the editing of documentary footage.*

Allan King, who looks like a rather "with it" long-haired Oxford don, was born in British Columbia in 1930. After a short time working in television in Vancouver he pulled off a major film success in 1956 with Skid Row, *his first solo effort. The film predates Lionel Rogosin's* On the Bowery *but has certain parallels in its examination of the life of the derelicts on Vancouver's skid row. It is a harsh, moody, honest film and marked the first time such subject matter had been treated on Canadian television.*

After leaving the protective shelter of network television, King went to London, where in 1961 he assembled a highly talented group of film makers under the cooperative banner of Allan King Associates. This group included Richard Leiterman, William Brayne, the cameraman on Warrendale, *and Peter Moseley, the editor of* Warrendale, The Train, *and the hour-long documentary* John Huston.

Till 1966 one could say King enjoyed a fairly solid reputation in London based on work for the BBC, work on sponsored films, and Running Away Backwards, *a description of American jet set living on the island of Ibiza. However, it was left to* Warrendale *to establish King's name in the international class.*

Warrendale *was commissioned in 1966 by the CBC as a portrait of a treatment center for emotionally disturbed children in northern Toronto. What King produced was not (as misinterpreted by many critics) a rambling discourse on a method of treatment, but an explosive communication of the nature of the experiences of the children at the center. In spite of its power and brilliance, it was banned by the CBC and the BBC because of the obscene language used by the children and the violence of a number of the scenes. These "problems" did not stop it being awarded the 1967 Critics' Prize at Cannes.*

If one wants to compare King to other cinéma vérité exponents, two points seems to stand out very clearly. First, I would maintain that films like Warrendale *and* A Married Couple *show a much deeper and more personal concern on the part of the film maker for his subject than is seen or felt in most other vérité films. The second difference lies in the fact that, unlike Al Maysles, Ricky Leacock, or Don Pennebaker, King is no cameraman. His vision has to be translated through the eye of others, and yet there is still a unity to all his films. Possibly his talent lies in conceptualizing, organizing, directing, and a certain flair in guiding the editing.*

Yet these things are not enough; there also has to be the ability to draw out the inner truth of the subject. This is one talent King certainly possesses, an ability to capture and present an extremely honest grasp of the subject matter even if it limits his "artistic" scope. Finally there has to be communion, credibility, and feeling. And all these qualities King has. Perhaps that's why after seeing Warrendale *Jean Renoir called King one of the greatest film artists working today.*

Q. Can you talk a little about your background?

A. I was born in Vancouver, B.C., in 1930. I went to the University of British Columbia and took honors philosophy. I then drove a taxi for nine months, went to Europe for a year and a half, traveling, hitchhiking—the sort of thing that one did then—and finally got a job in television in Vancouver as a production assistant. I did live television for two years, but in fact after six months switched primarily to film. The first film was *Skid Row*, then three or four more in Vancouver. Then I left Vancouver.

Q. What were your jobs in these films, director, producer, worker?

A. Yes, director. We were very lucky out there, because there weren't very many experienced people in the country and television expanded more rapidly than the availability of trained personnel. I was also very heavily involved in film societies in Vancouver when I was a teen-ager, so one got to see just about everything that was of interest to see. After the Vancouver stint I went abroad and started independent production, first in Spain; I then settled in London and built up an office and production group there. I came back to Canada in 1967, and I've been here ever since.

Q. How does your group work? As a cooperative?

A. More or less. Basically we all function as free-lancers, except that we work together, are grouped together in one house, and pay a small percentage of our fees to the house. We all have shares in the house, and the house owns the equipment.

Q. How did the concept of *A Married Couple* arise? What was the first sparking point for it?

A. I'm not really sure. I don't think there is ever a single point. I suppose the first point of real action was when I was pretty well to the end of *Warrendale* and wondering what I was going to do next. I knew there was a spot open for an hour and a half film on television at that time, and I thought I would like to do a film about a marriage, about a married couple, recording them over eight to ten weeks, to get some sense, in a way that I don't think has been possible before, of what happens between a couple. One knows about such relationships from one's own experience; one knows from a certain kind of observation of friends which is pretty limited; and one knows from parents, from literature, drama, the arts. But those are all different kinds of knowledge, all useful in their own particular way. I thought it would be fascinating and illuminating to stay with the couple and observe.

Most particularly, I was concerned with a marriage in crisis and wanted to observe the kinds of ways in which a couple misperceive each other and carry into the relationship anxieties, childhood patterns, all the things that make up one's own personality and character. But these inevitably distort the other person and make true intimacy or true connection difficult. As that difficulty gets greater, conflicts and tensions develop in a marriage, so that it becomes less and less rewarding. That is what I wanted to explore. It was something I had been absorbed with since childhood. It had struck me, even when I was a kid in the thirties, that marriage didn't seem to be the kind of rewarding thing in reality that I read about in books or fantasized was going to be mine when I grew up. It puzzled me that people always seemed to get less from marriage than they wanted. My own parents separated when I was a kid, perhaps that gave me a particularly exacerbated view of marriage and made me rather more skepti-

23

A MARRIED COUPLE Second Cost Estimate	
CATEGORY	BUDGET
General Personnel	$ 13,300.00
Cast	5,000.00
Crew	6,310.00
Equipment	6,062.52
Lighting	3,172.50
Stock & Processing	29,200.00
Sync, Screen, Transcripts	4,725.00
Editing & Finishing (*Incl. Answer Print & One Release Print*)	15,880.00
Travel & Expenses	4,632.00
Titles	1,500.00
Music	1,500.00
35mm Blowup	5,500.00
Insurance & Legal	2,000.00
Promotion	14,000.00
Contingency	9,883.02
Interest on Loans	—
New York Trade Screenings	—
	$122,715.22
Contingency 10%	18,407.00
	$141,122.22

cal or more pessimistic or more aware of, and anxious about, conflicts and difficulties in marriage than say a child whose family had been fairly secure.

Q. As the concept grew, did you have any particular friends or individuals in mind who you thought would be suitable for the film?

A. Not exactly. Billy and Antoinette, whom I ultimately chose, were possibilities, as were many other friends; but first I started talking to a lot of couples I got to through psychiatrists, social workers, and various counselors. Altogether I talked fairly intensively with about ten couples. I didn't, during that early period, talk to Billy and Antoinette. Finally, I decided I would talk to them and see if they were interested.

Q. What was their reaction to the concept of living with a camera?

A MARRIED COUPLE
Final Cost Summary
As of December 31, 1969

PRODUCTION

General Personnel	$ 20,620.08
Cast	7,724.10
Crew	7,627.25
Equipment	17,819.19
Travel & Expenses	6,965.36
Stock & Processing	52,066.94
Editing & Finishing (*Including*	
Titles, Music, Blowup)	38,716.74
Insurance & Legal	3,721.50
Miscellaneous Exp.	7,485.09
Promotion (*as per budget*)	14,000.00
	+4,857.59 excess
	$176,746.25
Overhead 15%	26,511.95
Total Production Cost	$203,258.20

A. They had been fascinated for a long time with the idea of being in a film. At one stage or another in their lives both of them had dabbled in amateur or semiprofessional theatre, and many of their friends are in the arts, so it always interested them as a possibility. When they knew I was making a film about a marriage in crisis, or a marriage in conflict, theirs was not in that critical a stage, or at least they didn't acknowledge it. When I finally approached them, Antoinette was ready to be involved in the movie, but Billy was very reluctant. He said, "Our marriage isn't that much of a crisis at the moment, so you would have to make a film simply about an everyday marriage." My own supposition was that the conflicts I sensed to be there, were there, and that they would emerge.

Q. One is very conscious in the film of the style of repartee, and wit of the dialogue which goes on about nonessential things. Was this in the back of your mind when you ultimately chose them?

A. I guess it was the major factor—it was the plus that offset the minus that I was concerned about, plus the fact that they can be very funny, and very playful with each other, verbally anyway, and so that was a great advantage. I think a film like this, unrelieved by any lightness, could be very powerful; but it could also run the risk of being overpoweringly depressing and heavy.

Q. Can we go now to preshooting production problems, planning, that sort of stage.

A. I had already chosen the cameraman during the year I was looking for couples and raising money. I had Richard in mind and Chris to do the sound. I needed Arla Saare to do the editing. I seem to work in a similar sort of pattern every time I set up a film, or once a film starts to go. Once I've had the notion and decide that is what I want to do, I work out a budget. The first thing to see is whether the project is financially possible, and then where I am going to get the money. So I was occupied with that pretty early on, and went through various attempts and routes to finance the film.

First, it was going to be done as a three-country co-production for television. When the Canadian element, the CBC, dropped out, I decided to raise the money privately. A friend of mine thought he could do that and had a go at it, but it didn't work out. So then I went around and simply borrowed money. We set up a company in which the shareholders put in the investment to pay the heart of the cost of the production. They basically put up $75,000 to $85,000, and we sold television rights to follow theatrical distribution in Canada and in England, which made the balance of our production budget. And at that point we were set. Actually, as the film developed we went way over budget. One of the difficulties is that if you take a year to raise money, your budget is already 10 percent under right off the bat. We were budgeted at $130,000 to $140,000, and we spent $203,000. This was partly because we went over in time, and partly because we shot a lot more film than I had anticipated.

Having sort of settled the financial questions—raised the money— we finally decided to ask Billy and Antoinette. After they accepted we worked out a fee for them, which was basically union scale and came in the end to about $5,000 for the two of them, plus a small percentage of the profits of the film. Though I have generally no particular commitment to a way of working or an ideology of working, I decided not to intervene in this film, not to direct, not to ask or require anything from Billy and Antoinette, but to allow them to take any initiatives that they might wish to take; this "nonintervention" also covered Richard and my sound man Chris Wangler. We would simply spend as much time as we could physically manage with the couple and record when we felt like it.

We established also that, while we were all friends and knew each other, it wouldn't work if we had dinner with them, or if Antoinette was obliged to make coffee or provide the kind of hospitality that one normally extends to people in one's house. We decided to dispense with all this and to avoid conversation with Bill and Antoinette as much as possible, so that interactions of that kind wouldn't interfere with our ability to observe and record.

q. In making *Warrendale* you spent three or four weeks with the cameras on location without doing any shooting; did you employ the same method here?

a. In *Warrendale* it was necessary for me to find out something about the children because I didn't know them very well. I didn't know them at all when I started, and they needed a fair amount of time to look at me and get used to me and decide where I was going to fit into their lives. With Billy and Antoinette, that amount of time wasn't necessary; but we did need a bit of time not so much to get them un-camera-conscious or unselfconscious, but for them to work into more intimate feelings, the kind of real expression of strongly felt things. That took a lot of time. What we did do was spend about two weeks with them lighting the house. We could have probably done it much faster but we sort of puttered and fiddled around.

q. Can you be more explicit on the lighting?

a. As with *Warrendale* we lit the entire house, which was basically the way we did most of our shooting. We had our own power source from the mains. We put a whole new power system in really, so that we could go in first thing in the morning and throw the switch and the whole house would be lit. Actually it took a fair while to work out a lighting pattern that allows you to shoot 360 degrees and shoot so that you are not hitting your own lights or throwing shadows and all those kinds of problems; there is a certain amount of trial and error to that. Also, you can't really anticipate what are the most frequent patterns of movement until you've spent some time with people and get an instinctive sense of where they are going to move and when. That all took about two or three weeks. We also had to adjust the house a bit, and do some decorating. The front room was all walnut paneling, which is very, very dark and just soaked up light. So we put in light paneling instead.

When Billy and Antoinette went on a three-week holiday to Maine and Vermont we followed, taking an extra lighting man. We had him go three days before to rig the two physical locations so that they would be all set, and we would just have to trim, so that again we would have the least possible technical interference with the lights.

q. Can we get into the actual shooting, and so on?

27

A. Clearly the ideal would be to spend twenty-four hours a day at the house, but that would have meant two crews and you would split your style. While there were variations, basically our pattern was to spend as much time with them as they were together with each other. Richard and Chris and the camera assistant would go early in the morning, turn on the lights, go upstairs, and be around when Billy and Antoinette woke up. We would stay through breakfast until Billy went to work. Sometimes, though not often, we would stay with Billy or with Antoinette and Bogart, and sometimes would go with Billy to work and film at work. But the general pattern was to leave them at half-past nine or ten o'clock. Richard, Chris, and David would go home and get some sleep and a meal, and then come back about four o'clock to be there at five o'clock when Billy came home. Then they'd stay all through the evening until Billy and Antoinette finally went to sleep, and then back again the next morning. Of course, weekends were very tough. They would start at five o'clock Friday afternoon, and they would get maybe seven or eight hours sleep and time off in the middle of Friday night, Saturday night, and Sunday night—that was very exhausting.

For the first three or four weeks I was around the house a lot. Later, I found it worked best for me to stay away. A director in that sort of situation is a bit irrelevant. You need enough time to observe a lot of things and you drop in; but there is no need, I find for me at any rate, to stand and tell a cameraman "point here, point there, turn on here, turn off there." All you do really is interfere.

Q. Did you discuss with Richard the kind of things you were looking for?

A. I know Richard's style, and he knows my style, because we have worked together for years. So the question of style has been worked out over a long time. We had talked about the problems that anyone has shooting dialogue between two people with one camera, whether to pan back and forth and so on, before we started filming; but it was difficult for Richard to dictate where the camera was going rather than have it dictated by the dialogue. But he very quickly got onto that. What would happen is that we would talk a great deal about the rushes. Either he would see them, or certainly I would always see them. We'd say this or that didn't work, or that seems to be working very well, something seems to be happening here, how do you feel it; and so we would do a great deal of talking on the phone, or before or after work, or wherever it was necessary, so that we could check with each other on what we felt was significant.

In the end I very specifically gave Richard a credit as associate director, because the contribution that he made to the filming was so very, very important. There was no way of doing that kind of a film without an exceptional person shooting, because he had to make the basic choices of when he was going to shoot and when not. We talked a lot about strategy and something about tactics as we were working, but often it was the choice that Richard made; in a very real sense he is the associate director.

Q. How much does the camera interfere? How much do people put on for the camera?

A. It depends on the cameraman. If you get a dumb, insensitive, obtrusive cameraman, the interference is enormous. If you have a sensitive, intelligent, quiet, responsive, unobtrusive and unjudging, impersonally critical cameraman or camera crew, then not only is the camera not inhibitive, but it stimulates the couple to talk, in the same way an analyst or therapist does. You can talk if you want to; you don't have to talk if you don't want to; you do what you want. If you choose to put up smoke screens, or you choose to put on a dialogue, or you try to hide something, this would be evident to anybody with any sort of sensitivity. It isn't possible for people to produce material out of thin air irrelevant to their character. Whatever occurs is relevant to the character, and it gives us that overall sense we have of the person. So I felt for a long time that we were not concerned with the question, "Is it the real person?" or those kinds of questions. These are really ways in which an audience or some elements of an audience tend to evade the actual feelings they are getting from the film. "Is that really real?"—what the hell does that mean? Either the film means something to you, or it doesn't. On the question again of interference, I think it is well to allow the person to express stuff in perhaps a little more concentrated period of time.

Q. Did you sense that anyone was putting on an act for the camera?

A. There were various places in the film where they do, but there are two kinds of acting. If you ask, "Are they acting for the camera?" you can say, "no," and a little while along you would have to say, "yes." It depends on how much space you have in which to explain. They performed for the camera in the same way they perform for friends. Friends come together, and often they would get into fifteen minutes of bantering back and forth, teasing each other; they'd have a mock row, or they'd set up a whole line of dialogue which they could carry for fifteen or twenty minutes as a way of entertaining themselves and their friends. You can see them do that in the film.

The only thing one has to remember is that we all, at all times and to varying degrees, perform, or perform as if we were different people. At different times we are different persons with different people. I am aware of myself behaving a little differently with a businessman, with a student, with a critic, with my office staff, with my girlfriend, or with my parents. Each of those situations provides a different context and you behave differently. Ideally, when you are totally your own person, you are always the same; you are a consistent character throughout, in all transactions. But that's not the way most people are most of the time.

Q. Did Billy and Antoinette impose any restrictions on you? Obviously you would be getting some very intimate material. Did they see the rushes, or did they only see the final print?

A. Billy wanted the right to veto anything that he thought was unbearably embarrassing. We had a long protracted negotiation about it, and I was profoundly reluctant to allow them to do that—oddly enough not so much because I really felt it would be exercised, but because I thought they would in fact deprive themselves of some of the benefits which would occur from the filming. If they were going to have that right, there would be some area of cheating in the film and some area of withholding. However, Billy felt that he could not be uninhibited, could not be free, unless he had some protection. Oddly enough, Antoinette didn't ask for that until Billy had thought of it; and so she said if Billy has it, I want it. In fact, the right wasn't exercised. I didn't allow them to see any film except a little bit to show them that there were images on the celluloid, and it was going all right. I didn't allow them to see any film until we had finished shooting, and then they screened all seventy hours.

Q. At that stage did they want to cut anything out?

A. No, they didn't. They didn't have the right of editing or anything like that.

Q. Now, if you can come to the point of selection. The film is mainly Billy, Antoinette, and Bogart; one sees very few friends except for an evening when Antoinette goes out with her girlfriend and on the occasion of the party. Now, friends must have been over at other times. Was this limitation a choice on your part?

A. Yes, the stuff with other people just didn't work out. It wasn't significant. If you want dramatic structure, you want interchanges with other people if they are significant. But there wasn't very much happening with the other friends. For instance, Antoinette was not having an affair with the husband of one of their friends or one of the couples they were friendly with. Had she been, of course, that would have been very pertinent to the film. But just having people over for dinner usually ends up with no more than a scene of people sitting down and having dinner, and it's not very interesting.

Sometimes something explosive will happen at a party, particularly if there is a camera on. People get angry at the lights and so on, or resent other people being the focus of the film. In the first party we filmed, in Toronto, nothing very significant happened. The party in Maine was different. If I were using this technique again and I wanted to involve more people, then I would have to find a particular way in which they were interacting with the other people in the film so that episodes would occur which were emotionally significant.

Q. Let's move on to editing and structure. You shot seventy hours, and you use an hour and a half. Were the choices difficult regarding what to omit?

A. I can't remember—my memory is a bit foggy. I have a bad time once I've cut a sequence out; by and large, I forget it even existed. Yet when you're looking at a rough cut and you argue about what's to come out, you say, "I can't take that sequence out; I've got to have that sequence"; but once you take it out, you very seldom miss it. However, I can't remember very much; I can't remember sequences, but there must be some which we had in and then took out. It was really much more a question of tightening sections and making them work as sequences and, more than that, making the overall structure work.

Q. Is the final film in chronological order?

A. No. The opening of the film was shot about two-thirds the way through; the breakfast scene was shot halfway through. Basically, the main arch of action is at the end of the film when they wake up—after they have had that moment of intimacy when she's sitting on his lap crying, and they wake up the next morning and have a great fight and he throws her out of the house. That whole passage happened the week before we finished filming, and it was what we were waiting for. Not that it had to be a fight; it might have been a very happy episode. But you wait for one significant arch of events that hang together and give you a core. The holiday, and when they're at the lake and so on, and the party around that—they all occurred very early in the filming and are actually unrelated to the rest. All I do is take episodes and put them into a dramatic structure that works for me.

Q. So you are aiming towards a kind of emotional fiction?

A. Yes. It is very often the case that episode *a* is put together with episode *b* to produce a feeling of *c*, when in reality they don't have that connection. However, if feeling c doesn't have a feeling relationship or isn't true of the characters, then it won't work. What I'm doing is finding conjunctions of events which create for me the feeling I have about that couple and about life, and what I want to express.

One has to be very, very clear. Billy and Antoinette in the film are not Billy and Antoinette Edwards, the couple who exist and live at 323 Rushton Road. They are characters, images on celluloid in a film drama. To say that they are in any other sense true, other than being true to our own experience of the world and people we have known and ourselves, is philosophical nonsense. There is no way ninety minutes in a film of Billy and Antoinette can be the same as the actual real life of Billy and Antoinette.

Q. Did they make any comments on the time rearrangement in the final film?

A. No, because they clearly understood that we would do that. But it was hard at first for Antoinette to handle. For example, there is very little shown where she is very giving or very tender; there is very little shown of how she is with other people, which is often very warm; very little is shown of how she is with her child or the fact that she's a good cook. At other times and in other circumstances, she is all those things. In the middle of a major crisis or conflict, she couldn't be very giving and much of the time was very tense; it was a very tough time. So she comes out in the film—or rather as the character in the film—as someone caught up in those devastating demands of that moment.

Q. Can we come back to the dramatic structure and your preparation work with Arla. I am thinking of your problems of reordering the sequences in order to gain maximum dramatic effect, and the things you look for in going through the rushes.

A. First, I think you perceive certain kinds of things, certain things that happened that week and seemed to be something that was a consistent preoccupation, say of Antoinette or Billy. First of all, we went through all the material twice; we went through all the rushes as we were shooting and we went through it all once or twice after that, and then chucked out fifty hours.

Q. What were you looking for when you went through the material?

A. Stuff that connects with other stuff, episodes that connect and illuminate each other. Stuff that contrasts, and stuff that is alive. The trouble with a lot of shooting is that nothing happens, so it's aborted; or you miss half of it because you come in late. You end up with a set of sequences which are alive and are funny, moving, sad and have

A MARRIED COUPLE
Notes Made from Inspection of Footage

ROLL 273

Tape 143

806

Bedroom (a shade hot) 2 shot W By. on bed Ant. standing beside Ant. exits to hall returns to beside bed. MCU By. pb to LS Ant. to By., to Ant. back to By.

BEAUTIFUL.

806

MS By. pb to Ant. she explains phone call while standing at door holding handbag. pan to By. She doesn't want to discuss what's bothering her, she just wants to be away from By. right now. He accuses her of not wanting to talk because of cameras. She says she's going to Mary Jane's, wishes she could just go without telling him where but thinks that would be unfair. She exits.
By. calls to her "Honey, are you sure you wouldn't rather stay and talk?" Long hold on By. he finally gets up.

807

Ant. in blue coat in hall pan to By. coming into hall from Kitchen and goes up stairs LE into kitchen.

808

same LS Ant. comes into hall and goes out front door. Hold on door.

809

From porch – car pulls out of driveway and moves off GOOD BRIDGE

MOS WS By. sitting on rug legs outstretched back to camera listening to Beethoven's 9th – crane up Merton in BG. BEAUTIFUL SHOT

ROLL 274

810

Reverse angle WS By. in same position Sound in – music up – CU By. nodding to music Merton enters shot, licks By.'s face then lies down in front of him.

810

change angle WS By. and Merton – listening to music 2 shot in MCU Ceiling rosette – MCU Merton with By's head resting on his body EXTRAORDINARY

811

Focus up on CU carafe – CU Merton mock growling – By. shouts commands to freeze, Merton obeys. ALL GOOD WITH DOG

812

CU foot pumping up plastic furniture, slow PB to WS By. in TV room TV Audio BG. GOOD TIME BRIDGE

812

By. sits on blue couch to watch TV in LS pan to TV side view

813

Change Angle MLS By. slow PB yellow chair in foreground obscuring slow ZI to TV

MCU Bog. asleep in crib through rungs BEAUTIFUL TIME BRIDGE
slow PB to full crib then crane up to full shot Bog. asleep
Nice shot

MS TV – By. pulls out plug and walks into bedroom – WS By. on unmade bed – he leaves hold on bed MS By. at dresser

WS By. standing by bed – pan round to LS dresser, By. walks into shot to get tobacco. GOOD TIME BRIDGE

MLS By. washing feet in bathroom sink GOOD TIME BRIDGE

814

LS alarm clock showing 1:30am – By. undressing – naked, he gets into bed slow ZI to CU By. reading newspaper FRAMING CROOKED
EYEPIECE TWISTED??

815

he gets out of bed and returns with paper (darker than previous)

816

change angle MS By. reading in bed.

816

change angle same action

from living room into hall (Nice light) waiting for Ant.'s return
She comes in front door carrying package – walks through hall returns to hang up coat in closet – change angle (still from living room) Ant. enters shot and goes upstairs. RUN OUT
slightly out of sync

emotional values. Those are what you start with, and you then try to find an order to those events in which the feelings are amplified, and amplified and amplified, until they've reached a peak. Then you try to resolve them again—rather I suppose in the way you construct a piece of music.

Q. Can you tell me how you work with Arla?

A. Basically, it seems to me that the director and the editor always perceive things a little differently. The director's notion of what's happening is different from the editor's. But as I say, I chucked out about fifty hours, so we had about twenty to work with; if Arla felt she needed something or was stuck, she would go back into that 50 hours. But we then basically screened the twenty hours; we had a list of what those sequences were and a rough idea of what the order of events would be. The twenty hours represented roughly twenty sequences, twenty episodes, and each was roughly an hour long.

We would sit down in the morning and go through an hour. I would say what I liked and what I thought the shape was, and Arla would say what she liked and what she thought the shape was; we would usually very quickly agree on the rough shape of the sequence. Then she would go ahead, pull it out and cut it. The next morning we would come back and screen the rough cut of that sequence, and decide that such and such worked and such and such didn't, or what needed ordering or how we could fix it; and then she would do that, or sometimes she simply set it aside and we would go on to the next one. Arla works extremely quickly, and we would tend to do almost a sequence a day until we had the rough assembly; and then we started polishing.

Q. How long did the assembly take you?

A. The assembly, which was about four or five hours, took about six weeks. Then we were stuck for a month trying to get a shape that would work, and we tried juggling it this way and that way.

Q. Can we tie it down to specifics. What were the alternate shapes you had in mind?

A. It doesn't seem so much like alternatives because you either have the feeling it works or it doesn't work; and if it doesn't work, it's not an alternative, and you keep juggling around until finally it does. But for example, there are two or three major fights in this film. There's the first little fight about the harpsichord. This is a joke fight, but it sort of sets up many of the key strains that emerge later in the film. There's the car fight which is a very bitter fight, but isn't violent and sort of has a semiresolve to it, and is left with a hooker at the end of it. Then there's the fight where he throws her out of the house.

The harpsichord scene isn't a major fight—it's just sort of a way into the film. If you have one big fight at the beginning and one big fight at the end, and the first one is sort of left open and unresolved, all through the middle part you wait for the threads to be picked up. There may be all sorts of little threads in the middle which are significant; but you are really waiting to see what big thing is going to happen next, so it's a matter of how you get those threads to develop and amplify each other.

The biggest problem was to put the car fight where it was able to pick up the threads of conflict, so that the earlier clues were expanded and amplified. Another problem was how to make Antoinette's desire for other relationships apparent, rather than merely talked about. She discusses them with her girlfriend, but the discussion is transferred into action when she starts the flirtation with that guy in the red shirt at the party.

Q. You get the development of intensity of their arguments, which serves to increase the tension; but you also have several other sequences, which in a sense could be placed anywhere—the holiday sequence and an explanation of Billy at work. How did you play around with these in the order?

A. It is largely how much relaxation you want from your tension, and so it's merely a matter of gauging the emotional charge or the degree of relaxation that you want before you build to a higher degree. The choices, ultimately, have simply to do with relaxing and heightening tension.

Q. Jack Gold, the English director, has said that when he does a straight documentary, he may have twenty sequences. He then puts those on cards, and in a sense he edits the cards. Do you work at all in this way?

A. I just jot ideas down on paper that feel right—this, then this, then this—and you work out a sequence; and then you think, "but if I do that, this isn't going to work here because it's too early, or it's too late, or it doesn't connect with what follows after." Then you try another juggle. And whether you do it on cards or you do it by numbers on a piece of paper, it is the same process.

Q. I asked you before whether Billy and Antoinette had the power of censorship. Now I am wondering if there were times when you were using your own taste, saying, "No, I've got this scene, but I don't really think it should be used as a matter of taste." Can you give me some examples there?

A. Well, at that time, Billy had been going to a psychiatrist to help resolve some of the problems he was having. I recorded four sessions with the psychiatrist, and they were absolutely fascinating and indeed hair raising, as there was some extraordinary material involved. But I decided not to use the material; in some ways it was like a red herring. When a person is talking to a psychiatrist and talking about something that they feel is quite horrific that they've done, an audience may seize upon that and jump to all sorts of conclusions about the person, conclusions which are misleading or allow them to classify the other person or to depersonalize the other person. So I didn't use these scenes. They were very tempting, and there was a lot of revealing material in them, but I felt they were misleading.

Q. Billy is very funny when he is reading some advertising. Did you catch much of him at work?

A. We spent two, three, four days with him at work, and there were some other funny passages; but you are really looking for that passage that you can get in a minute or thirty seconds which stands for all the things. There were several other episodes, but those were the best ones. There was a long talk with some guy in Saskatchewan. They were planning a centennial campaign for Saskatchewan, and Saskatchewan wanted to look like Expo, but for only $200,000 or something like that, and the dialogue was very funny.

I was a little unhappy about a couple of sequences that technically didn't work, showing Billy's strength and his forcefulness with other people, because he's rather a different person at work than he is at home. At home, at that point anyway, he was a little more insecure about various kinds of things than he was at work. That extra dimension would have been nice to get included. We did do one other thing. I had a screening with some friends, thirty or forty people, when I had the first sort of rough cut. This was in order to see it with an audience and get a sense of the way other people responded. I did it again with the final cut and then once more, and they were very helpful. It's not so much that people can tell you how to fix a film or what's not working, but you get the sense of an additional perspective, which is very helpful.

Q. Can you remember any of the things said after the rough cut?

A. Yes. There was a lot of imbalance in the reaction to Billy and Antoinette. At one time, people were generally much more responsive to Antoinette, and then there was another point at which they were much more responsive to Billy, and I wanted a balance. It is still the case in the final film that it almost acts as a Rorschach test. People either identify with Billy or with Antoinette, or reject them both, or think they are both marvelous; and you get everything in between that. But you eventually have to decide what is the balance for yourself, and part of that you get from the way the audience is responding. It's also very helpful where jokes are concerned—what's working, and what's very funny to you but is not funny to anybody else; how much pause you need after for the laughter to subside, so that you don't lose lines. We finally blew the film up to 35 mm when we had a cut that was one hour and fifty-seven minutes. I knew it was long, but I had gotten too close to the film to decide how much more to cut it, and how much could come out; so we blew it up at that point, and had a number of screenings in New York with other people. Then I cut another twenty minutes, and got it down to ninety-seven minutes.

Q. Was this basically just shortening sequences, or did you take sequences out?

A. Shortening. We didn't take any sequences out; we just tightened up the slack. I took out parts of sequences—after the major fight, after dinner, and after their very funny episode when Bogart picks up a little piece of shit on the floor, which is an extraordinary reliever of the tension of the moment. There was another sequence when they are talking on the bed upstairs; the telephone rings and Antoinette wants to answer it, but Billy doesn't want her to leave the bed and get out of the discussion that they are having, and they have a fight about that. It was a fascinating exchange, but it was just one too many; and I thought, I just cannot take one more fight, so I took it out. In order to tighten up another sequence I cut one bit that I really regret. Billy and Antoinette are in bed the second time in the film. She has been in her bed, and he takes her into his bed. He wants to be intimate with her, and she rejects him; I shortened it a bit and in consequence lost a passage where one really experienced more strongly the anguish and humiliation that Billy felt in being rejected. One still gets a lot out of the sequence, but it is a little diminished.

Q. You said you went way over budget. What were the things that blew up the budget?

A. We were budgeted for seven weeks of shooting, and we shot for ten; we were budgeted for 80,000 feet of film, and I shot virtually 140,000 feet—those were the major things. My own time was double what I said it would be. Editing time wasn't as much as we had anticipated. Our lighting costs were more; we had the trip to Vermont and Maine which wasn't in the budget. Promotion costs were a lot more than I had anticipated; I had budgeted $14,000 to promote the film, and I spent $30,000.

Q. When you finished the film, how did you go about selling it? You said you had a certain number of precommitments on television, but these commitments pay relatively little. How did you begin to get the money back?

A. It wasn't too much of a problem in Canada, except for the amount of time required to do it and the number of speaking engagements and screenings you have to have. I find with a film that it helps a lot if you get out to many locations, wherever the theatre happens to be —St. Catharines or Belleville or Ottawa or Windsor. You go along to see the film, to see the press, and so on; it all helps. The main problem is getting good distribution. This wasn't much of a problem in Canada because we had that settled. But we had a long, long battle with censorship in Ontario, which was very costly and took a lot of time.

Q. What were the problems brought up in censorship?

A. The language, which was virtually unprecedented in Canada. There had never before been so much swearing in a film in Canada— that was really the crux of the problem. The first censor to tackle it had a great deal of difficulty deciding whether it was going to arouse a great public reaction and whether it was within the tolerances of community standards, which is the real basis of most censorship.

Q. How did you eventually win them around? What were the compromises?

A. I made three cuts in Ontario. I haven't had to make any cuts thereafter in any of the other provinces so far, and no cuts in the United States because there just isn't any censorship there any more—or at least no government or state censorship. The key to persuading the censor was that after it became a public controversy, it was clear that more people were going to be upset by the cuts in the film than would be upset by the language in the film. It tends to be a political thing.

Q. You said Canadian distribution was easy; what about American?

A. America was much harder, and we still haven't found an adequate solution to the problem. I have also found greater difficulty with the film in the United States, and I am not quite sure why. I noticed very early on that our screenings in New York had quite a different flavor than in Canada; people seemed to find the film more threatening, personally threatening, personally heavy and painful. I would guess this could be, particularly in New York, because personal relationships there are more strenuous and less secure, and therefore the film seems more painful. In the early American reviews, for example, there was virtually no mention of that fact that the film is very funny in the first half, virtually no mention whatsoever.

The reviews have been of three kinds: from young critics, very responsive and very good reviews; from sort of middle-aged critics or middle-aged married people, an intense involvement in the film, but the reviews tend to say as much about the reviewer as they do about the film (at least that is what we drew from between the lines); with older critics, and this particularly affected us in New York with Judith Crist and a couple of others, a rejection of the film as ugly and the characters distasteful. There was a total inability to take in the film and accept it. In Canada, audiences are a lot more open and easy, especially if there is a very large house, which somehow socializes the experience. In the States, there seems to be a great taste for fantasy at the moment; everybody seems to want an escape. *Easy Rider* is enormously popular. It's a good film but I often wonder how much of its appeal is that it romanticizes and fantasizes an experience.

Q. Has the film covered its costs yet?

A. No. It will eventually in Canada and in England. What will happen in the States is still very much up in the air, but I am not terribly optimistic.

Q. This question of using vérité technique and the nonfiction drama, where do you think it is going from here? Do you think you will use the process again?

A. I think I will probably use it on my next film—I am quite sure I will—but more as a way of setting up and recording that kind of feeling exchange: the kind of dynamic that arises out of direct interchange between the characters and the film. But in the next film, I don't think the people will have had actual past relationships with each other. They will be characters that I've deliberately put together in a film, and asked to interact and interrelate.

The next day . . . Mailer had the opportunity to
watch Leiterman at work. Whenever he saw Mailer
he would smile. This would seem part of his photographic technique. He would always smile encourag-
ingly at his subject. After a while one was glad to see
him.

NORMAN MAILER DESCRIBING RICHARD
LEITERMAN IN "ARMIES OF THE NIGHT"

In England in August 1969 I saw some of the raw footage of Dubrovnik Festival. *I liked it but paid no attention to the name of the
cameraman. I likewise paid no attention to the credits when I first saw*
High School. *It was only when I was viewing* High School *a second
time in order to discuss it with Wiseman that I realized the photography was done by Leiterman. Thus, the fact of using three films by
Leiterman in this book is accidental—but it is a coincidence I'm very
happy about.*

*Today, Leiterman must rank as one of the five or six best direct-
cinema cameramen in the world, being credited with such award
winning films as* One More River, Running Away Backwards, *and*
Lynn Seymour.

*Leiterman, born in 1935, is the youngest of six children and grew
up in nothern Ontario and British Columbia. At different periods he
has been a logger, garbage collector, beachcomber, and truck driver.
Apart from a brief session at film school, his real entry into film dates
from the late fifties when he began a continuing association with
Allan King (later Allan King Associates). According to Leiterman
the big break came in 1964 when he signed on as second cameraman
on* One More River, *a film about the civil rights movement shot in
Mississippi and produced by Richard's elder brother Douglas. From
being second cameraman Leiterman went on to shoot 80 percent of
the film, which eventually won a Canadian Film Award.*

Since 1964 Leiterman's films have included Running Away Backwards *(1966), a film about expatriate life in Ibiza;* Saigon: Portrait of
a City *(1967);* Will the Real Norman Mailer Please Stand Up *(1968);
and* Margaret Mead's New Guinea Journal *(1968). He also shot* Dubrovnik Festival *(see p. 215) and* High School *(see p. 66), and in
1970 completed a Canadian feature,* Going Down the Road.

Leiterman is at opposite poles from the spectacular jazzy camera-

man of fiction. He is basically rather quiet and reserved about his work until one makes contact. He then becomes very warm and totally open, and one begins to understand the easy contact he has with his subjects. Of all the directors he has worked with, Allan King probably knows him best and has this to say about Leiterman: "Richard is not as flashy or spectacular as many cameramen who work in vérité, but he is incredibly secure in what he sees and responds to. He has a unique vision and great integrity. He never grabs at a subject. He doesn't push but responds to what is happening in front of the camera, with the result that he gets more respect from his subjects than anyone I know."

Q. How did you happen to get into films?

A. Getting into film was something I didn't decide on. Film has never been anything that I really thought about as a life career. I didn't finish university; I went two years and then bummed around Europe doing a number of jobs. I met Allan King in Europe, and the work he was doing then was documentaries for the CBC—very low budget—and I asked him if there was some way I could get on with him. It seemed like a pretty good thing. He traveled a lot, and I was interested in traveling and seeing a lot of people. It's kind of a joke now in documentary or films when people say, "Oh, aren't you lucky to be able to travel so many places, and meet so many fantastic people, and do so many interesting things!" But then, it seemed a pretty romantic idea. Anyway, Allan didn't have anything for me at the time and suggested maybe I find a film school and get the basic grounding, as I had no idea of what still photography was about, let alone movies. He suggested the British Film Institute, suggested trying to get in with the CBC or NFB, and things like that. At any rate, I came back to Vancouver and took the university's first summer course on "be your own film director in six weeks."

It was Saturdays and Sundays for six weeks. They had an old Bolex, and a Bell and Howell, windup. Stan Fox had set the course up, and it was in its first year. So I went to that and learned basics about film—what made an image on a piece of film, how it was cut, rewinds, all that. It was a general, basic, all-around course, and we turned out a little seven-minute film. They asked us why we were in the course, and I firmly said that there were a lot of things that could be done a lot more interestingly, more artistically, and better than were being turned out by people in documentaries and news and things like that. I did the course, bought my own little Bolex windup with some money I had, and shot a couple of news stories out in Vancouver.

They were just freak stories. One was a storm. I lived at the water-front, so I just went out the front door and shot some waves, sea gulls, and water pouring down, and sold it to the Vancouver news for $35. I thought it was pretty terrific, an easy way to make a dollar. During the next couple of months I tried to do more of that, but I didn't have any luck. CBC wasn't interested, and there weren't any more freak storms. So I went back to the job I had, which was out in the tug boats.

Meanwhile, I had written Allan and said if there was any chance that I could get on just for subsistence fees, just as second camera assistant or whatever, to let me know, and I would come over to London. I told him it wouldn't cost him any money and I did know something about the business now. I was very lucky. He called back about two months later to say I could come in as second cameraman on one of their CBC documentaries about the common market. So I got on second camera with an Auricon which I had never seen before and didn't know how to use. Allan said if it worked out it might be worth-while for me to stay in London. If it didn't work out there would be enough money for me and my wife to get back to tug boating or whatever. However, it panned out nicely. I stayed in London; I got a credit by CBC news in London and did a fair amount of work for them.

Q. Was most of this photography self-taught, or did you learn from the other cameraman?

A. On the first job, the one with Allan, the senior cameraman was a very good, a very painstaking lighting man; and as I had never done any lighting as such, he took the time to show me the basic lighting setups—how to put a back light in, and a fill light down the hall if you're shooting one room and seeing through to another. So it was kind of an apprenticeship except that I wasn't looked on as an apprentice. I had to learn and shoot at the same time. It came very easy somehow, I don't know particularly how, and it worked out extremely well.

Allan's films would come up about once every six months or so, when he would get one of his own productions going; so in between we were shooting news for CBC out of London and Paris, or we'd go to Germany. Shooting news was interesting; I think I learned more about how to shoot a documentary in the way that I felt a documentary should be shot. The stuff I had done previously for CBC on documentary was kind of a setup deal where you have person *A* walk from here to there to show you what was in the background, which might be called *C*; they would sit down on a chair, which was already prelit, and go into what was supposed to be spontaneous talk about whatever the social problem was. That wasn't my idea of doing documentary.

Q. What year are you talking about?

A. This was in 1961. Basically, we would go out to do a story, find out where the action was, and shoot it, and shoot it as many ways as possible. You had to be fast. You had a lighting setup to do; you had to go bong, bong, bong, and have your lights up. The guy came in and you shot it. You tried to frame it right; you tried to make it look as nice as possible; and ten minutes later he was gone. If it was action news, you worked the same way. There was no director to tell you where the action was; you were on your own. Sometimes, you'd have a sort of briefing and off you would go, with an Arriflex or whatever, and shoot it; it was the kind of experience which I found invaluable in learning how to shoot straight documentaries.

Q. What were the key documentaries you shot during 1961 and after?

A. The one I liked best was a profile on Lynn Seymour, a Canadian ballerina who was working at Covent Gardens; I shot it and Allan directed. That worked out very nicely; she's a lovely girl, and it went well. You did walk-in, you did portable sync, all kinds of things. In 1964 I came over to America and shot *One More River*, which was directed by my brother for Intertel. I guess that was the first long show that I did on my own. Doug was there a lot of the time, but a lot of the time there was just Beryl Fox and myself scooting around the Southern states, looking for it. Then I got into a series of Intertels, for NET. One was on the color problem in Britain called *Colour in Britain* directed by Mike Sklar. Then we did schools in England and America, which was a deadly show.

Q. Did you work free lance the whole time?

A. All this time I was free lance. I've been with Allan King Associates since it originated in England, but on a free-lance basis. I worked for the company, but I could also go out and hustle on my own. I could work for whomsoever I wished. I'm not under any obligation to Allan King Associates. This has always been the way with all of us in England.

Q. Can we get on to *A Married Couple*. Can you tell me how Allan approached you and discussed the problem with you?

A. This was after *Warrendale*. Allan said the next film he did he wanted to be a real film about a married couple. It sounded like a very interesting idea, but I wasn't sure whether it would come off or not. I wasn't sure how I would feel about walking into a couple's house and filming and recording them.

Q. I gather it was fairly clear from the beginning that it was to be a marriage in crisis; how did you feel about that element?

A. It was a bit upsetting to me. Due to my being out of town an awful lot on various assignments and various pictures, I did not have the ideal marriage, although it's going well and we have overcome a lot of differences. But to go and observe some married couple in some kind of difficulty—well, who needs that? I could just shoot in my own house. It did seem to me, though, that perhaps out of this would come things that would be particularly interesting, not only to myself, but to a large audience especially in America, where marriages seem to be off and on, in and out, almost like the tide. If we could get something down on film that would be good, that people could look at and say, "All right, they're not much different from us, and they are still making it, and if they're not making it, why aren't they?" They could look at themselves through Billy and Antoinette and find out why some of the niggly things blow up into such great things. Maybe it's a kind of visual therapy. Basically that's what we came around to, and said, now let's do it and be as real as we can. When Billy and Antoinette were chosen, I felt, well, that's fine, I know them. I knew them from when we lived in Spain, but it wasn't a close knowledge. They are both vocal, somewhat inclined to be exhibitionists, but pleasant, and they seemed right. I guess I would sooner have gone into their house than into a stranger's.

Q. Once they agreed that you could shoot there, how did you set up preparing the photographic side of it?

A. That was difficult. The first two weeks we were around, testing and thinking. We wanted to be able to shoot anywhere in the house, and we wanted to be able to go indoors and outdoors, and not be too affected by changing film stock or magazines. That was pretty much the reason for using the fast Ektachrome daylight stock, so that I could go in and out, and could make use of the daylight coming in the windows as supplementary lighting. We set up lights around the house, and made special brackets to fit in the living room, the dining room, and upstairs. We tried to hide them behind closet doors and hang them from the ceiling; we put blue dichroic filters over them to balance with the daylight coming in the windows. It was a trial, but I still couldn't get enough usable light dichroics after setting it all up because the dichroics take away approximately one-third of the illumination. There just wasn't enough light in the house; but to put any more light in would have cooked us, literally, because it was summer and it was hot. We therefore went back to the method of using tungsten, taking the dichroics off, gelling all the windows with filters, and using tungsten light inside. So we ended up shooting on tungsten film; when we went outside, we had to change and put a conversion filter on.

One of our basic things was to make it as natural as possible. Using key light or fills or anything like that was pretty much impossible, because we never knew where the action was going to take place. My next move was to put my lights in the places where I *could* put them, which were in the corners of the rooms, mainly to allow me to shoot all around the room and in any direction without catching light. The odd time I caught a flare was when they were hung from the ceiling and from corner brackets. There was no key light; it was all fill. Well, let's say it was all key light with some bounced light for fill, consisting of 1,000-watt adjustable floods in three of the four corners, going in towards the center of the room. In addition we bounced minilight 650s from the ceiling and had photofloods in the practical light fixtures like table lamps and stand lamps. In the living room I guess we had about 4,500 watts, including some Lowell lights which I found most practical because you can put a 500-watt flood in and gauze it a bit, and you can fill out areas and hide that light just about anywhere.

It was very hard to get any kind of dramatic feeling in the rooms because we didn't know where the action was going to be. I didn't want to have to go out and start turning on and off lights when they moved to one corner rather than another; so then the thing was to try and position oneself where the light was best. Also, during the first two weeks of testing lights and testing Billy and Antoinette, I was also testing for where I could shoot and get good results.

Q. Can you say something about choice of camera?

A. We started with the brand new professional Bolex 16 mm self-blimped camera, which had just come over here. It has motorized zoom, mechanized focus, and detachable magazines, and it all seemed very fancy and very new and very nice. It took a while to get used to it—it's basically a whole different concept because it is all on fingertip control, rather than manual control. There were certain things wrong with it: the zoom and the focus were on the same motors, and if you wanted a slow zoom and a fast focus, it was impossible; you could only have a slow zoom with a slow focus and vice versa.

During the first days that we used it, we got a particular scratch on the film, and we took it back to the Bolex people. They looked

45

through it, couldn't find anything wrong, and gave it back to us. It ended up that the gate was not set up to use the thicker, softer emulsion stock of 7242; it was too narrow to allow the free passage of the film. The camera we finally chose was the Eclair, which was ideal in fact for the job. When they brought it out years ago, it had certain problems, and that's why I never used it before. I only used my own Auricon, which I cut down and remade into a shoulder camera. It was balanced very well, and that's why I didn't like the Eclair because its balance is all forwards, although it is the most comfortable camera there is on the market today for portable hand holding.

But I didn't want to use the Auricon because it was even noisier than the Eclair, and it didn't have reflex viewing. The Arriflex BL is just too hard to hold. I don't like being encumbered with shoulder braces or belly braces of any kind, and the weight of it is certainly something that you can't comfortably hold. It's just too impractical. The brace means you can't get down to get low-angle shots, and you can't bend and get the high-angle shots. You're strapped into shooting straight in front of you.

Q. What procedures did you set up with Billy and Antoinette?

A. We went in with a kind of ground rule that we would have no communication with them, nor would they communicate anything to us. We put up an invisible barrier between us, Dutch, myself, and Chris the soundman. If we came at any time, they were not to act surprised or to change what they were doing to something else, and they would not make any exception to what they were doing just because of our presence. If we walked in in the middle of the night, so we walked in in the middle of the night; and if we didn't come that day, we didn't come that day. It was just to get them used to us being around, whether we were fiddling with lights or whether we were following them around with the camera; it also served the purpose of getting them used to our presence.

Q. How natural were they before the cameras? Did you see a change in them from the beginning to the end? Did you notice things that you would say were put on for you?

A. The presence of the camera tends to distort at the beginning of any real filming. People are trying their best to be normal people; but in doing so, I would think that the majority of them find they are acting. We certainly noticed this in the first two or three weeks, but the first two or three weeks are not in the final cut of the film.

Q. Can you give me specific cases?

A. Some of the dialogue that they would come up with, you could tell that it was for our benefit. Some of the antics that they went through; they are both, as I said before, kind of exhibitionist people. For example, Antoinette might be downstairs in the kitchen and Billy would make his entrance, maybe from work or from upstairs watching television. If we were filming Antoinette downstairs, he would make an entrance with a terrific wisecrack, or a smash-bang, or bring a beer bottle down and plunk it down in front of Antoinette to make sure that we knew he was there and to feel that he was making his entrance in the finest possible way. I think that there were times when Antoinette might have worn a little less makeup towards the beginning of the film. She wasn't quite her natural self; she was doing a fair amount of primping, I guess, mainly when we weren't filming. They were aware of us; they were making jokes to fill time; they couldn't sit quietly for any length of time as normal people would do. Even Billy and Antoinette will sit quietly and not say anything to one another, but in the beginning their time was nearly always full of conversation.

Q. How was the child in the film?

A. Bogart was excellent. We explained to him the first day we were there what we were going to do: We were going to make a movie in his house; and when we brought the cameras and sound gear in, I explained to him what the camera was, and I let him look through it. But I told him once we started working that he was to leave us alone; and Chris did the same thing; he let him listen in the earphones, and told him that we didn't want him bothering us. Billy and Antoinette also told him that he was to leave us alone. Bogart did pretty well. Every now and then he would get bored, feel that he wasn't getting enough attention, and he would come over and try and poke his head in the lens but it was very seldom and certainly not on a crucial occasion.

Q. How long did it take before you think they became relatively natural?

A. I think it was during the third week. They just seemed to slow down, things weren't so rushed or nervous, and they didn't make so much noise. Maybe they weren't quite so funny when there was no need for it.

Q. How did you get yourself a pattern for shooting and what was your relationship with Allan at this stage?

A. During the first few weeks, Allan was around the house quite a bit, and he would sometimes go down to the office and screen the previous day's rushes. When he was actually in the house, just sitting in the living room or dining room trying to be inconspicuous, it became very difficult for him because he was just sitting there; he had

47

nothing to hide behind—he wasn't doing anything. He couldn't make himself useful in any way and was just an extra person. Chris was fine. He could sneak behind his Nagra or fiddle with it; even if he wasn't recording; it was something he was doing rather than sitting nakedly. And I was behind my camera, and could polish the lens if I wasn't shooting anything, or could just sit there. But Allan's presence was a bit inhibiting to Billy and Antoinette because he had nothing to do except just be there, kind of observing. And because he had nothing to do, he was more liable to be brought in or looked at in a way that asked, "Are we doing the right thing now?"

Q. To come back to the selection of what to shoot; you have five or six weeks at the beginning which then extends. When do you know when to make your choice, to turn on and turn off? When Antoinette and Billy are together, it seems obvious that you are there; but when they are separate how do you know which one to stay with?

A. It was very difficult to start with. I was first trying to see if there was any pattern to what they were doing after dinner. Did Antoinette always go and do the dishes, or did Billy sit down with a magazine, or did he go upstairs? They didn't seem to follow any set pattern, so a lot of the time it was a case of who was doing what. When they were separate, Billy would be upstairs or at work; when they were both in the house, it was a question of who was doing the most interesting thing: how valid was it to what we were doing; was it good to have; should be cover it; how well will it develop.

I think these are the key words in the kind of shooting we were doing: "Will it develop into anything?" and secondly, "Can you possibly use it for a cutaway, or maybe just a silent music-over sequence?" Are they doing something alone which can be used to show something significant about their joint lives; or can it be used as just a simple little sequence by itself of something beautiful and softening. So you take it from there. Perhaps we would shoot Antoinette in the kitchen for a while, but we wouldn't know what Billy was doing upstairs; so we would make sure to first cover the sequence of what Antoinette was doing, and then we'd beat it upstairs and see what Billy was doing in case we needed some of that to go with what Antoinette was doing.

Q. Normally, if you are working as the photographer, you concentrate on what is within your frame and the director can concentrate on what is being said; here, you had to combine the two. Had you done much of this kind of thing before—was it an extra problem?

A. I must say that I have kind of conditioned myself to do it, because this is the kind of filming I have done and have done well. It's a matter of anticipating a movement, anticipating what's going to come next, where your dialogue might come from. You find if you shoot a classroom in a similar way you immediately sort out the guys who are going to be the first to put their hands up. You sense this so that you can almost get there before them. But it's hard because you're not ready most of the time. You just try to outguess them, or first-guess them.

Q. Could you say something about shooting with only one camera, and things only happening once?

A. When shooting with only one camera, there are no chances for retakes; there is no chance for questions being asked again—it is a one-shot thing. And you also have to cover yourself so that the film will cut. On many occasions Billy and Antoinette would get into a discussion across the room, one sitting on one side and the other sitting on the other side. You cannot bear to be continually panning back and forth unless the action needs it, unless the action really necessitates it. If the action is fast and furious, you can only gain by some quick pans back and forth; but basically if you can see something starting, if you can anticipate that this is going to be an argument, and this is going to be a fairly important argument—they have been needling around, they've been at it for awhile, and they've settled themselves in for it—then you have to cover yourself and listen very hard to what they are saying. You try to get what is important to be in sync on frame, and when you can you sneak off and get the silent cutaways of the other one, and try not to lose too much important sync dialogue.

Q. There are a number of very intimate sequences in this film, such as the bedroom sequences. Did you find the camera interfering with the reactions of Billy and Antoinette?

A. In the first bedroom scene, both of them were very self-conscious about us being there, and whether they should or could make love before us. The first intimate scene in the film was actually the first time that we did any long shooting in the bedroom, and there was a certain amount of tomfoolery. The lights were very hot, and I really didn't have them set the way I would like to have had them, had I been able to shoot up there previously or had more time to reset them. It was a very hard, overall light, not at all a dramatic light, and here were Billy and Antoinette in bed—with Billy trying to get sexy toward his wife. He didn't know how far he was going to go, and she certainly didn't feel like she wanted to have anything to do with it. It was a time when I found that the camera was at its most noisiest, and that the floors squeaked every time we moved to get another angle.

Q. Where, in fact were you shooting from?

A. I was shooting from bedside, very close to bedside. I guess I wasn't more than four feet from the bed at any time, except for wide cover shots which I went back and shot through the door. Christian, I think, was as embarrassed as they were or I was, and was trying to get the sound without being any closer than he needed to be. It was my first encounter with that kind of a scene in a real situation, and I just found that it wasn't going to happen. There was nothing more going to happen. They weren't going to make love for us, or for themselves—it was too difficult—and I decided that there was not much sense in staying on any longer with them.

Q. How could you judge when it was appropriate to shoot in the bedroom?

A. Well, when they had a particularly good day and felt very kind towards each other, I sometimes sensed I might get something important upstairs. For instance, the night they got the stereo set, and were having a marvelous time, and were both very happy. Without really thinking about it, we knew that we would stay. You could stay to a point, but when there was nothing else coming, my reasoning was that you had to leave. Otherwise you were forcing them to do something that perhaps they didn't want to do, and if you got it, how real was it? If they had made love for us in front of the camera, I would have wondered how much they were forcing it and whether it was really necessary; and I think that my whole thing is that it wasn't really necessary—at least not within our film. There were many happier times that were easier to film that come across with more "togetherness" than the bedroom scene.

Q. When you weren't filming and were just sitting around, at what point did you make a decision, "let's turn it on"? Can you give me an example?

A. The dinner table was one of the biggest action spots for us. Dinner might start in the usual manner, but it was the place where most things were discussed. We never missed a dinner or evening meal. The events of the day would be gone over, and you'd get the scene. You would shoot cover shots just in case something came up, and you wanted the table with them bringing the food on. We would make sure we got some cover shot so as to set whatever outfit they were wearing, and to try and keep some semblance of continuity. Billy might come on with "Well what did you do today?" You could almost sense when this was going to happen, and we'd shoot that. Then they would go on idly about Antoinette, maybe she went to Mary Jane's, bla, bla, and you could tell there wasn't anything.

I guess a lot of the times we missed the important question from either one or the other. The food for the dog sequence comes to mind. Billy was angry when he came in—he was angry from work, I can't remember why, but I know he was angry—and I knew that something was going to happen. We didn't shoot for awhile, and it was kind of a silent meal, not like usual, and I guess maybe it was second sense, or maybe I just turned on because he was chewing his food rather strangely. It's something you watch for.

Q. There are two or three things that look as if they might have been set up, and I wonder if you can comment on them. One is Billy always appearing in his underwear; the second thing is the scene where Antoinette is scratching her crotch in a pretty unladylike way; and the third one is the shooting at the Café de la Paix, where Antoinette talks about sex to her girlfriend.

A. Billy was quite comfortable wandering around the house in his altogether. When he comes home from work, he immediately strips; this was a ritual almost with him. He wears red shorts, I guess he has seven or eight pairs of them. They weren't set up for us by color co-ordination or anything like that. He said, do you want me to wander around naked, or do you think I should wear a pair of shorts; and our feeling was, that unreal as it might be, let's cover you up in pair of shorts. But it certainly was not set up, and I am sure if Billy had had his way he would have been naked most of the time. The first week we were shooting, we were there for morning wakeup and Billy got out of bed and tramped around the house, went down and called the dog, and then went out in the backyard and played with the dog—all this completely naked. We felt that maybe that particular thing was set up for us—maybe he was doing it for our benefit—but it was just Billy acting normally.

Antoinette scratching—I guess she did a lot of things like that, and I suppose it was her nature. There's another scene of her pulling the hair under her armpits that one critic took exception to in New York. It is a thing Antoinette does. Her scratching her leg or her crotch, I never took it as anything else. Maybe she was trying to provoke Billy; but she has a number of mannerisms like that, and maybe it is part of her makeup as a woman who likes to do these kinds of things to provoke, or maybe it's just a nice feeling for her.

Café de la Paix was set up. We asked Antoinette to invite one of her friends whom she confided in, so that we would have a background on their marriage.

Q. Did you tell her what to talk about?

A. No, not in any real terms. We told her that we would like the two of them to talk about Antoinette's feelings. Perhaps her friend, Mary

Jane could question her on this. We wanted them just to talk about the background and present feelings of Antoinette towards Billy and thought that perhaps this could be brought out by a second person. We shot an awful lot that afternoon, about two and a half hours of them chit-chatting. I had a pair of earphones because I was back too far to hear what they were talking about; I tried to pick my shots and anticipate where the action was going to come from. Allan was also listening on a set of earphones. At one time he did in fact interrupt, when their conversation was drifting, and asked them to get back to what was more pertinent, which was the subject of Billy and Antoinette.

Q. Once the filming was beginning to develop, did you see the rushes, or did Allan ask you to concentrate on any one particular thing or another?

A. I guess to begin with we had fights. We had fights over color stocks, we had fights about what we should be filming; but they weren't fights, they were just talks. Finally we did get it over with one night when I asked Allan what I should be shooting, and he said, "What you are shooting is really fine, but you're being a bit hasty; you're not staying long enough with the subject—you're not staying long enough for the sequence to develop. Be a little more selective, be a little more steady, in terms of holding onto a subject before you go back. Don't be so anxious to cover yourself because you're missing what might be a lot of the real action; you can afford to stay on Antoinette even if she is not saying something and Billy is, but try and *think* more." He's good like that; he will seldom call you down, but he will make it seem that maybe you're doing the wrong thing or you're being a little hasty or something like that.

Q. What did you find the most difficult scene to shoot?

A. The most physically difficult, as far as setup of the thing goes, was the car fight where they are in the living room. One is on the red couch, and one is on the gold couch; neither was in a particularly good position for light, and the spread of the room was too great to follow the dialogue easily on camera or mike. Chris was using the 804 microphone, and he would have to move it around and try to anticipate them; he couldn't follow my directions because sometimes I was picking up or getting ready for a reaction shot while the dialogue was still going on, and I wanted him to stay on the active line while I got ready for the reaction. I couldn't shoot it standing up because the angle just didn't look very good; I couldn't cross the axis at this point to get a new angle because there was no way of doing it continuously, and without interrupting their line of thought. If I walked in front of them, or walked between them, I didn't feel it would have done any of us any good. They would have been broken a bit just because of it, although they would have covered well I am sure.

The one blessing of that whole sequence, which went on for about an hour and a half, was when the phone rang, and I could follow Antoinette out. At the phone I could then flip around and shoot the reaction of Billy and still have enough time to get back to Antoinette hanging up and saying goodbye. I could then take up a new angle as I followed Antoinette back into the room.

I guess the second most difficult scene was the bedroom sequence where they are both trying very hard to get to where they're at, to a point almost embarrassing to both of them; and I had a feeling myself that they weren't getting anywhere. They would break and go down and have a coke or something, and I would follow them down, and I felt very sad and very sympathetic to both of them.

Q. What about the shooting of the party?

A. Had we been able to use the party in Maine, maybe just as a half-hour film by itself, it might have been great because there were a lot of things happening. There was this guy Bill painting away, and Billy was taking photographs of Bill painting; plus there was a party going on in the other part of the building and people were being very intellectual and doing all kinds of hand movements, drinking and smoking, and it was fine that way. But when it came down to Antoinette's flirtation with the chap in the red shirt, that was hard, because we had to establish them sitting there; we had to establish that the rest of the party was going on, and there was a terrific clatter that Chris had trouble with. Meanwhile, in the back, Billy was going somewhere or doing something when a lot of the pertinent stuff between Antoinette and Red Shirt was taking place. Billy in fact, was disengaging himself from the whole party and doing his own thing, taking stills with his camera.

Q. Had you forewarned the people at the party?

A. Yes, we asked them to have a party, and get their friends around. It was set up for the purpose of filming the contemporaries that Billy and Antoinette socialized with, to let the audience know that their friends were a bit kooky. But I am sure there would have been a party sooner or later.

Q. Could you say something about filming what I call the "record love sequence"?

A. This is one where they got the stereo set and the Beatle records.

They had bought a hi-fi; Billy brought it home, and they talked about getting the records. We shot them right through, from the beginning of Billy bringing in the cartons and opening them up, and there was an air of excitement. They hadn't had any kind of record player in the house, and they both dug music, so it was kind of exciting, and it was going to be nice. They put on the records and started dancing. The dancing is great; the music is great; how can anything be any better —but how could you do the shots without getting in their way. We did all the usual shots, low angle shots, shots up between them, holding the camera above them, getting close—I guess that's where the window came in for variety. The particular choice of where the music stopped fitted in quite well, and using the music, through the window to me was very exciting. That was just a beautiful sequence!

Q. What about arguments between a cameraman and director in the sense that the cameraman thinks he has a magnificent series of shots, and the director doesn't want to use them. Was there any sequence you would like to have seen used purely from a photographic point of view?

A. Yes. There was another dance, done that same stereo night, which I liked very much. They were just kind of fooling around, and just swinging each other round and round; and I framed so that you would see Billy's full face framed grinning away, and the next moment with a natural wipe of hair or something, you see Antoinette coming in and filling the same frame, and I went across her, and you get them going away from each other. I argued a fair bit about those, and Allan had them both in to start with; but there wasn't room for them, and he took that one out. I am glad he left in the one he did, but I was sorry to see the other one go. Another one was in Maine, down by the waterfront of the little town they were in. They were walking around, looking at boats, and the color of it seemed just very soft. It was a bit blue—it wasn't color-color, but had a very pleasant atmosphere to it.

Q. In terms of color did you tell Billy or Antoinette what to wear?

A. No, only on a couple of occasions for continuity's sake. Allan would ask Billy to wear a particular suit and shirt to the office, and maybe he would ask Antoinette to come downstairs in the morning wearing a particular dressing gown or housecoat to try and keep a bit of continuity from a scene that he had seen in the rushes that he felt might be quite pertinent.

Q. Are there any things about the photography or direction that we haven't gone over?

A. I guess the most significant thing in that kind of shooting is the trust the director has in the camera crew, and the confidence that the cameraman has in the director, that the director is telling him the truth, that what he is doing is right or wrong. There's also the question of trust and confidence between the crew and the principals. I guess one of the nicest things in this regard happened at the end of shooting, when both Billy and Antoinette said, "We could never have done this film with anyone else," which meant to me that we had done the right thing.

Arla Saare

Arla Saare is recognized as one of Canada's top film editors, with work covering a broad range of styles from the CBC's "Telescope" series to the cinéma vérité problems of A Married Couple.

Arla Saare was born in Finland, emigrated to Canada with her family at the age of eight, and grew up in Nelson, British Columbia. She graduated from Vancouver School of Art and became a medical photographer during the depression.

About her entry into film she says, "Just as I left art school the Vancouver General Hospital was running a vigorous campaign against tuberculosis and needed an artist to do charts and graphs. I then moved on to developing X rays and taking clinical films. So it was all a kind of happy accident."

In 1942 Saare joined the Canadian National Film Board under John Grierson and, after some initial work in animation, settled into the editing department. Saare stayed with the board till the early fifties and then moved back to Vancouver to work with directors such as Ron Kelly, Gene Lawrence, and Stan Fox. It was during this period that Saare met Allan King and cut his first film, Skid Row *(1956).*

Besides being principal editor of "Telescope" for a number of years, Saare has also done a number of shows for Intertel. Of these the best known is probably Three Men, *a profile of United Nations secretary generals Trygve Lie, Dag Hammarskjöld, and U Thant. Since the conclusion of* A Married Couple, *Saare has been principally engaged on a film by Peter Pearson about eastern Ontario. This is one of three films commissioned to mark the opening of the new Ontario Pavilion in Toronto harbor.*

Q. Though you are very well known as an editor, I understand that you entered films in an entirely different capacity. What in fact was your first film job?

A. I started as a medical photographer in a hospital. During the war I applied to the National Film Board which was being organized under John Grierson and started as a cutter; I then went into the optical and special effects department (fades, dissolves, special effects of all kinds, shooting animation) and shot some of McLaren's early animation on the animation stand. When the CBC started in Toronto in 1952, I applied there as an editor and worked for a year cutting news, news magazines, sport shows. Then when Vancouver television opened up, I transferred over, and it was there that we set up a small, very active film unit; Ron Kelly was there, Daryl Duke, Allan King, and various other young film enthusiasts. After a while, most of the film work came to be based on Toronto, so I left the CBC and came here as a free-lancer. At that point, I worked mostly on CBC shows for three years. I was doing "Telescopes," which is a documentary style centered mainly on some prominent person—a profile. I did various shows, *Open Grave* for instance, hour-long shows for Intertel, a nature series, and so on.

Q. How long have you been associated with Allan King?

A. I met Allan in Vancouver in 1954 where I later cut his film, *Skid Row*. Then when *A Married Couple* came up, he asked me if I would cut it; but the CBC wouldn't release me, so dear old Allan waited for five months for me to get free of my contract.

Q. Could you give me your method of working with Allan on this film.

A. I suppose in a sense this was quite different from any other kind of film I've done, because Allan had screened all seventy hours of the film many times. The first ten hours were not acceptable technically, and possibly also from the point of view of the two people involved; and so when I first began to work with Allan, it was rather strange. Normally, I screen a film with a director, and if he has a point of view, or a structure, he explains it and lets me carry on; after a rough assembly he looks at it, makes some changes before the fine cut, and then the film is frozen. But in this instance, I found it rather curious that Allan and I would sit here, and he would say, "Well now, roll 102 has some interesting stuff, let's look at it." He wouldn't look at the film on the Moviola, but would watch my reaction to it. He knew pretty well what he wanted, I think, but he was interested in having a fresh point of view, maybe even a woman's point of view, I don't know; but I could see him watching me rather intently, and if I reacted favorably, it was put aside, and we would say then, "Let's use this."

Q. Can you recall some of the favorable and unfavorable reactions?

A. I suppose what always interested me in screening the rushes was the sense of humor through the whole thing and the quickness of the repartee. I would often laugh uproariously at the Moviola, certainly on the opening, when Billy and Antoinette close the door on the outside world, and start talking about the harpsichord. I felt that was a very good opening because it showed both of them sort of egging the other on and laughing at each other, and just seeing how far each could push the other.

Q. You said a moment ago that you couldn't use things because they were technically wrong, but also because they are wrong from the point of view of Billy and Antoinette. Can you think of anything which you considered was wrong or in bad taste and therefore not used?

A. I can't think of anything that was in bad taste. I'm simply speaking in terms of interest within a situation. Something would develop and not carry through; a great deal of the film was very boring. For instance, the general routine of the marriage—the cooking, the cleaning, and reading the paper, the tantrums of little Bogart, people calling—all that sort of general routine that had to be covered in order to get a broad picture of their married life. Some of it was good but a lot of it was extremely boring.

Q. Okay, so you take out ten or so hours. Where do you go from there?

A. Then we started to pull out all the things that interested us, and to assemble them. We tried right off to have some sort of vague general order, or general structure.

Q. Did you order that structure, or did Allan compose that structure?

A. Allan did it originally, in order for us to have a starting point. He said, "Now I think we might begin here, and go on to here, and here," and so on; and certainly, at the very beginning, his structure was wrong. From the show biz point of view, he felt that right off the bat we should have a violent argument. However, we could see in our first three-and-a-half-hour screening that it was too violent. Possibly four of us looked at the very rough assembly of all the material that Allan and I found interesting, and it was apparent even before we pared it down that our major problem was going to be structure.

Q. So you pulled all the interesting material, and cut it into sequences without having any idea as to the eventual order?

A. Yes, we cut it into sequences because of the way it was shot— possibly ten minutes on one segment without a camera stop. Allan and I would view it on the Moviola and say, "Out of this ten minutes, the first three minutes is good, and then it goes flat, so let's take out a minute there, and pick it up again, and pick this up"; and out of the ten minutes, we would possibly end up with five minutes, without any sort of refinement whatsoever. The segments we chose had to interest us from some point of view—humor, violence and antagonism, tenderness, whatever.

Q. You then have twenty or thirty segments which you can label violence or humor and put on rolls?

A. They weren't really labeled violence or humor or tenderness; they were labeled, strangely enough, "Argument about a harpsichord" or "Lunch at the Café de la Paix: Antoinette and her friend" or "Playing horsey with Bogart" or "Petula Clark, dance record."

Q. How did you decide on the beginning and the end of the film?

A. Well, the beginning remained pretty much the way it was originally. It was very difficult to find the beginning. It's so much easier in a film that is structured from the very beginning; in one minute, you can set a scene. When there is no structure, when it is vérité, it takes much longer because the scenes aren't shot in that way, and therefore, you have to find some device.

Q. You start with the discussion about the harpsichord. Had you any alternatives for the beginning in mind?

A. We had about three. Allan originally thought we should begin right off the bat and show an argument. Then he also toyed with the idea of beginning with that wonderful scene where Antoinette is sitting on Billy's lap and they are playing *The Magic Flute*, and she is weeping. Allan wanted to begin with that but then he thought, that will put off the average movie going audience. Who knows *The Magic Flute*, and what kind of arty film is this? So we stayed with the discussion about the harpsichord at the beginning. It was a little stilted, but I think it had humor to it; and right off the bat, they go upstairs and go to bed. We begin to see a little bit of their problems about marriage, because Antoinette doesn't want Billy to bother her. Of course, at that point, we have to see what the house is like, find the child, see the dog, see what kind of a job he has, what kind of a person she is. This originally was quite long, and involved the boring mechanics of setting the scene, what kind of house they have and so on, and showing their status.

Q. How much does Allan work over you, and how much does he leave you alone?

A. Normally, directors and producers leave me very much alone; but in this instance, because Allan was so conversant with the whole topic of the marriage in crisis and I'm a single person, I never argued with him, because I could never find anything to argue with—except possibly later on. At our first screening with a large audience (maybe thirty people) it was quite evident that the film was sympathetic to Antoinette, and Billy was terribly unlikable. And so at that point, Allan said, "We must soften Billy, get more interesting stuff of Billy, and cut Antoinette down a bit, so there will be more of a balance." Then Allan and I looked at all the materials that we had discarded and were able jointly, and with no argument, to say, "This is just great; he looks fine here; he's sympathetic, funny, a little pathetic."

Q. Can you give me an example of material which you added to make Billy appear more sympathetic?

A. There's a wonderful scene where they have unpacked their stereo equipment and are playing records and dancing. They are both very gay and having a lot of fun; and then at the end of it, they go upstairs and to bed, and he sits on her bed and says, "There are only three things in life I want—fame . . ." (fame is what he wants most—I've forgotten the other two), and she says, "Not me, I want people to like me." He says, "You're such a liar; you want fame too and want everyone around to say, 'There she is, there she goes, the beautiful Mrs. Edwards.'"

Obviously she is very desirable to him at that moment, so he picks her up and takes her into the master bed, and pleads with her to please stay there but she says, "Why do I have to stay here? Why can't I sleep in my own bed? For weeks you let me sleep in my own bed." Billy is still pleading with her, and she says, "That was the answer when we first got married, that was the answer—separate bedrooms," but that was ten years ago. So he was very pleading and very soft and I think it gave a full dimension at that point that we needed very badly.

Q. Are you saying that the whole of this sequence was only inserted at a later stage?

A. Yes. It's a beautiful sequence, and I don't know why we didn't include it earlier. I suppose we were so interested in the car fight, and that terrible fight that still sends shivers up my spine where he throws her out of the house. Another sequence we added later was that charming sequence about the new regime—"There's going to be a new thing in this house; we are going to sprinkle spiritual lux around"—that was added at a later time. In effect, we were adding a gay, later sequence and a little gay, soft, sympathetic to Billy sequence.

Q. What were the other sequences that were filmed, but which you decided not to use?

A. There was one sequence that I was desperately anxious to have in. At the end of the party in Maine, they go to bed; it's four o'clock in the morning, and Antoinette says, "Bring the clock," and he says, "What do you want the clock for?" and she says, "So I can see what time it is when we get up," and he says, "I'm not going to bring it," and she snuggles down in bed and says, "Bring it," and he says, "I won't"; she says, "You jerk." The whole sequence was so gay and so delightful that I hated to lose it. I suppose it was mostly the quality of the shooting and the iron bedstead; and it was so obviously a cottage, and they had had a good time at the party, and most of all Antoinette was so delighted to go to bed so late and wanted that clock so badly, and he wouldn't bring it.

Q. Allan said it was very difficult to cut the party sequence; can you explain why?

A. The party sequence gave us more trouble than anything else because we were trying to show Antoinette being very interested in another man. When we were looking at the rushes of her talking to this other guy at the party, they lasted for a good hour. Antoinette was putting on for the guy; he was interested in her; and there was the play of hands, the unconscious play with wedding rings, and she was looking terribly sexy. Looking at this, it was so obvious to us that she was putting herself on for this man, that she was fascinated by him and he was by her; but when it came to cutting it down, telescoping it into four or five minutes, nothing worked. The sex part didn't come out, her dress slowly falling off, and this playing with wedding rings—nothing worked. I had it cut, I would say four times, and put everything back where it was originally; we looked at it again and tried to find other segments of it that would bring out this strange sort of interlude. But we couldn't make it work.

Finally, we made it work by having Patricia Watson come in and look at it with us again; strangely, in the end it did work, but not because we used the most sexy scenes, but because we used lines that had no real meaning at all. Pat suggested this business of taking sentences that really had no meaning, and putting them together so that we weren't following what they were saying so much as just watching. Originally, our problem had been one of trying to make their conversation make sense.

Q. Can we talk about problems of structure?

A. I would say that, next to the party sequence in Maine, structure gave us the most trouble. We had three or four or five major ingredients. We had the car fight which was terribly important; we had the record-return fight, which was important; we had the lovely, tender scene that was important. Originally, the tender scene followed a party in Toronto; that party was shot by Richard, and he obviously wasn't interested in the party.

Q. What do you call the lovely, tender scene?

A. Where she is sitting on his lap and they are playing *The Magic Flute*. It now follows the sequence in Maine, so of course we had to move that around. But the party in Toronto, as far as I was concerned, was a disaster; I couldn't make anything work in it, and it wasn't important anyway. We had trouble placing the tender scene, but it made sense to us to have it follow the party in Maine. In other words, you can make what you like out of why she is crying, after her session with the other man. As a viewer and as an editor, I would say that when Antoinette is sitting on Billy's lap, weeping, and we hear the lovely *Magic Flute,* we take it—or I take it, as I think most of the audience takes it—that she regrets the session with the young attractive man whom she has just had a strange conversation with, and she regrets the misunderstandings and arguments that they have; and so in effect, she is weeping for everything that takes them apart from each other.

Q. This, of course, is fiction documentary, and you put things together nonchronologically. Do you think that the audience has realized this is not a chronological sequence?

A. I am sure that the audience doesn't realize this, and I don't see why they should. I don't see why we shouldn't present something that makes sense in some form of structure of our own, because we can all take out of this film what we choose to take out of it; but I think it's rather wonderful that we were able to make that one scene so poignant by having it follow a flirting scene—and she is a real flirt in that scene.

Q. Did you have difficulties with the ending?

A. No, there were no alternative endings. The problem was where to put the car fight. We juggled, I would say, for a good six weeks, Allan and I. We juggled the car fight; we had it early, we had it late, and finally we realized that we would have to have it within the first third of the film, in order to give the film strength and to give the film a meaning; because there were so many sequences in the film that were either just funny or routine, things that we had to get out of the way.

Q. Coming back to basic problems of cutting, if you have, say, a ten-minute sequence, do you work from a transcript on which Allan underlines, "cut from here to here"? Or are you just looking at the viewer, and say, "All right we'll take it from here, from this point to this point"?

A. No, Allan and I screened every sequence pretty thoroughly, and on the Moviola we made up our minds as to where we should begin and what segment out of that we would use. We had transcripts to work from, and of course originally we had chosen very long sequences; but after it was pared down, we were able to cut it rather finely. In fact it was very difficult to cut. Normally one's angle changes so often in a feature film. You have so many choices; you

A MARRIED COUPLE Second Draft of Sequence Order	A MARRIED COUPLE Third Draft of Sequence Order
	Act I
Harp	Harpsichord & To Bed
Make-up	Wake-up
Breakfast	Breakfast
Ext. Esplanade	Exterior Recording Session
Cafe	Recording Session
Psych.	House Cleaning
Supper Pre-car	Supper
Car Fight	"Who Drives Car" Fight
Exit Ant.	
Beethoven 9th	*Act II*
Ext. Rec. Studio	
Housework	Cafe De La Paix
Rec. Session	Martin Goodman
Horsey	Dance Class
Kitchen Discussion	Horsey with Bogart & Merton
Record Discussion	Supper with Kitchen & Records
Hi-Fi	Hi-Fi Listening
Ski Boots	Maine & Photo-Nite
Bed Rejection	
Poss. Psych.	*Act III*
Dance Class	
Goodman	Party Montage
New Regime	Tenderness
Photo-Nite, Inc. Res.	Record Return Fight
Tenderness	Supper
Right	Argument In Bed
Supper	Argument On Couch
Bed Fight	
Couch	

can do over-the-shoulder shots, you can go in for a close-up, you can get reaction shots, everything. But in this film, that was impossible, because the camera, although it was moving, didn't change framing that often; and so if we removed ten seconds here and thirty seconds there, it caused great problems.

Q. Normally, I would assume you would start your editing while the filming was still going on. So the editor can say to the photographer, I want this and this additional. Now here, the filming had been completely finished.

A. The filming had been completely finished, and the footage had been sitting for roughly four or five months before we started on it. But in no way was this a director's film. Allan will verify that he sat out in the hallway most of the time, because he didn't want to intrude. I think in only one instance was there any direction at all, any set up, and that was when Antoinette was in the Café de la Paix talking to her friend about her marriage. A lot of people have picked this up as one aspect of the film that doesn't ring true, that looks like an interview, and I think they are right.

Q. If you had been around while Richard was shooting, is there anything you would have asked him for which would have made your editing task simpler?

A. No. There was no way I could say, "Richard, get me that closeup of Bogart at the table, get me this and get me that"; there was just no way, with all the shooting that was going on, no way I could possibly have foreseen.

Q. What were the changes made between rough cut and fine cut?

A. Mostly paring out unessential setting-up scenes, mostly paring down within a sequence, cutting down the car fight (as fascinating as it was, I think possibly it is still a little long), altering structure. Where we have a beginning and an end, and how do we progress through it, how do we keep humor, argument, that whole very delicate balance of keeping a film moving. For a long time, we thought of having a flashback to Maine by using a sort of standard technique of showing slides, so we could see slides on the screen and then get to the holiday in Maine and the swim; but that proved to be too artificial.

Q. You said that this was very different from the way you normally cut a film.

A. Normally, cutting say a half-hour film for television, a director would come to me, and I would see with him possibly 10,000 feet of film, and he would say, "This is what interested me about this man, these are the things he said that I liked; I've shot this of him for you walking through the woods, and I've shot this, and I've got a shot showing him painting, and talking about his interests and his hobbies." It would then be up to me to structure it from there, and I would always have complete freedom except for a few changes that the director or producer would suggest. Within three weeks, the film would be finished, and it would be mostly my structure. But *A Married Couple* was so different because it needed the director and myself to talk constantly about the impact of scenes, to discuss structure, to cut it down where we felt either one was being maligned or not being fair to another person. It was much more a twosome in this marriage film than any other film I had worked on.

Q. What would you say was the biggest satisfaction you got out of this film?

A. When Allan first showed me the rushes and asked me if I would cut it, he showed me the car fight; I listened to it and I was horrified. I was taken aback by the language, taken back by the arguments; I really disliked the couple. But at the end of the film I knew that under my hand we had isolated segments out of two people's lives, in a rather cohesive order; and it showed Billy and Antoinette in a very sympathetic light. I think the film has charm, humor, violence, and that they are two very ordinary, very wonderful people.

2

High School
Frederick Wiseman

Fred Wiseman talks of his work as being a search for the cultural spoors of our society. So far he has four films to his credit in the search, each of which has managed to stir up more than its fair share of anger, praise, condemnation, and enthusiasm.

All of Wiseman's films deal with key institutions in American life. Titicut Follies (1967) looks at an asylum for the criminally insane; High School (1968) is a documentary about an urban middle-class school in Philadelphia; Law and Order (1969) shows the routine activities of the Kansas City Police; and Hospital (1970) illustrates the activities of a New York hospital, giving particular emphasis to the services offered to the poor.

One soon sense a similarity in style between all the films. They tend to be austere. There is no music or narration, and although they are sensitively shot there is a minimum of flamboyance and camera high jinks. And although the subjects differ, one also becomes aware that all the films are really examining the same thing, the way power is exercised and manipulated in the institution on show.

In spite of the fact that the films are sometimes quite stark and bleak, they present a depth and plumbing of human experience which may be hard to beat in the field of the documentary. They are also all curiously ambiguous, with no easy commentary to guide the viewer to a "correct" perception of the subject.

This ambiguity runs right the way through High School. The sequences are seemingly neutral. A girl is reproved for wearing a short skirt to a prom; it shows disrespect. Students need permission to make telephone calls. "Casey at the Bat" is read in an uninspired way to a listless audience. A boy who protests his punishment is told to accept it, "to establish you can be a man and take orders."

At the end of the film the school principal reads a "thank you" letter from a G.I. ex-student and says, "When you get a letter like this it means we are very successful."

North East High, where the film was shot, is a school parents and teachers want and are proud of. Value systems vary. Wiseman keeps quiet, and the viewer has to make up his own mind whether he is for or against the system.

Wiseman's career spans both law and film. He was born in 1930, graduated from Yale Law School, and served in the army from 1954 to 1956. During the following two years he practiced law in Paris and from 1958 to 1961 taught at Boston University Law School, specializing in criminal law and forensic medicine.

Although there was a mild flirtation with cinema in Paris, Wiseman's real entry into film dates from 1964 when he produced The Cool World, *which was directed by Shirley Clarke. In 1967* Titicut Follies *won documentary first prize at the Mannheim Film Festival, and both* Law and Order *and* Hospital *have received Emmys. Slowly one begins to understand why Pauline Kael wrote, "Wiseman is probably the most sophisticated intelligence to enter the documentary field in recent years."*

Q. The first documentary that you did was *Titicut Follies*. What inspired the choice of a mental institution as a subject of study?

A. When I taught law I used to take some of my students to a maximum security prison called Bridgewater, which is on the outskirts of Boston. I liked to take them there, as well as to the other prisons and courts in Massachusetts, because I thought they should have a complete idea of all the processes and situations in whch their clients and themselves could possibly be involved. Following this line of thought, I considered it right that they should have a look at all manner of institutions where their clients could possibly end up.

At Boston University Law School a lot of the students go on to become assistant DA's and DA's and judges in Massachusetts; yet most of the people working on the prosecution end of the system have little idea of where they are sending people, and the defense lawyers don't really understand what they are trying to protect their clients from. I felt, however, that a knowledge of the prison system and mental institutions was certainly as important as reading dry, dusty old court decisions. So that's how I got to know Bridgewater, and the idea of making the film grew out of that experience. I got to know the superintendent and started negotiating with him for permission to make a documentary.

Q. Was anyone willing to back you financially on the project?

A. Not in the beginning. I had to get credit from the labs, borrow equipment, and borrow money from the bank to buy the film.

Q. You seem to have plunged in feet first, from law to film. How does one go about that with so little film training?

A. I don't really know. One goes about it because one wants to do it. You do it because you must; because you're stupid enough and naive enough to take the chance. And because you think you may like doing it.

Q. Did your lack of technical knowledge bother you?

A. Not really, because I felt I knew what I wanted to get. There seems to me to be too great a mystique attached to film making. You certainly have to master a lot of the technical aspects, but film is not a science and it doesn't require three years of monastic preparation.

Q. Most television films are shot with a certain audience in mind, and also have distribution assured before completion. What was the situation with *Titicut Follies?*

A. Nobody was interested in the film till it was finished. I approached NET who wanted to buy it, but by the time they made up their minds to go ahead, a lawsuit had started in connection with the film. The Public Broadcasting Laboratory almost ran it as its first show.

Q. How did the lawsuits arise?

A. There were three basic issues. First I was accused of having breached an oral contract giving the state the right of censorship of the film. Secondly, it was alleged that the film had invaded the privacy of one of the inmates. That suit was brought in the name of the superintendent as guardian of the inmate. Thirdly, it was argued that a trust fund should be set up whereby all the receipts of the film would be held in trust for the benefit of the inmates. I won on the third issue, but lost on the first two, and the trial judge ordered that the film be burned. Luckily that decision was stayed pending appeal. In the end the Massachusetts Supreme Court ruled that the film had value, but only for professional audiences such as doctors, lawyers, judges, students, and people interested in custodial care and related fields.

What the Massachusetts Supreme Court said, in effect, was that the film could not be seen by a merely curious general public. Now this was the first time in American constitutional history, so far as my lawyers have been able to dscover, whereby a publication of any sort which has not been judged to be obscene has been banned from public viewing. It was the first time any book, movie, or play was found to be acceptable to one audience and not another. However, a petition for certiorari, which is a request of the Supreme Court to hear the case, is now pending before the United States Supreme Court. As the contract problem has been washed out and the trust fund matter settled, the only issue that's left is whether first amendment rights, guaranteed by the Constitution, can be circumscribed in this manner.

Q. What permissions did you have to get when you were doing *Titicut Follies?*

A. I had permission from the superintendent. I had permission from the commissioner of correction. I had an advisory opinion from the attorney general of Massachusetts, and I had the strong support of the then lieutenant governor. However, some of these men turned against me when the film was finished, with most of the trouble starting two or three months after the superintendent and the attorney general had seen the film.

Q. What happened after *Titicut Follies* and before *High School*?

A. The public trial part of *Follies* took place in November and December 1967, and the decision was rendered in the first week of January 1968. It was a bit dispiriting, but in the spring of 1968 I received a foundation grant to do what ultimately became *High School*.

I originally had permission to do the film in one of two high schools in Boston. Then came the *Follies* trial. One of its side effects was that though the superintendents of schools said they were personally willing to do the school film, the boards of education were upset and considered they couldn't go ahead for political reasons. I thought after the *Follies* that I would never be able to make another documentary.

I then contacted a friend of mine who is a consultant to and friendly with the board of education in Philadelphia. This friend of mine in turn called the superintendent's office at half past four one afternoon and asked whether a documentary might be made of the Philadelphia school system. Nine o'clock the next morning he called me back and said I might be able to do it, and should go down and see the people in Philadelphia. So I traveled down, visited a number of schools, picked out North East High and began work on the film.

Q. What other ideas had been in your mind at that stage besides the *High School* project?

A. What I'm aiming at is a series on American institutions, using the word "institutions" to cover a series of activities that take place in a limited geographical area with a more or less consistent group of people being involved. I want to use film technology to have a look at places like high schools, hospitals, prisons, and police, which seem to be very fresh material for film; I want to get away from what I consider to be the typical documentary where you follow one charming person around or one Hollywood star around. I want to make films where the institutions will be the star but will also reflect larger issues in general society. In other words the specific issues that I'm filming, such as institutional management, should be very relevant by analogy to some of the larger issues around us. It is, in a sense, like being on the track of the abominable snowman. You're looking for cultural spoors, but you're looking in a well-defined area.

Q. Did you have any preconceived notions of what you would find in the two high schools you picked out?

A. Not really. I knew I didn't want to do a black school, because that scene had been overworked. There were all these heart-rending stories about the problems in a black school, all of which were and are true, but there was really nothing more to be said about it. I felt it would be more interesting instead to have a look at what was thought to be a good school, and to see the kinds of values being taught to the students. I really had no preconceived ideas since I hadn't been back to visit a school for years.

Q. Did you do much research into literature giving the background of schools today?

A. I tried a couple of the sociology books but I don't understand the language. I found one writer whom I thought was good, Edgar Friedenberg, but this wasn't a book research oriented project. I tried to make it a kind of expedition where the product of the expedition is the final film. The film is both a theory of and a report on what I have learned. The film is a kind of natural history. I think it is a terrible mistake to go into a subject like this with a set of views which you impose on the material. What is important is to be able to respond to the material, and not distort it to fit a preconceived view or a stereotyped notion.

Q. You call your films "quests for natural history." If I find a dinosaur, I'm likely to regard it as typical of a certain species. Do you see any dangers of your films being untypical of the wider areas of the subjects you're studying?

A. I wouldn't know what's typical or untypical in film, or in anything else. My films are totally subjective. The objective–subjective argument is from my view, at least in film terms, a lot of nonsense. The films are my response to a certain experience. To the extent that people who are acknowledged experts (however one becomes an acknowledged expert) recognize similarities between what they find in my films and in their own work, that's all well and good. But what I want to avoid is any of the films being considered the definitive statement on the material or on the institution in question.

Q. What caused you to finally center on North East High?

A. The thing that really clinched the decision was the fact that by common consensus North East High was thought to be one of the two best high schools in Philadelphia. The other top school was all male. This made the setting slightly unnatural and, therefore, decided me in favor of North East High.

Q. You did the sound yourself on the film, but used Richard Leiterman for cameraman. Was there any particular reason why you chose him?

A. I met Richard, liked him, and he was available when I wanted to start. We discussed what we wanted to do, then just went ahead.

Q. There's obviously an organizational problem in planning a day's shooting, even in vérité films. How did you solve that problem, and what was your relationship with the teachers?

A. Once I got permission from the superintendent and from the school principal, I asked the principal to publicize the whole film project as widely as possible in the school. This she did by speaking to the faculty and to the whole school in various assemblies. There was also an announcement made in the school daily bulletin which said that no one need have his picture taken if he didn't want to.

Q. Were any limitations imposed upon you?

A. I never accept any. Sometimes after films are completed people feel retrospectively that they had a right of censorship, but there are never any written documents that support that view. I couldn't make a film which gave someone else the right to control the final print.

Q. Did you have a total opening to every classroom?

A. I was never denied permission to go into any class.

Q. How did you go about the daily schedule?

A. It was primarily a matter of casing the place. I went out a couple of days before we started shooting, but I don't think that there's any point in spending a long time nosing around without beginning shooting because something may happen which is the once-in-a-lifetime incident. In all my films, I've just gone in the first day and started. It's a combination of developing a theory about the institution, which you then set out to test against your actual experience.

A high school, like any institution, is a self-contained society and you have to hunt out the places where power is exercised. That's where you're going to find the real values of the institution expressed. In one way the film is organized around the contrast between the formal values of openness, trust, sensitivity, democracy, and understanding, and the actual practice of the school which is quite authoritarian. It therefore became very necessary to see what was being done by the principal, the vice-principals, and the dean of discipline. That was one side. The other was to see what sort of values came to the surface in the actual practice of teaching, in the history and economics classes, in home economics, in the gym class, in the lectures on sex, and so on.

In one way it was like being on an expedition. You have a formal sense of what the place looks like, and then you work from your judgment and intuition. You also quickly develop a set of informants. For instance, there's one sequence in the film where a woman teacher reads "Casey at the Bat." I found her through Michael, who is the kid who's lectured to about being a man by the dean of discipline. Michael kind of hung around and then came up to me one day in the corridor and said, "You guys have gotta go see my English teacher." I went to the English class and found the teacher doing a multiple choice test on *Hamlet,* which went something like this: "Hamlet hates Polonius———; loves Polonius———; is indifferent to Polonius———. Mark off the correct answer." We went back the next day and she was reading "Casey at the Bat." It was marvelous material, and I had to restrain myself from going back and filming her reading *Macbeth.* Making a documentary like this is in one sense a very rational process, and in another it's highly nonrational and intuitive. You've also got to be lucky.

Q. How much footage did you shoot?

A. About 80,000 feet. All the films have a similar range of 70,000 to 90,000 feet.

Q. How long were you there?

A. Twenty-two shooting days. Four weeks of school.

Q. In many other documentaries the structure very clearly imposes a beginning, a middle, and an end, and there is an obvious way of putting it together. Here you have nothing like that. How did you cope with the problem of finding the right structure?

A. It's a matter of the final film being both a report of what you find and a reflection of your experiences and feelings about what you find. So it's really a question of trying to think your way through the material. I've been at North East High for twenty-two days. I've got this great glop of forty hours of film, and it evokes certain responses. It's like a reality dream. I try to see the themes that are inherent in the material. For example, I'm interested in the contrast between the formal values and the ideology of the school, and the actual practice. The problem then comes in expressing this conflict not just intellectually, but also in concrete film terms. This also leads to another issue: How can I, as a film maker, express abstract ideas in film terms without being didactic.

Q. Can you give me an example?

A. One of the things that I felt most about North East High was the boredom, the mechanical nature of so much of the curriculum, and the tremendous indifference to all the things that they thought they were really doing. That's on the "feeling" side. Then the first thing that struck me physically about North East High was it looked like the General Motors assembly plant. So what I wanted to do was open the film with a sequence which would convey the grey physical setting, but would also give a mental idea of the indifference and the boredom.

Now it so happened that as I drove up the parkway to school, almost every day I heard a song by Otis Redding played on the radio called "Dock of the Bay." At the time I never really paid any attention to the song, but when I felt I wanted to start with one of those row houses in Philadelphia and the factory look of the school, the song started creeping back to my mind. I hadn't really paid any attention to the words but it's really about the American dream. It's about a guy who has left Georgia and gone to California in search of America. He's trying to find out who he is and what's going on, or what it all adds up to. And he's sitting on the dock of the bay feeling dreadful. He's at the end of the continent. He's traveled all over and it doesn't mean a goddamned thing to him! He's out of it! This is the black man talking in the most immediate way about the black experience in America. But he's also talking about the difference between the promise and what actually happened; and that seemed to me to be very relevant to the subject I was filming, so I put it at the beginning of the film.

Q. At the end of the film the principal reads out a letter from an ex-pupil, a GI, written while he's stationed on an aircraft carrier off Vietnam, about to land behind the DMZ. The letter expresses his love for his school days and complete satisfaction with "the system." When did that sequence take place in terms of your actual shooting?

A. It was a gift. It was the last day and the very last thing shot. That's what I mean by "you have to be lucky." There was a faculty meeting on the last afternoon I was there; I got up and addressed the faculty and thanked everybody for their cooperation and for the wonderful spirit we had there, and I said how much we enjoyed being there. I didn't do it in a mock way because they had indeed been very cooperative, and I meant everything I said. Then I sat down and the principal got up, started reading the letter; and we started shooting. So we got one of the best sequences in the film just as we were quitting.

Q. Did you have any idea she was going to read the letter?

A. Absolutely none. There it was, and it expressed the whole essence of the school. The boy has adopted the "correct" attitudes to society, and what does it matter if he has lost his own uniqueness along the way. It was also the perfect counterpoint to the beginning. You begin the film showing a factory process, and you end with a view of the perfect product.

Q. What sequences got altered most between rough cut and fine cut?

73

A. In the first crack at the film there was a lot more about the space trip. In fact, there was enough material there to make a whole separate movie on the space trip, which I may get around to doing, as it was a nice parody on the whole space thing. I also took out a sequence from the school show. They were doing *Carrousel*, and in the show there was some kind of encounter between the teacher and the students—but it was very arch, so I didn't use it.

Q. Many documentaries use the subjective interview or comment to get views of a situation. I notice in your films no one does that.

A. No. I don't use interviews. That's where you get all the formal, pompous bullshit. I'm more interested in trying to wing it and take a chance; I work on the assumption that when people are involved in a meaningful situation something quite penetrating and illuminating may emerge. In such a situation they are not going to make pompous statements about life in our times, but will talk naturally and easily. Your bullshit meter gets very sensitive to the setup interviews. It's much more interesting to wing it, get the actual stuff in, and then put it together in a way that relates to certain common themes.

Q. Do you ever find, after winging it, that you've got an interesting sociological study, but you haven't got a clue how it's all going to hang together?

A. You never know that till you finish. And then you're just making a judgment of whether you like the finished product. Naturally you hope that somebody else likes it, but that gets you back to the audience question. I think it's totally impossible to make a film with an audience in mind. I make a film to satisfy my own internal standards as to quality and integrity, and I try like hell to make it meet those standards. I wouldn't know how to make it specifically for the guy at Harvard or the guy at Iowa, because I don't know who he is. This thing of becoming a cultural arbitrator, of saying it's okay for this kind of guy and not okay for that kind, it's all nonsense.

Q. The most striking thing in your film is the noninvolvement and nonparticipation of the students. Some people have said maybe you just took noninvolved students to meet your thesis.

A. One of the most depressing things about the whole experience there was the total passivity of the students. It wasn't something I selected. It was around the whole place and I couldn't believe it. This was in the spring of 1968, just around the time that Johnson had withdrawn and the bombing of North Vietnam had been halted. McCarthy had won the New Hampshire primary. Bobby Kennedy was going in. King had been killed. There was a fantastic amount going on in the country of great importance. There was a lot going on in Philadelphia, but these kids were really out of it. The only lively bunch that I found were those kids in the scene toward the end of the film. That was in extra-curricular, in what they call "the human relations discussion club" that met after school. Those kids were easily the liveliest bunch, and they were all just about drop outs.

Q. What has been the reaction of the school, and what has been the general reaction to the film?

A. It's hard to say anything about the reaction of the school because it hasn't yet been shown there. The superintendent saw the film in December 1968, liked it, and showed it to the staff in the board of education building while I was present. And it was very well received. A few people said they didn't like it and that they thought it was biased, but the superintendent said it was an accurate portrayal of the school and schools like it across the country. Afterwards the superintendent asked me to work with him in presenting the film at the school. He said there ought to be some presentation, and we ought to spend two or three days up there, helping the faculty in preparing to discuss the film. I said I would be happy to participate.

I didn't hear from the superintendent until February 1969, when he said he wanted to borrow the film to show to his class at the graduate school of education. Then some national reviews began to appear which were very favorable to the film and quite critical of the school. When this happened the principal of the school announced in Philadelphia that she had a right of censorship over the film. Well, I still had the *Follies* thing pretty fresh in mind and could see it beginning to shape up like the old story. So my lawyers said, "Don't show the film in Philadelphia until she acknowledges she has no right of censorship over the film."

There were also a series of intermediate steps. We went down and showed it to the board of education and tried to negotiate with them to get the film shown down there. While we were discussing the film the superintendent played a very interesting and curious game, and it appeared that there was a lot of political pressure on him to denounce the film. So one day he held a press conference and denounced the film and denounced me, and yet the very same day he called me up and said that I shouldn't pay any attention to it. He said he had to do it for political purposes and hoped I understood. Anyway, the net result is that the film hasn't yet been shown in Philadelphia, though it's been seen in most other parts of the country.

3

Salesman
Albert Maysles

It's the greatest piece of literature of all time. . . .
The Bible runs as little as $4.95, and we have three
plans on it. Cash. C.O.D. And a little Catholic honor
plan.

PAUL, IN "SALESMAN"

*Albert Maysles, or Al as he prefers, is one of the best documentary
cameramen in the United States, "the greatest" according to Jean-Luc
Godard. He is also, together with his younger brother David, one of
the key North American figures in the development of cinéma
vérité or, to use a term they both prefer, direct cinema.*

*Maysles was born in Boston and raised in Brookline, Massachusetts.
During World War II he enlisted in the army and was assigned to
the tank corps. Following demobilization, he gained a BA at Syracuse
University and an MA at Boston University, where he later taught
psychology for three years.*

*Both of the Maysles brothers started in film in 1956, but in the be-
ginning followed separate paths. Thus, while David worked as a production assistant on two Marilyn Monroe pictures, Al went to Russia
to make a film on mental health care.*

*Their work as a team dates from 1957 when David and Al decided
to travel from Munich to Moscow together to make a film about the
aftermath of the Polish student revolution.*

*During the early sixties both David and Al were associated in ex-
perimental television projects for Time, Inc., together with Robert
Drew, Ricky Leacock, and Don Pennebaker. Al's main contribution
to all this was the shooting of* Yanqui No *and part of* Primary.

*In 1963 the brothers produced what was, till recently, their most
famous film* Showman, *a controversial hour-long portrait of movie
mogul Joseph Levine. This was followed by films about the Beatles,
Truman Capote, and* Meet Marlon Brando *(1966). In 1970 Al and
David, and Charlotte Zwerin also produced* Gimme Shelter, *which
featured the playing of the Rolling Stones and an alleged murder by
a member of the Hell's Angels gang. Apart from the "portrait" films,
the brothers have also produced a considerable number of industrial
films, and Al was invited to France to shoot one section of a four-part
feature for Godard.*

Salesman *(1969) covers six weeks in the life of four traveling Bible salesmen. One sees them on a typical day pitching wares in snow-bound New England and later swapping experiences in their motel. One follows them to a super sales meeting in Chicago, and later travels with them to Florida for more door banging, exhortation, and selling on the Catholic honor plan (an installment gimmick).*

As the film progresses it increasingly focuses on the personal crisis of Paul, a likeable man of 55. Paul has been selling for 22 years, but something has gone wrong. He is beginning to confront the failure of the dream of riches and independence, and it is agonizing watching him fall apart at the seams.

The film then is an intensely moving portrait of an ordinary human being, which also provides an insight into part of the American milieu. It's a slow and sometimes ponderous film to watch, but it illustrates some of the most interesting things about Al's work, such as his camera versatility and his extraordinary sensitivity to people and situations. It also demonstrates the fundamental difference between European and American exponents of vérité—the former being deliberate, obtrusive, and provoking and the latter passive and as detached from the action as possible.

The Maysles call the film "a nonfiction dramatic feature." Like A Married Couple *it is a move in a new direction. Besides broadening the whole concept of the feature, it also gets away from the usual vérité emphasis on stars or major crises to concentrate on normal and uneventful facets of the human situation.*

But it also provokes certain major questions. Would this idea of following the world of the ordinary really have worked if Paul's identity crisis hadn't occurred to give the film a focus. In other words, are the normal conventions of drama and conflict still essential to provide a structure for this more human and low-key movement of vérité. Maybe the answer will be seen in the next film of the Maysles which is scheduled to be a highly personal movie starring their mother, themselves, and the whole family.

Q. What did you do before you started making films?

A. I used to teach psychology at Boston University. I also had a number of jobs, including selling Fuller brushes from door to door. When I got out of college, I worked for several weeks as an encyclopedia salesman with the Encyclopedia Americana and discovered the whole canned speech that they used for their customers. I believed every bit of it, and it took me a week or two before I began to see that there was a basic deception involved in that kind of selling. So I quit in the third week, although I had made an awful lot of money. That adds some background to the film *Salesman*.

Q. Who taught you the rudiments of film making?

A. Nobody taught me anything about movie making. When I was a kid I had a little still camera that I bought in a hardware store called a Univex. The pictures were so small that the film size was called "00" and cost 10 cents a roll. After a while I vowed I would never take any pictures again until I could get decent equipment. That didn't come till 1954 when I took a friend's Leica out of hock for $200; in turn for that favor he said, "Take the camera with you on your trip to Europe," so I had a chance to take my first pictures with a decent camera. The following year I went to Russia and borrowed a 16 mm camera from CBS. I told them I was going to Russia, could get into the mental hospitals, and might be able to make an interesting movie. Mind you, I had never taken any movies before. I met the CBS people a week before I departed and they gave me 100 feet of film to practice shooting with. I shot some stuff, CBS processed it, and told me some of the things I had been doing wrong, which were fairly obvious to me; the fact that I wasn't holding the camera steady, the fact that I wasn't holding the shots long enough. That was my training and off I went.

My whole interest in making the film was as a discovery. It was something that nobody knew anything about; there was only one book in this country written on the psychiatry in Russia. I came back, showed the film to CBS, but they weren't very interested because mental health in Russia didn't have "political significance." I then finished the film on my own, got it shown on network television in Canada, and also sold it to a drug company. So I more than made my money back on it.

Q. You've said on record that you consider *Showman* and *Salesman* the best films you've done. Was *Salesman* your idea coming from your experience selling encyclopedias? Was it David's? Or did the two of you generate it?

A. We were always making lists of subjects for films, and one thing that had been on our list for a long time was a salesman's convention. But nothing got done about it. Then in 1966 David had a lunch conversation with Joe Fox of Random House Publishing Company. We knew Joe, because a little while earlier we had filmed Truman Capote, and Joe was his editor. Anyway, David told Joe we were looking for a nonfiction subject to make into a feature. We wanted to do in film what Capote had done in literature, with his novel *In Cold*

Blood. Now Joe used to be a book salesman, and when he said "why not film a traveling salesman?" that immediately sparked an interest in David; when David in turn told me of his conversation with Joe it immediately clicked with me as well.

Then David got to work writing letters to different kinds of selling companies—Geritol and the like—companies that sell you everything and anything. We thought of book salesmen too, although for my part I had been turned off the whole scene and would never have considered an encyclopedia salesman because the whole thing is such a low form of selling. Then David met a Jewish high school friend who was selling Bibles in Manhattan, and this turned us in a fresh direction. A Bible salesman was something different. Selling the Bible represented a metaphor of our time, which had ramifications reaching to every avenue of our culture. So that's how we happened to choose this subject.

Q. In the film your principals are salesmen for the Mid-American Bible Company. Was this the first company you contacted?

A. We hired a researcher to look into the various companies, and it was quite a long time before we found the right one. For one thing, although we would explain by letter or telephone what we were after, no one could really grasp the concept. They were used to scripted movies and so didn't know what they would have to do for this film. They were also very sensitive about how they would be portrayed, so it was very difficult to get them to cooperate or understand what we wanted to do.

Q. How did you zero in on the Mid-American Bible Company?

A. We got as far as talking to one salesman who we thought would be good. We went to Rhode Island, and he was terrific. He was a guy who had a confusion of roles. On the one hand he would talk about how the customer was a sucker; and on the other hand, he really wanted to be like his brother who was a high school teacher. He would have been great but his boss didn't want to cooperate, and without this cooperation we were dead. So we decided not to film him. Also, he was the kind of salesman who not only sold the Bible, but also sold magazine subscriptions, *Look* magazine, all that sort of thing. It was getting too diffuse and detracted from the pure Bible salesman idea.

I don't know exactly how we heard about Mid-American. David had heard of a company in Chicago that had some ninety salesmen on the road selling Bibles; and he contacted one of the owners of the company in Chicago. This was Kenny Turner, who is in the film. We met Kenny, and as we were interested in going back to New

England where we come from, David asked if Kenny had any salesmen in the New England territory. Kenny said, "Yes. We have four
guys; they work together," and almost with that there was a keen
interest on our part.

When we met the guys, we found out they went by names they
had invented for themselves—the Badger, the Bull, the Gipper, and
the Rabbit. That's very Irish, and even at that early point it warmed
the cockles of my heart. This was because although my father was
brought up Jewish, he lived in a totally Irish neighborhood and was
probably as Irish as he was Jewish. This also gave a peculiar twist
to the filming of *Salesman*, because traditionally the salesman is supposed to be Jewish, and someone from an Irish background like Paul
would normally work as a clerk at the post office or as some other
kind of government employee, which is what my father did. So there
was a curious kind of reversal of roles which accounted for my special interest in the thing.

Q. Did you go out with the four salesmen before you started filming? Did you get any feeling of their personalities in relationship to
people, or their problems or hang ups?

A. I would say that most of it was on a feeling level. We liked the
guys, all four of them, and we could see the potential from the start.
We looked into the Rabbit's face for example, and those eyes were
so extraordinary; he just looked off in kind of a dreamy way. The
four complemented each other. At first we didn't know for sure
whether Paul would be the main character or whether it might be
Charlie the Gipper; but we knew that one of them could and would
be, so we were sure we had a major character.

Q. What were the reactions of Paul and the others when you suggested the film?

A. They were kind of amused; they didn't know quite what to make
of it because they didn't think they were worth it. They couldn't
understand a film being made of their lives, because they seemed to
be so ordinary. I guess almost anybody would feel that way because
the whole history of movie making has been to portray extraordinary
things, and no one has felt that much confidence in looking at life
itself and finding the extraordinary in the ordinary. But one person
who expressed the idea sixty years ago was Tolstoy. His first reaction
to the movies was when somebody came to his home in Moscow in
1906, saw him sitting on the porch, and shot some home movies of
him. They showed him the stuff a few days later, and Tolstoy said,
"That's it! We don't have to invent stories any more; we have an
instrument now where movies can be made of ordinary people, of

Russia, in ordinary situations; and we don't have to invent stories any more."

Q. After the men had agreed to appear, what financial arrangements or general arrangements did you make with them? Did you tell them how long you expected to shoot?

A. We figured we would need maybe two or three months, and we ended up using six weeks. We told them we would need to be with them for three months, on and off, and they agreed to that. I believe we paid them $100 each, and they signed a release; we also agreed that we would pay their expenses—not all their expenses, but things like the trip to Florida. Their expenses, in fact, came to something between $10,000 and $15,000, so it was a very sizable chunk. There were two factors; we didn't have much money to give them, but what was even more important, we didn't want to make an arrangement that would make them feel like performers.

Q. Can we get into the actual filming and its problems?

A. It's pretty simple. You just ask the guy what's coming up, and you look into his schedule. He doesn't know the kinds of things that are going to make good film for you; so to a certain extent you have to act intuitively. Each salesman would have a hundred cards of people's addresses that he would pick up at the beginning of the week, and he would say he was going to such and such a person today and we would go with him. We had a terrific advantage in filming four people rather than one, because we could break away from one person and give him a rest and pick up with another one.

Q. How did you get over the problem of knocking on a door and suddenly confronting a stranger, not only with a Bible salesman, but also with a cameraman?

A. You have to know and impress on yourself that it's not going to be a problem; you may be wrong, but you have to feel quite confident that your presence isn't going to adversely affect what's going on.

Q. What did you say when you knocked on the door of the potential customer?

A. The salesman would knock on the door, and I would have to make a judgment right then and there whether to start filming at that moment—which I did sometimes—or whether to put the camera down. Then maybe he would start chatting, and I would be filming. Then, not long after that, Paul or Raymond would introduce us by name and we would explain why we were there. The explanation would usually run something like, "We are making a film for movie theatres and television about this salesman and the three people he works with. We're following them from house to house, and we never know exactly what's going to take place; but we are very interested in the job and find it very likable, and the purpose of the film is inventing more than just a human interest story." That took me maybe thirty seconds. Most people at that point would then say they understood, even though perhaps they didn't; but we would try to explain honestly what we really were about, and that was enough. Then when the whole filming was over, maybe twenty minutes or thirty minutes later, they would say, "Tell me once more what this is all about," and then we would explain and give them a release form which they would sign.

Q. I am interested in the technical problem of filming a scene with just the one camera, and your difficulty in trying to follow actions and reactions. How do you approach all this?

A. Well, I don't think in terms of actions and reactions. I don't think in technical terms at all, but rather of what I really want to get, and what I really want to get is a front head-on look at the person who is talking at the time. I'm not thinking of an artistic shot or an artistic composition of shots, though that's important. I suppose that approach makes the editing more difficult, but I feel that it is one of the reasons why the human content of the film is so strong and so totally convincing, because my concentration is on what I feel I have to get of the person, rather than some artistic thing I'm trying to prove. In none of the shooting, for example, do you have any views that are from high up or from low down. There is one shot where I'm looking down on a card table, but it was shot that way because that was the best way to get the coverage and not because I wanted to be artistic.

Q. What was the size of your crew?

A. The crew consisted of just David and myself. I did all the lighting and David handled the Nagra tape recorder.

Q. How did you manage your lighting? Did you use a sun gun and bounce light?

A. I have a light on the camera which is a sun gun with a 1,000-watt bulb in it. When I entered a home I would just plug it into the wall and flip it on. I also had a battery on me so that I could use the same lamp with a 250-watt bulb, and flip that on if necessary. You remember the scene where I follow the guy out of the house at night and into the car? Well, I couldn't walk out of there and still use the light plugged into the wall, so I flicked on my battery power, followed him out of the house, and as he pulled the car out of the garage I was still shooting with the sun gun. All of these things were one time efforts—never any reshooting.

Q. What film stock were you using?

A. Plus X and double X which I would rate at 125 ASA, which is normal for it. Very occasionally I would push it a stop. As for shooting ratio I think it was as high as forty to one.

Q. What would you say was the biggest problem or problems in the shooting?

A. The biggest problem was money, but more specifically, having only 400 feet of film in a magazine is a pretty big hang up. I should have had 1,200-foot magazines, but they get too bulky.

Q. In this kind of intimate filming do you think the cameraman affects or alters the situation?

A. I think he always does. The problem is to handle it so that it becomes more of what the scene is rather than something different.

Q. Did your four salesmen ever deliberately play up to the camera?

A. No, I don't think so. Certainly not while the camera was on, because the moment that occurred, I would turn the camera off.

Q. I was wondering about Paul? He seems to have these monologues specially put on for the benefit of the camera.

A. That's a little special. That's where I would say our presence made him more of himself; the monologues are the kind of thing he is doing all the time.

Q. You said if Paul or the others tried to do something specially for you, you turned the camera off. Can you give me an example of that?

A. To tell you the truth, I can't remember any time when they actually tried to do anything special. I would say that there were many times when I didn't film because it would have been in bad taste, for example some of their conversations about their wives or something like that.

Q. On this question of Paul and his monologues, did you ask him questions to get him going or was it all purely spontaneous?

A. If you knew Paul, you would know that he repeats himself a million and one times, and the one thing he would always repeat was his description of the other guys. The only time we may have prompted him was when we filmed him in the automobile. We started by asking him about the guys, and then he took off by himself. It was when we were down in Florida with him, and all the filming had been finished, except for that. But that automobile conversation is the only exception. Normally, we completely left the scene alone.

Q. Were there any situations you would liked to have filmed, but for some reason or other you couldn't?

A. We once went out with the fellows before we began the film and saw them laying out their Bibles in front of a church. That was the only thing that the Bible company didn't want us to film. That forced us to make a decision—did we want to go ahead with that restriction and make the film. We thought quite long about it, and then decided that if it really was going to be the only restriction, then we would take it. However, not being able to get that, we had to get other material which made it quite clear as to how they got their potential sales leads, so that was okay. But visually, the scene in front of the church was fantastic, and I regret that we couldn't do it.

Q. Were there any discussions before or during the film between you and David as to what should be in or what should be out?

A. No. I firmly believe that a person is always revealing himself. What we get is an infinitesimally small percentage of any one man's life, so it is very selective. People say, "You're being very selective," as if to say that what we get isn't characteristic of the person. If that were so, if the handicap was so great that you could never really get anything characteristic of an individual, then you might just as well throw away every perceptive still photograph that was ever made. And here we are getting twenty-four frames a second—our images are far greater in number than in the still photographs.

Q. We were talking earlier about your switching off when you thought it would show a certain lack of taste to continue shooting. It's a very stark film in that sense, but it doesn't really go outside the confines of these men selling the Bibles, it doesn't go into their personal history or background. Was this limitation deliberate on your part?

A. We had an extraordinary entré to their lives, and we made use of that. We had footage of each of the men who is married, and of Paul who is separated. We had footage of them and their families, but we didn't use it primarily because it didn't help the film. In fact the inclusion of such stuff might have hurt it. Staying as small as we did made the film much tighter. Now some sociologists might say, "But we don't know that much about them," but they are wrong. By watching Paul on the telephone with his girlfriend you learn as much about how he relates to women, whether it's his wife or anybody else, as you would in all the stuff that we had of him with his former wife. Let me give you a reverse example. We were with Paul on the night that his daughter got married. We filmed the ceremony and all of the goings on between him and his daughter and his wife, which were very interesting; but the stuff that's in the film really is more revealing of him as a person with women and children than that material. So I think our decision to exclude it was correct.

Q. Can you tell me something about your difficulties in selling the film? Have you recovered your money yet?

A. If you have a very commercial film, you have no problem, that is if the person who is a potential distributor thinks that it's going to make a lot of money. A film like *Salesman* was more difficult because nothing like that had ever been done. Of course, that is usually what the distributors want—they want something new but they want something old. There's a paradox. There were all kinds of objections that the distributors raised in seeing this film—it was too depressing, too realistic for the public, and so forth. So we had to distribute it ourselves, in commercial theatres and at colleges—and we're doing pretty well.

Q. What was the reaction of the four salesmen when they saw the picture?

A. There was a lot of laughter, more so than from the rest of the audience. They saw it on the opening night in a full theatre, and a lot of the other people were annoyed with this group of people who were overreacting to the film. But there were other things. I know Paul cried at times when he saw it. My main impression is that they were amazed at the mass of material, and that there was so much in the film of their lives. It was very difficult; they had tried to imagine what the film would be like and couldn't. Once having seen it they were very much impressed with it. Whether it changed their notions of selling or not, I don't know. I don't think it did very much. In fact, after one of the screenings at the theatre, Ray the Bull walked out with the audience, and a man came over to him with his wife, recognized him and said, "My wife would like to buy a Bible," and the Bull said, "You mean it?" When they both said "Yes," Ray walked over to his car, pulled a Bible out of his trunk and got $50 on the spot.

Q. How did the Bible company respond to the film?

A. I'm not sure whether they were pleased with the film or not. As salesmen, they like to present everything in a positive light, but when they saw the film they recognized a certain depressing quality in it. They thought it was too bad that Paul, the star of the film, wasn't a very good salesman. But then the other three were, so they were fairly happy.

One of the main disappointments in much critical discussion of vérité style films is the failure to accord recognition to the part played by the editor in the success of such films. Too often a mass of brilliantly shot but basically unordered material is dumped into the lap of the editor—material that resembles the all-embracing notes of some primitive ethnologist—and it remains the editor's job to make sense out of the chaos and order out of confusion.

The editing of vérité material is certainly one of the most arduous and taxing tasks in documentary today. It requires not merely a competent editor (dozens of which abound in England and the United States), but a rare quality of sensitivity which is quite hard to find—a sensitivity which one sees in the work of Peter Moseley in Warrendale, *and which is very characteristic of the editing of Charlotte Zwerin.*

A number of people had mentioned the name of Charlotte Zwerin to me before I actually met her. Robert Hughes spoke highly of her work on Robert Frost, *and Terry Filgate told me she was one of the best editors in New York, with "a marvelous eye for discerning the hidden qualities of the material." Neither mentioned she was honey blonde and looked more like an art student than an extremely experienced film editor.*

Charlotte Zwerin was born in Detroit and educated at Wayne University, where she studied English literature. "We also ran a little society looking at classics, otherwise there was very little film activity in school. That was in 1952."

Following graduation Zwerin worked as a photographer on medical films, like Arla Saare, before moving to New York where she found work as an assistant editor on a Forty-second Street burlesque film. "I think it was called Strip Show *and was the first editing experience I had. Actually I was working for nothing at night, after I finished my regular job. At the same time I enrolled in City College Film School, but found I learned so much more actually working in the editing room that I dropped the course and just went from there."*

After a few small commercial jobs Zwerin went over to CBS. "I started there as a film librarian and assistant editor, and gradually went over to working on 'The Twentieth Century' series. I think I may have stayed at CBS too long, but I loved working with stock footage. It was really fantastic."

From CBS Zwerin went to NBC to work on the NBC "White Paper," series and to ABC to help edit the Churchill series. This was followed by a year associated with Leacock and Pennebaker, and the editing of Robert Hughes' feature length documentary Robert Frost: A Lover's Quarrel, *which received a 1964 Academy Award.*

Apart from some industrial promotion films, the larger proportion of Zwerin's recent work has been on vérité films for the Maysles brothers, and when I interviewed her she was in fact working on their film about the visit of the Rolling Stones to San Francisco. Among former films she has edited for Albert and David have been What's Happening *(1964), the coverage of the Beatles' trip to the United States;* With Love from Truman *(1966), a visit with Truman Capote; and* Meet Marlon Brando *(1966).* Salesman *(1967) is credited as a film by the Maysles Brothers and Charlotte Zwerin.*

Q. What were the first rushes you received?

A. They were from the meeting in Boston, when the road manager comes out and gives the four salesmen a pep talk. That batch was followed by the road selling in Boston and various sequences showing what these guys did all day long; what it was like to be on the road in snow and rain, and live day in day out in hotels.

Q. What was your reaction to these rushes?

A. I was terrified. I felt that nothing was happening. It was all undramatic and flat, and I got the impression that the people being filmed were withholding everything. And it was very painful. I began to get more of a sense of the thing in the later rushes. The sales meeting was particularly hilarious. Screened through, without any cuts, it provided a staggering portrait of the American dream, and the kind of shabby things people give themselves to so completely and totally.

Q. Did David and Al share your reaction, that a lot of it was flat and undramatic?

A. I was alone, and viewing the rushes for quality, because David and Al were still on location and needed some feedback as to what they were getting on film. It was strange. They would call and get excited about this fantastic scene they had shot, and I just didn't see it. Gradually it began to dawn on me that because they were so much part of the situation—because they were living with these four salesmen and experiencing their lives at close quarters—their enthusiasm was based on everything that was going on. But this total experience which they felt just wasn't there on the film. So it became a kind of funny problem, because when they would call, I had to show an enthusiasm I just didn't feel; it got so that I just dreaded the next call.

If I had been filming, I don't think I would have had the courage to go on as they did. But they saw and understood what they were getting, and I didn't; it was because they were living the experience and knew that eventually all the pieces would fit together, whereas I was seeing the film reel by reel, and knew nothing about the final stages.

Q. Do you think this "separation" from the shooting has any advantages for the vérité editor?

A. One of the really important contributions of an editor in a vérité film arises from the fact that he only sees what is on the screen. The cameraman will tell you that a great deal of what he gets in shooting depends on his relationship to the subject, but whatever is happening between himself and the person he's shooting distorts the event for the cameraman; he can't see the scene in perspective. But the editor has the advantage of knowing that something either *is* or *is not* conveyed on the screen. His immediate reaction isn't blunted by any personal knowledge. For example, Paul eventually became the center of the picture but I didn't know him, so I had no feeling about him. As a matter of fact I disliked him a little bit when I saw him in the rushes. I thought he was a bit self pitying, which was the opposite of what David and Al felt about him. But I think this removal from the scene helped my judgment and helped me to understand more clearly what the viewer would feel.

Q. How did David's closeness to the scene and your remoteness affect editing decisions?

A. The two seemed to balance each other, because I think I would have been a great deal harsher with the material if David hadn't been able to tell me his feelings about the four salesmen. They were feelings I just didn't have.

Q. What happened when David and Al returned from shooting?

A. David and I started structuring a story about four salesmen, very much in the order the thing was filmed. That's something that is a necessary part of cinéma vérité. When you start pulling events out of chronological order, their relationships fall apart. Something is said down here that can't be said up there, and any kind of juggling is very touchy—you stay away from it.

Anyway, we started with the four salesmen story, and it took a long time because we started off in the wrong direction. We spent about four months trying to make a story about four people, and we didn't have the material. Gradually we realized we were dealing with a story about Paul, and that these other people were minor characters in the story. Al made me understand Paul's character a bit, because of his own feeling of the Boston background. In Boston, you're Irish, or you're this or that, and the Irish tend to go into the civil service. But what touched me is that Paul believed in himself as a kind of independent free spirit. He wanted to avoid the civil service job and being locked down to a pension after twenty-five years. He thought he had avoided all of that, and was going to pursue the American dream of independence and wealth and working for oneself. But watching him in the picture, it just wasn't so.

Q. How did you proceed after settling on Paul as the main figure?

A. The first thing was to concentrate on Paul, and go to the scenes that had a lot to say about Paul. So that automatically eliminated a great deal of the other stuff, and the shots of the other salesmen. We also worked towards the sales situations that best revealed the character of Paul. There were a lot of scenes of Paul going into a house and selling books; but naturally, because of the people he met or because of his mood, some were much more revealing than others.

Q. Can you think of any scenes where David and you differed regarding their inclusion?

A. There are a couple of scenes that are in that I didn't want. I didn't like the scene where they changed the flat tire; it never communicated to me what it did to David. And there's the scene where Paul gets lost in Florida. I don't know if you have ever been to Florida, but it was really typical of Florida. Somebody started to build one of these Ali Baba cities around the late twenties; and then the depression came, so what you're left with is that marvelous city hall, and all of the streets named, ready, and waiting. My first impression was that the scene was getting very heavy handed in its humor, but I think David was right to press for its inclusion. It provided a certain relief that the audience needed; it was a kind of slapstick treatment of an event that in reality only merited a one-line funny.

Q. Can you recall sequences that were totally excluded, not just trimmed, after the rough cut?

A. We left out the wedding of Paul's daughter, and a sequence of Paul going back to Boston by train. Those sequences were actually shot after the end of the main filming, but they didn't work in to the direction of the film. There was also one scene Al shot early on, showing Charlie and his family at Christmas; but we realized very soon that this was not the proper line for the film. Also all the salesmen had a problem of stiffness and shyness in front of a camera; and whereas they were willing to cooperate about selling, they simply did not want to reveal anything about their personal lives.

We also left out part of the film shot in Chicago. After the super sales meeting the road manager had suggested that Paul and the others go to visit Feltman, the man who makes the speech at the dinner, "the world's greatest salesman of the world's best seller." I think he believed it might help the image of the company, or something like that. But it was just a beautiful scene of total awkwardness, proving again what both David and Al say, that if you try to do something that people don't normally do, it will stick out a mile.

Q. Did you ever ask Al for certain shots to help the flow of the editing?

A. Yes. As I began editing I found I needed certain establishing shots, and Al went back and got them for me. I think these shots included things like exteriors of the motel in Boston, and some stuff around the Florida motel.

Q. I'm interested in the question of continuity in editing vérité style films. Did you find this much of a problem in *Salesman*?

A. Sure, it was murderous. Al goes into a place and has so many things to think about—lighting, reasonable camera angles, how to shift position without falling over everybody—that, consequently, he can't really consider how its all going to edit smoothly. We talked about this problem all the time, and sometimes I got very angry when I felt that he wasn't really trying. But his job was very hard.

Q. Can you give me an example of a sequence that was very difficult to edit?

A. One of the funniest but also most difficult scenes, was when Charlie and the Rabbit go in to sell a Bible to this old Irish lady and her daughter in Boston. The two women were marvelous characters and very amusing, but the sequence drove me mad for a couple of months because Charlie and the Rabbit kept shifting around from the piano, to the coffee table, to the door; they went all over the place, and Al couldn't do a thing about it. He obviously couldn't tell them to sit or stay rooted to one spot, but every time Al cut away it looked as if Charlie and the Rabbit had gone to another house. The lighting of the room was also maddening and didn't help the cutting. The salesmen were in one end of the room which was black, and were wearing dark clothes, while the two women were sitting on the couch wearing very light clothes in a very light situation. There was no room to get back and get an establishing shot, and after looking at the rushes I was left with the feeling that the two groups weren't even in the same room.

Q. At one point in the film you crosscut between Paul on the train and the sales conference. Whose idea was that?

A. That was mine. I felt it was important to show the kind of pressure that Paul felt from both the sales manager and the sales situation in general, and also to set him apart from the three other salesmen, so that he assumed a greater prominence in the film.

Q. How long was the rough cut?

A. About two hours.

Q. What things did you sharpen up or change in going from the rough cut to the fine cut?

A. The selling situations were whittled down to show more of the other salesmen's relations to Paul, so that the only scene you get at the end where Paul doesn't appear is where Ray goes to sell a Bible and the couple play the Beatles' record in the background. The scene illustrates quite a lot about Paul, as it shows the ease with which Ray handles the selling in contrast to Paul's awkwardness. We also added the introduction and naming of the four salesmen in the beginning of the film. This was done because when we showed the picture to other people we discovered that the characters weren't sufficiently defined for them, and they were continually mixing up two of the salesmen.

I found these screenings much less useful than David. In fact it reached a point where they were driving me crazy. Any group of people in screening situations like that begin to feel they are called upon to offer their advice, you know, "I didn't understand this," or "I don't get that"; and if you put all the advice into a hat and try to restructure the picture to cover every point, you find it's hopeless —you can't. You accomplish nothing. I still feel that the picture suffered to a certain extent from the fact that we tried to convey information that just wasn't really necessary.

Q. At the end of the film one sees Paul standing very forlornly in the doorway. Did you ever have alternative endings in mind?

A. No. The scene where Paul sits on the bed was always the ending of the film. It was the most moving thing I saw in the rushes; he is trying to go off into his little Irish song and dance, and he can't even do it any more, and you finally know that he knows it too. It seemed the only way to end.

Q. When you finished, were you happy with the general rhythm and framework of *Salesman*?

A. I was very happy with the general structure of the film, but wasn't happy with the pace of it; I don't think anyone is. I think it is a difficult film to view. It has some excellent things but it isn't very easy for you to look at; it comes across at a very slow and rather undramatic pace. But if you finally care about Paul, and you care about what has been happening and what it all represents, then the picture becomes very meaningful and very rewarding.

91

Television Journalism

4

This Week

Jeremy Isaacs

One of my objects in film making has been to try and seize an audience which may not want to know about Vietnam, or race problems, or people poorer than themselves and persuade them to watch throughout the program, so that at the end of the broadcast they may have learnt something both intellectually and emotionally about the subject.

JEREMY ISAACS

Jeremy Isaacs was born in Glasgow in 1932 and educated at Oxford, where in 1955 he became president of the Union. He entered broadcasting in 1958 as a researcher for Granada Television, and a year later was producing current affairs programs such as "Searchlight" and documentaries on the General Strike and the Irish problem.

In 1963 Isaacs was made chief producer of "This Week," a thirty-minute television magazine, which he ran for two years, before moving over to the BBC in 1965 to become the guiding hand behind "Panorama." These two programs, along with "The World in Action," were for a number of years the top status current affairs magazine programs of the BBC and ITV, drawing in audiences of between ten and eleven million people each week.

Both programs reported from all over the world on subjects as various as the future of Africa or poverty in India. Both had the capacity to respond quickly to pressing issues, and both occasionally took direct reformist paths. Outstanding examples of such attacks were John Morgan's report for "Panorama" on the homeless of London, and "This Week's" bombardment on the subject of drunken drivers.

In his book Factual Television *Norman Swallow offers an interesting comment on the differences in styles between "This Week" and "Panorama": " 'This Week' gets into the story much faster, but to some extent the lack of an anchor man destroys the program's personality. 'This Week' is slicker than 'Panorama,' but less homely and possibly less friendly. Yet its technique is arguably more in keeping with the mood of the time."*

Besides the difference in the number of items in the two programs, which Isaacs discusses, both programs also interpreted the function of current affairs broadcasts in opposite ways. Under Paul Fox, for example, "Panorama" tended to add comment and analysis to direct

weekly news. Where Isaacs differed was in seeking a broader defini-
tion of current affairs, so as to allow a coverage of events outside the
strait jacket of the weekly or even monthly happening.

Whether a current affairs program succeeds is largely a question
of the ability and driving force of the executive producer. During
Isaacs' tenure of the hot seat at "This Week" and "Panorama," both
programs became absolutely compulsory viewing for most of the
news conscious and politically aware people in England. Since leav-
ing "Panorama" in 1966 Isaacs has moved from current affairs to fea-
tures and is presently controller of features at Thames Television.

Q. How did you get into television journalism?

A. After university and the army I thought of either newspapers or
television, and eventually ended up with a British commercial television company called Granada. The first thing that struck me was
that people were trying to make a distinction between television and
film. They used to say, "We won't have a film unit and we won't
make films. We're a television company and therefore we make television." But it very soon became apparent to us that if you could
only operate in the studio, you were hopelessly limited as a journalist.
You could discuss issues in the studio, you could even try to hear
what ordinary people had to say in the studio. But all this took place
in such a stilted and abnormal atmosphere that it was quite clear to
me that it was going to be impossible to report on current events,
either in this country or abroad, unless we used film. So eventually
we began to go into film. From then on a very large proportion of
the programs I've done have been on film rather than studio based.

After about five years of working with Granada as a producer of
various network current affairs shows and also making a few compilation and documentary films, I was invited to become the producer of a weekly current affairs program called "This Week." It
was produced for Rediffusion, and at that time was ITV's only
weekly current affairs offering. "This Week" used both film and
studio, and was a hard-news-oriented program. It ran for half an
hour a week and tried to be topical. This it did by running two, three,
and sometimes four items in any one program. But already, before I
got there the producers were being more and more tempted to use
the entire half hour to deal with one big subject of major importance
—and there were certainly enough around.

Q. What was your attitude towards this movement?

A. I seized upon this trend and codified it. I said, "That's what we're
going to do, and anything else, any subdividing of the program, will

be the exception." I also wanted to get current affairs out of the studio to stop it from becoming an endless pat-ball debate between politicians, experts, pundits. I wanted to get out and find how political decisions and diplomatic decisions and international decisions affected ordinary people both in this country and abroad. That meant film. So very soon I found myself in the business of trying to make weekly half-hour films. But it never became all film because the budget didn't allow it. Thus, for the last year of my two years at "This Week," we were making two films out of every three programs. So the schedule went: one foreign film, one domestic film, and one studio-based program.

Q. How large was your production team when you were working on "This Week," and how was it divided?

A. I had a team of maybe four reporters (because all our films were made with reporters), four or five directors, and three or four researchers. These last seemed to me absolutely crucial elements in the film-making process. Each director also had a production assistant. We used a four-man film crew, and I suppose that I had access to two four-man crews most of the time and whenever I wanted could hire additions. Finally we had two cutting rooms, with two editors and assistants and a block booking in a dubbing theatre on transmission day which was Thursdays. Most of this came to me free, that is to say it wasn't part of the direct budget. In addition I had a direct budget of something like £3,000, or $7,000, per week which had to cover stock and processing, all fares, travel, and subsistence. That was, of course, a few years ago, and budgets are much higher today.

Q. I assume you must have had some regular production meeting to plan policy?

A. When I came to "This Week" there was a meeting every Friday to discuss what went into the program the following Thursday; this was in the days when the program still had more than one item in it. People had diaries in front of them, "futures diaries," and they used to say, "Something might be going to happen in Nicaragua this weekend, can we go to Nicaragua?"

This tendency of always *responding* to the news or to predictable dates seemed to me a rather pointless activity. It meant we were responding to exactly the same news that triggered off everybody else and had to work in a frantic rush before even starting on the story. Certainly working on that kind of a schedule we would never get anything like a thorough look at the subjects we were dealing with. So I abolished the weekly conferences in that form and begged people to forget about diaries and just to start making a list of subjects which were urgent and important, rather than merely topical from day to day. We still had a weekly transmission framework, but what we were moving away from was a weekly production schedule. We were saying that we wanted to make half-hour films; since such things could easily become very expensive, we, therefore, had to be absolutely certain that the film was worth doing before we embarked on it.

Q. That seems to entail a movement towards much greater planning and research?

A. Right. The first thing I did was to employ researchers, not as frantic "fix-it" men, but as people who would go, investigate a situation, and draw up a report on the content of the story and on the form the treatment might take. They were based in England and would investigate the story abroad. However, the decision to send a researcher abroad, which might entail airfare to California, was often so expensive that one was pretty well saying, "We're going to do a program and we're sending a researcher not to find out if the program is on, but to lay it on, so that when the crew arrives and they've had some sleep, they can start filming."

We inherited in this part of British television a really impossible situation where nobody blended together. And indeed, the situation to some extent still obtains today. This was because we were a current affairs outfit, working as current affairs journalists, but were formed from two utterly distinct and disjunct sources. We were made up, on the one hand, of journalists with great experience on Fleet Street and no knowledge whatever of film making and, on the other, of film makers with some experience either in film or television and no knowledge whatever of either journalistic techniques or the content of current affairs. It now works very much better because, after a great deal of kicking and heaving and suggesting to people that they go and work elsewhere, we are left with directors working in current affairs television who are primarily current affairs animals, whose whole interest in life is what is happening in the world and who have also acquired a mastery of the technique of film making. But, nevertheless, in this company, Thames Television, we still like to work with reporters because we believe that reports should be personal reports.

Q. A lot of the executives on the American commercial networks would argue that television should avoid taking sides, and that its function is always to be "neutral" and "objective." You obviously have a different approach?

A. I don't believe in the objectivity of television. We try to be fair, we try to be balanced; but the viewer is entitled to know whose voice he's listening to in the commentary and to form some appreciation over the months and years of what the person's attitudes are.

So we still have directors working with reporters, and we still have a great deal of preparatory work done for them by a researcher, and we are a very top-heavy, clumsy team. We still have four technicians when we might be better off with three (in some situations, usually war situations, we film with only two), but we're still a caravan when we ought to be a car.

Q. Did the movement towards the use of light weight 16 mm cameras and crystal sync affect the way you shot your programs?

A. We now shoot 16 mm sync. It is scarcely believable but in 1965 we were still shooting on 35 mm. Shortly after that we started shooting on 16 mm and blowing it up to 35 mm for cutting and transmission purposes, because all our cutting-room equipment and our dubbing theatre was geared to 35 mm and not the smaller gauge. Eventually however, we became wholly geared for 16 mm; we shoot everything we can on 16 mm using double system sound. At the moment there's pressure on us to shoot striped film in two-man-crew situations, what the union regards as a short crew. But I'm against this and am trying to resist it. To my mind it would mean a serious loss of quality, particularly a loss of sound quality, if we adopted it for half-hour film making.

I ought to explain that, although I had the use of a studio every Thursday night for transmission, I decided not to use it. This meant that the man who had formerly introduced the program from his studio chair had to leave. As a result we tried to find some way of building into our half-hour film the background information which the "link man" had provided in the studio. What in fact I was asking my people to do was to make a half-hour self-contained film under a great deal of pressure which would tell viewers a complete story. We wanted to tell important stories very simply and very clearly. We were aiming at the mass audience that reads the *Daily Mirror*, we were not aiming at the audience that read the *Guardian* or *The Times*, although we were delighted if they chose to watch us too; after a time they began to do so. But basically we wanted to present issues that people could identify with, and we wanted to do that even if we were talking about countries a very long way from England.

For example, we were very interested in the Catholic Church and birth control. But we didn't want a debate between theologians. We wanted to show what the ordinary Catholic mother in a poor slum in Liverpool felt about birth control. So, we would send a researcher up to Liverpool (in this kind of case the researcher was often a girl), and she would spend a week tramping a poor parish. She would talk to doctors; doctors would direct her to patients. She would go to the Family Planning Clinic; she would talk to mothers, some of whom were in such utterly desperate straits that they were prepared to talk openly to a television camera about their problems with their husbands, their problems with their doctors, their problems with their children, and their problems with their priest. Nowadays, this seems almost a cliché of television journalism; but when we did it we were the first, and people were riveted to their screens because they began to see issues presented as they actually affected ordinary people.

Q. How would you proceed after the initial research?

A. In a film like that, a researcher might spend a week in Liverpool, she would then write a piece of paper for me saying, "these are the people we could film there; this is the time it would be easiest to get them. I can lay all this on from next Wednesday." I would then send a film unit, a reporter and a director, to Liverpool. They might have a day to acclimatize themselves, to have a quick look around, and then they were off. They would have about a week in which to make the film, and they would shoot at a fairly high ratio because this kind of film involved a great deal of talk, and talk takes up a lot of space and time. I suppose that some of their stuff was shot at a ratio of nearer to twenty to one than ten to one. I would view the rushes with film editors back here. Later I would be joined by the director and the reporter, and we would then put the lists together and put the film on the air.

The editing process itself was always a fairly rapid affair. All we had were two cutting rooms, and it was almost impossible to start work on a film for the week after next without some sort of special dispensation. This meant that cutting a Thursday film was a process that didn't really begin until the preceding Friday. And for practical purposes that often meant Monday, giving us just four days. Our aim was to have a fine cut ready by midnight on the Wednesday, and give the reporter the shot list to read immediately when we finished. He then had to write the commentary through the night or on Thursday morning for recording on Thursday afternoon. We would then dub on Thursday evening, and the film would go straight from the dubbing theatre into the telecine machines and onto the air. There were hair-raising occasions obviously when reel two was still being dubbed when reel one was actually on the air. But we only once got a second or two of black between the two reels.

Undoubtedly, as we went on with this, we became more and more aware of the limitations of cutting and dubbing at this pace. There was also another important point. We were beginning to work with directors of higher calibre, cameramen of a better quality, cameramen better able to handhold and to make use of the new techniques that lightweight equipment was making available to them. Our all-round efficiency was improving; and we began to wonder whether we oughtn't try to elongate the cutting and dubbing process as well, because film which had now taken a great deal of time to research properly and a certain amount of time to shoot was losing a lot of its finesse and potential as excellent material because of the rush to complete the editing.

This is a problem which we haven't completely overcome, although we do now have more cutting rooms and therefore the pressure is off to some extent. Now, very often, we complete cutting and even commentary writing and recording well in advance of transmission, although we still tend to dub very late.

Q. It must have presented quite a problem to keep the program unified and controlled in the face of so much pressure?

A. In the early days the pressure of the schedule was so overwhelming; the work required to make a decent job out of a half-hour film was so concentrated, pressurized, and demanding that I felt that the only way of getting the program on the air, under the pressure of the deadline, was to have somebody very, very firmly in command. All arguments between the film editor, the director, and the reporter as to whether this bit of sync should be left in or this sequence should come before that sequence, or this shot should stay in instead of that shot—all these arguments were resolved by me in a prolonged shouting match that rose to a crescendo all through Wednesday and Thursday.

Q. Looking back over the programs you did for "This Week" and "Panorama," is there any one broadcast that stands out in your memory as giving you particular cause for satisfaction?

A. I think, even to this day the film that I am happiest to have had anything to do with was a film for "This Week" that we made in a very great hurry at Christmas 1963. Over the four days of Christmas in 1963, one hundred and twenty people in Britain died on the roads and those figures were available within hours of the Christmas holiday period being over. Christmas knocked us completely out—I mean the labs closed down, nobody was at work; and knowing that this hiatus was going to enter our lives, I had some sort of standby program ready for the following Thursday. However, when I came into the office on Friday I knew that I wanted to do a program about the road deaths that Christmas so I said, "We will make a film and we'll put it out next Thursday."

We knew that somewhere there was available a very convincing breakdown showing how alcohol was a causal factor in road accidents. We also had available a sequence showing what effect the drink laws in Sweden had on holiday makers at a carnival time, and by happy coincidence this film clip showed Sweden on New Year's Eve.

Between Friday and the following Thursday we traced the relatives of the people who had died on the roads over Christmas. We asked them to talk about how their husbands or wives or children or parents had been killed, and we asked them for photographs of the people they had lost. We asked motorists in the streets about what they thought about drink and driving, and what did they think about the one hundred and twenty people dying on the roads in four days. Some of them gave astonishing answers. One man said driving was sport, wasn't it? What was wrong with that? We asked people who were campaigning for a strengthening of the laws on drinking and driving to talk to us; we also spoke to defenders of the status quo. To crown everything we went into a London pub on New Year's Eve, whose car park was jammed with motorcars, and talked to the people drinking in that pub about how much they had had to drink and how they were going to get home that night. When they drove away from the pub, we stopped the cars as they drove out of the car park out into the main road and asked the drivers if they felt capable of driving. They said, "Yes," but they obviously weren't.

I also did one other thing. I went to the top of the fire brigade tower on the south bank of the Thames. Beneath it I lined up one hundred and twenty people to form the message, "Christmas '63" and started the program with a high shot of one hundred and twenty dots forming these words "Christmas '63" on the quite white ground beneath us. As the camera zoomed down a little bit, the people looked up and we said that statistics were meaningless, that the dead were people, people like Mrs. Jones of such and such. We then projected a picture of Mrs. Jones and said that at five o'clock last Wednesday she was crossing such and such a high road when she was knocked down and killed. We then took a great thick cross animated onto the photograph of her face, and as brutally as we could blotted out her face. After that we intercut pictures of the victims throughout the film. To end we had an interview with the minister of transport. This was done live from the studio. I've never seen anybody so shattered by a film as he was. After him we had someone singing *Where Have all the Young Men Gone?* over pictures of road accident victims.

It was an overt propaganda film and had more impact than any other film I've ever done. It gave me more satisfaction than any other film I've ever done. I've no doubt at all that that film and other films like it helped to change the law in this country, because on our program the minister was saying that he was powerless to bring in legislation that would prevent people from drinking and driving because public opinion wouldn't stand for it. There's no question in my mind that public opinion was influenced to change the law partly by seeing our film.

Q. You've mentioned that you don't believe in the objectivity of television. Would you mind discussing the whole question of biases, propaganda, and the pressures on a current-affairs producer?

A. Everyone in television in this country has some obligation to be impartial. We try to be objective; and we have an obligation which we observe to present both points of view. But you can't make a good film which presents both points of view. All films are statements by the producer or the director or the reporter because they involve a process of selection. Therefore, one tries to be fair as a reporter but as a film maker there is no question that films that mean anything are statements by the people who make them. And we often find that some of the films we make infuriate some of the people who watch them.

For example, it's impossible in this country to make a film about Israel and the Arabs which attempts to do any kind of justice to the Arab point of view, without infuriating a large number of people who really do not want to see an impartial film at all. When we do the Middle East, we try to be as objective as we can. On the other hand when we go to a country like South Africa or Soviet Russia we often make a film that very few people in this country would disagree with, but which may, nevertheless, seem to the defenders of the regime to be wickedly unfair. This is, I suppose, because the range of political opinions and attitudes in the team of people making the film, which is very considerable, doesn't extend so far as to include someone who is actually in favor of apartheid or anyone who is in favor of Soviet Communism in its harshest posture.

On the whole, we prefer complaints afterwards rather than pressure beforehand. Of course, there are pressures; it's just up to us to resist and to know that we are telling the truth as far as we humanly can.

Q. Was your work for "Panorama" in the same vein as your work on "This Week"?

A. When I was doing "Panorama" for the BBC, I was trying to do, perhaps less successfully, the same thing for the BBC that I did for "This Week" which was to turn "Panorama" into a one-subject program, such as sending people to Vietnam to make a fifty-minute film. Again it seems commonplace today, but in those days neither "Panorama" nor BBC's nightly current-affairs show "Twenty-Four Hours" nor any other British outfit made current affairs films that long about one subject.

Q. You mention your Vietnam film which, as far as I remember, had a rather devastating effect on normally complacent English viewers. I am curious about how the rushes affected you and what extra you feel was achieved by doing one hour on the subject instead of a series of short pieces.

A. I remember watching the Vietnam rushes coming in, and they came in great swatches. For weeks you have nothing, and then you suddenly have thousands and thousands of feet to view at once. Among this endless footage I remember being absolutely shattered by one sequence. It took place in a center where the men, women, and children who had lost arms and legs were having artificial limbs fitted. They were keeping up a sort of incessant yowling and crying and moaning, and the staff at the center was trying to cope with this. The victims were asked through an interpreter if they knew what had hit them. They said, "No, they didn't." As I ran out into the corridor, sensing that this film was going to have extraordinary impact on people because I had never before seen anything so harrowing, I suddenly realized it might be legitimate to put that sequence after a sequence of interviews with American pilots who admitted that in dropping their bombs they didn't know where the bombs fell.

It wasn't just a matter of an editing gimmick; it was rather a question of trying to get a deeper point of view. A lot of the newsreel film one saw from Vietnam was concerned with this action on that day and that action on this day, and it was news reporting. Nobody tried to put the war together; nobody tried to find out how it affected the people of Vietnam, and nobody tried to provide any composite picture of the war as it affected the soldier and the civilian population. So we were among the first trying for this deeper and wider point of view. It was a necessary move, and one which in my opinion made the impact of the news documentary in England much greater.

5

What Harvest for the Reaper?

Morton Silverstein

Appearances are deceptive. At first glance Mort Silverstein looks like a walking apology for Madison Avenue. The shirt has red stripes, the blazer is immaculate, and the hair very carefully groomed. Such are the externals that make it hard to believe that between 1966 and 1970 Silverstein wrote and produced three of the period's most probing television documentaries.

Silverstein was born in Brooklyn in 1929, became an early high school dropout, and was sent to military academy, "as was the fashion when kids were sufficiently screwed up in Brooklyn. Before entering college I thought what could be a greater fantasy than a military academy and chose Miami University, where I developed a good game of tennis but not much more."

Silverstein's first job in television, except for a brief period in an army radio and TV unit, was working for "Night Beat," an interview show which starred Mike Wallace and was under the general guidance of Ted Yates. When "Night Beat" went off the air in 1958, Silverstein took up free-lance writing for the New York Times and ABC radio.

This period was followed by the production of several documentaries for NBC, a short film-making assignment with the United States Information Agency, and work for Westinghouse television which "allowed me to express all the things the USIA wouldn't allow me to say." From Westinghouse Silverstein moved as a documentary producer to National Educational Television, which has been the base for his most recent work.

What Harvest for the Reaper? *(1967) is certainly Silverstein's best film prior to* Banks and the Poor *(1970).* For an hour it follows the fortunes of a group of black migrant workers who are recruited in Alabama with promises of tremendous pay "up north." Not one man realizes that after paying for food, for rent, and for the bus to and from the daily job and after giving the crew chief a percentage of his pay, he will be lucky to be left with $1.75 a day. Few understand that*

---

* Banks and the Poor, broadcast by NET in November 1970, was being edited when I wrote the above.

the vision of a trip with Santa Claus will in reality turn out to be a modern version of slavery. After six months the migrants complete their work in the strawberry and potato fields and prepare to move on, possibly even more dispirited and broken than they were in June.

Though the pace of the film is occasionally slow and some of the incidents repetitious, these are mere quibbles in a film which as a whole is both moving and profoundly disturbing. Most critics praised the film, but a few remarked on what they claimed was Silverstein's failure to provide perspective. Some thought he should have generalized more, while others argued he should have provided more facts on the economic situation and on the failure of law enforcement.

My own view is that the facts were sufficiently brought out, and that in any case a social documentary is neither an MA paper nor a governmental report. Sometimes a situation calls for details to be left aside so that an uncluttered truth can emerge from a disgusting social situation. As Jack Gould wrote in the New York Times, *"Eight years ago the late Edward R. Murrow cast the spotlight of television on the plight of the exploited migratory worker. Last night Morton Silverstein of NET did a superb sequel."*

Q. What kind of shows did you do when you first came to NET?

A. I was working on a series called "At Issue," and the first film I did in 1963 dealt with the Christmas boycott following the bombing and killing of black children in Birmingham, Alabama. I did quite a lot of films for "At Issue"—mostly with Larry Solomon as editor—all of which tended to become exposés of political, social, or economic injustices, like *Death on the Highway*, which named by brand the unsafest cars on the market, and *The Poor Pay More*. Later we made *The Great Label Mystery*, which showed how large manufacturers defraud supermarket customers by fraudulent weights, fake packaging, and so on. We did other shows on the double standard of justice for rich and poor, and a program on the high cost and questionable quality of American medical care.

NET was and remains a good place to work because there are no external pressures; we aren't responsible to advertisers, and our mandate is to tell the truth. So when we were doing *Death on the Highway*, many people at CBS said, "Sock it to 'em." They knew they couldn't possibly do that kind of show, because the automobile manufacturers were among their principal sponsors.

Q. What sparked your interest in the plight of the migrant workers?

A. NET public affairs head Don Dixon assigned me to search around for a film topic in late 1966, and I came across a mention of the terrible situation of migrant workers in Long Island. These were workers who were brought up to Long Island from Arkansas and other places in the south, stayed for the summer, and returned home often poorer than they arrived. It brought Edward R. Murrow's *Harvest of Shame* very much to mind, and I was struck by the fact that in spite of the furore over the film, so little had changed in the intervening years.

I began to look into the topic and met with people like Lincoln Lynch, who was formerly director of CORE on Long Island. Lincoln put me in touch with people working in community action groups out on eastern Long Island, and after talking with them I went round and began to look at the different camps for myself. I began talking with people—the workers, the foremen, the bosses—and gradually began to get some feel of the subject.

Q. Did you ever consider shooting a large number of camps to get a very wide picture of the situation?

A. No. It seemed to me, right from the beginning, that the best way to do the film was to concentrate on this one single migrant labor camp on Cutchogue, Long Island, and to film the men's lives through one entire agricultural season. This way I could catch them arriving and doing strawberry picking in June, and could stay with them till they left in December after the potato harvest. I felt that by concentrating on a single group of black migrant workers, a single crew chief, and a single group of farmers—who seemed to me to be the modern equivalent of the slave masters of old—we would be able to attack the monumental injustice of the system more articulately than by citing many examples throughout the nation, which was the technique chosen by Murrow, David Lowe, and Fred Friendly. Their device was powerful, profound, and effective in its own right, but we preferred to make the story of a single camp the prototype for the national tragedy.

Q. What made you choose the Cutchogue migrant camp?

A. It was suggested to me by Lincoln Lynch and somebody else. Lynch knew the black crew chief of Cutchogue, a man called Andrew Anderson, and introduced me to him; my problem then was to persuade Anderson to let us film at the camp.

Q. What was the function of Anderson as crew chief?

A. He was the intermediary between the migrant workers and the farmers. He recruited the workers, brought them up from the south, allocated their work, supervised their lives, paid them at the end of the week, and so on.

Q. Was Anderson suspicious of what you were going to do, or did he suspect that the picture of the camp might reflect badly upon himself?

A. No. I think he agreed to let us film because the man simply had a large ego and also truly felt in some vague way that he was really being generous to his men—that he was being some kind of benevolent despot.

Q. Did you have any problems in getting permission from either the migrant workers or the farmers to make the film?

A. Both of these points presented difficulties but from opposite points of the spectrum. Anderson had said we could go ahead if we got the permission of William Chudiak, head of the farmers' group that ran the camp and used the migrant labor. When we went to see Chudiak only his wife was at home, so that permission had to wait. Meanwhile, I started filming at the camp, knowing that I'd got Anderson's go-ahead. But then came a problem with the workers.

It was Sunday, and we wanted to film a church service on the camp. However, there was a new minister who wanted to take a vote among the migrants as to whether or not we should be allowed to film. He said, "Talk with them first, and then we'll vote on it." I respected this attitude, but it made it very awkward for us. How could I tell the migrants that my sympathies lay with them without letting Anderson know that we were out to expose the system. If I had told them the film would be sympathetic to them, Anderson would probably throw us out of the camp. Anyway I made some kind of a speech, and while I was waiting outside with the film crew for a decision, a truck pulled up in front of us, and a burly guy clambered out and started yelling, "What the hell are you guys doing here. You're trespassing, and get the hell off my property."

This was Chudiak, president of the farmers' co-op, but I didn't know it at the time and had to figure out, first, who is this guy; second, what do I say to prevent the whole show from disappearing then and there; third, how can I prevent him from learning what I'm really doing but still tell him a sufficient amount so that I won't feel forever guilty of having lied; and fourth, how can I keep the trust of the migrants, the crew chief, and gain the confidence of this guy, all at the same time. Luckily, as I was talking to Chudiak, the minister came out and said the workers had given a positive vote. So that was one problem less.

Q. What did you finally tell Chudiak?

A. I told him I'd talked to Anderson, and had also visited his—that's to say Chudiak's—home and talked to his wife. At that he softened up a bit. Then he said, "If this is going to be another show like Murrow's, then to hell with it. That was just about the biggest lie I ever saw." He then went on to give a long discourse on the difficulties of the farmer, constantly telling me, "The trouble is that no one knows *our* side of things." I professed to be very interested, as indeed I was, and said, "That's the reason we're here—to tell the truth and get the farmers' point of view." Which is just what we did. We told the truth and we got the farmers' point of view, by which they subsequently hung themselves. Chudiak calmed down, said he would think it over, and take up our request at the farmers' meeting later that week.

Q. Did you try any preliminary "softening" of the other farmers?

A. I got a list of about half a dozen farmers who sat on the board of the labor camp, the so-called farmers' cooperative, and called them up and said, "We are doing a film and are concerned with your point of view. Can we come out and talk to you about your problems as a farmer?" Then for the next three days we shot several thousand feet of perfectly unusable film of the farmers discussing potato beetles, machinery difficulties, crop spraying, and other irrelevant material. Occasionally, however, I would throw in a question about the quality of migrant work and would get predictable angry responses which were very useful for the film, such as the farmer who said that the migrants weren't human beings but merely two-legged animals. After the shooting session I'd urge them to tell Chudiak what they thought of our interview. The upshot was that the board met the following Wednesday and gave us permission to stay the entire season and do the film.

Q. Did you ever tell the migrants specifically what you were doing, and what the purpose of the film was?

A. I told a few of them in confidence, and they were very helpful. They also became aware of my point of view when I interviewed them off camp. These interviews had to be done away from the main center because the crew chief had a lot of spies around. In fact the whole film was done with a great amount of secrecy, with the crew becoming a very tight family unit. There were reports of guns around the camp, and we had to be prepared for violence from the farmers or the local version of the John Birch society. All this produced a feeling of working under a cloud, and kept reminding me that the film could be aborted at any moment. But this atmosphere never seemed to bother the film crew, and whatever success the film had is the result of the collaboration, commitment, and courage of everyone in the unit.

Q. Did you prepare any formal outline for the film?

A. I knew I wanted to shoot a diary-type film. Having decided to use one camp and one season to tell the story, all that remained was to pick the best footage of each day and put it aside for film editor

Larry Solomon. Later, when we were much more familiar with the entire process of the dehumanization of the migrant worker, both Larry and myself would go through the footage again in chronological order and choose those sequences which best illustrated the true story. In many ways it was the easiest documentary I have ever done, because it was an on-going story and because we had the time to trace the entire agricultural season from June to December. It was not an issue-oriented show like *Justice and the Poor*, which was spread over many locations. Here we had a single location with a single story that best expressed the issue, which was the physical and spiritual brutalization of men.

Concerning the outline, then, I knew we would probably start with the recruiting stage down south, just before the potato season. We could show the men being recruited; we could establish the crew chief; we could show what the men do, the church service, the opinions of the farmers; and slowly I believed we would be able to move on to the loneliness of the men and get the feelings of what their lives were like throughout the season. That much was written down, or semiformally devised for structure.

Q. Did you scout out the situation very much before shooting?

A. Yes. I went down with my cameraman, Guy Borremans, in April before the camp really opened, and started looking at visual possibilities. There were no people in the camp. You could just see structures and shacks and the buildings being painted some sallow yellow color. We saw some discarded toys and dolls lying in the mud; we saw a few kids and generally managed to get a feeling of the tragic ambience of the camp even before it opened.

Then in June 1967, after the camp had opened, we returned for the first stretch of filming of seventeen consecutive days. I learned what the schedule was—what time the men got up in the morning, how they were fed, how they were assigned to the day's labor, how they were loaded onto pickup trucks or buses and carted out to the farmer's field, and so forth. I saw what happened in the fields, what their work was like, what they did when they came back, what payday looked like; and I started jotting down my idea on shooting the whole thing.

At the beginning, I watched very much over Guy's shoulder. I very much respected his work, but there's a difference in the way a director and a cameraman feel the need to select material. I felt very possessive about the show, and so I stayed at Guy's shoulder much of the time, though eventually we reached such a singularity of purpose that he probably could have shot much of it without my instructions.

Q. Although the film starts with the recruiting process, I understand that you shot the sequences fairly late in the year.

A. When we arrived in June the first group had already been recruited, so we had to take the September group and use it in the film as a flashback. Anderson, the crew chief, had always promised that we could film him actually recruiting in Arkansas, but he skipped out without telling us. When we found this out we took a plane and flew down to Arkansas, and in effect surprised Anderson as he got into Forrest City.

Once we started filming, the local police, who were Southern red-necked prototypes, assumed that we were "outside agitators" and tried to intimidate not only us, but also the storekeeper into whose store the crew chief would go to try to find men to go up north. They also tried to intimidate Anderson and pulled up with three prowl cars, which probably represented the entire Forrest City police force. It really scared the hell out of this sleepy, almost pre-Civil War town.

The police went very slowly through our credentials and said, "No more filming. Who gave you permission to do this? Most people ask *us* before they film," and so forth. Fortunately, by that time, we had shot everything we needed; but it was a clear attempt to intimidate us and, more important, to frighten the black crew chief Anderson, the storekeepers, and the people being recruited in order to keep them in their place.

This was the first time that I ever saw Anderson as anything other than a villain—that is to say, that my sympathy was split for the first time when I saw Anderson in the role of a black man in a white Southern town. I felt sorry for him, but then I said to myself, "Wait. This is a man who is exploiting other men," so to me he had no color then, but at first when the police came around, he was to me, an oppressed black man in the white South. Of course, the truth was that Anderson himself was as much a victim as he was an instrument of the system, a system which made him—a black man—exploit his brothers.

Q. There are no family relationships seen in your film, nor does one ever get a sense of the social relationships formed between the migrants. Was this a deliberate omission on your part, or were these things just nonexistent?

A. There is no family life. The men are mostly spiritually burned out, and they don't form relationships between themselves. There's an absence of social life. The men work in the fields, they come back to the camp, they buy twister wine—at exorbitant prices set by the crew chief—and they stay bombed most of the time or lie around until the next day that they are chosen for work. There is very little conversation. There is no shop talk; there is no "What the hell are we doing here? Let's band together and get ourselves out of this hell hole." There is very little awareness of their plight, and there is very little spirit or energy to correct that. Because of those characteristics, there is very little interaction between one migrant worker and another.

Q. Did you have to go back after your main shooting to get many fill shots, or scene-setting shots?

A. When we got to the end of our filming, we realized we needed a number of extra things. I had been unable to get a lot of these shots earlier, because I wanted to be very careful in the first phase not to blow the whole show by letting anyone know what we were doing. So, at the last shooting we went for interiors showing how the migrants lived in their shacks, the kind of rent they paid, the lice-ridden blankets they had to sleep on, and the fire hazards of living in a despicable shack. We showed how they ate, how they survived, how they were paid, and how the crew chief would double the normal price of the wine and the meagre food that he sold to the workers to make an extra profit.

We also needed an establishing shot of the camp and looked at the place from various angles trying to find a view that would embody the sense of enslavement and of being in a concentration camp, which in a sense it was. The men had no mobility; they were threatened if they left the camp. Finally, we found the symbolic view on the rise of a hill. We looked through the lens and saw the barbed wire in the foreground against a blurred background. From there it was possible to zoom in slowly on the camp, through the barbed wire, and reveal the claustrophobia of being disenfranchised.

Q. You have one subjective shot, where the camera is dragged through the fields and brushes aside the corn, or whatever is growing. Was this shot with a purpose in mind?

A. We were showing a lot of farm fields and had to find new ways of coverage. At the time we didn't know what we would use it for, but thought it might come in handy. During the editing we thought it might serve for match dissolves of the same land in June and in October; but it didn't work. Finally, in a segment in which James Johnson, one of the migrants, talks about going from one location to another and how his life was continually on the move, we decided that we could do a very good cutaway from him on camera and float the description of his travels over the subjective shots of the camera moving through foot-high grass. The shot seemed to corroborate visually the introspective talk.

Q. You have a discussion between the farmers at a meeting Was this specially arranged?

A. No. The farmers met fairly regularly and allowed us to shoot half their meeting. This was filmed in November at the end of our shooting schedule; and having nothing to lose, I could ask them questions which would have had us thrown off the camp in June.

Q. Were you worried during the filming, that there might be too much repetition of sequences, such as the men going out to work?

A. That was very much on our minds, and Larry Solomon and I were quite worried that if repeated too much we would lose the viewer. In the early sequences of the show, there are two very similar episodes; in the first the workers are being driven off in a bus, and in the second they leave in a pickup truck. What saved the second sequence from being redundant was that the men were being picked up in a truck by the farmers, whereas the first time it was Anderson who was doing the arranging and loading the men onto buses. So the actions were dissimilar, but it was still a little too alike for comfort. However, the second sequence served the function of allowing us to establish Chudiak, Al McBride, and some of the other members of the co-op, and it also gave a good lead in to the helicopter shots of the fields.

Q. Did you use a researcher to help you on the statistical evidence presented in the film?

A. I had a researcher, Lynne Littman, who took down my notes and queries at the end of the day. I would say, "We were at an auction today with farmer Lindsay, and he made such and such on his strawberries; let's check the difference between what he gets a crate, and what the migrants get." Or I'd ask her to find out how many migrants there were in the county, what trade union legislation there was—a million questions like that. I needed all this information, but I didn't want a statistical script; I wanted to write a script that would match the emotional quality of the footage, and one that would also supply the occasional explanatory footnote where needed. What I wanted the film to convey was the misery of the migrants' experience and the outrage I felt, along with others, at this situation. Many of the migrants were silent and afraid, and we had to become their voices.

Q. The narration has a very colorful emotional style. Were there any particular influences on you in evolving this manner of writing?

A. There were two kinds of inspiration: my own experiences and personal feelings after being six months at the camp and the works

113

of James Agee, particularly *Let Us Now Praise Famous Men* which was written about sharecroppers in Alabama. Agee's prose has an extraordinary rhythm and cadence of its own, and also a great sense of compassion for the lives of subjugated and exploited people which makes you identify with Agee's perspectives. I felt many of those same perceptions, and so tried to emulate ways in which he would say things. I used Agee's style as a goad to my own creative impulse, particularly in my opening narration about the "parched, bloodless, cotton bankrupt southern town" and in the closing section where we talk about "this legacy, these odors, these noises, these silences."

Q. A film team departs, but very often individuals who have been outspoken on behalf of the film are left behind to face the angry reactions of people they have offended. Did that happen to any of the participants in *What Harvest?*

A. You try not to leave people behind who can get hurt. But inevitably some good people *are* left behind. One of the people who helped us a great deal was the Reverend Arthur Bryant, who sits on the Suffolk County Human Relations Board. Mr. Bryant has been trying to get legislation passed which will enable the migrant workers to be part of the National Labor Relations Act. In the film he's called "a sick man" by the farmers, but this hasn't stopped him showing the film right in the Cutchogue section of Long Island. He's received intimidating and anonymous phone calls and obscene threats; but he's a gutsy guy, and this doesn't seem to have deterred him. In every show you need people who are compassionate and honest and concerned, and you realize in the end that *they* are the principal heroes, not the guys who come with a film crew for six days or six months and then vanish.

Q. One wonders what the film has achieved and whether it's changed anything?

A. I think the documentary must be an instrument of social change, or it is not worth the raw stock it's filmed on. This film led to some changes in the sanitation and housing laws in New York state; it also brought in a New York state legislature committee to investigate conditions at the camp; it aroused the attention of a congressional committee which investigated the camp and the migrant condition generally, and it also engendered the interest of the U.S. Senate Committee on Migratory Labor. It got enormous attention in the national press; it helped change a few laws; it kept Anderson out of the camp for a few seasons—but that's all.

Nothing basic has changed. The oppressive system still continues. We personally tried to follow up on the film in whatever ways we

114

could, by testifying before the Senate committee at their invitation
and by showing the film to concerned groups; but one soon gets involved in other social outrages in subsequent film work.

You know, that's one of the luxuries of someone who makes documentaries. You go through experiences that are shattering, or depressing, or inconvenient, or physically uncomfortable, or distressing emotionally, or whatever, but it's only done temporarily.

So we were at the migrant camp for six months, to which I say
"big deal"; so we did a film, but we're not the migrant worker. He
didn't travel back to New York to discuss over a good lunch what
he was going to edit that day; he didn't go back to a decent motel
when he was through that day. He's still traveling along on the high-
ways in unsafe buses run by crew chiefs; he's still traveling to Florida,
heavily in debt, trying to work that off on a citrus crop, and then
being carted off to the northeast and back to the potato fields again.
And what are we doing? We're on to another show. It's the luxury
we have and the guilt we must bear, and the obligation that we must
continue.

My first meeting with Larry Solomon was in 1968, in a rather crowded television studio in Jerusalem. Larry had come to Israel Television for a year to advise on the formation and training of editing teams and, when I spoke to him, was in the midst of a month-old battle trying to do away with bureaucratic practices and bring order out of chaos. During the following nine months, Larry edited two half-hour documentaries of mine, as well as five or six shorts. Thus there was ample opportunity to get to know and appreciate his capabilities as an editor.

Larry exemplifies the creative editor at his best. He stimulates, suggests, and encourages. He has a merciless eye for the filmic cliché and seems to be constantly searching for new creative solutions to filmic problems. He is an editor who will take risks, and in the type of loose film we were doing it was quite clear to me that Larry, as editor, was just as much author of the final product as I was as director.

Naturally we often differed on interpretation and approach. However, I can recall several occasions on which Larry's suggestions for reshaping a set of sequences gave an excitement to a picture which would have been missing had a lesser editor merely cut to my outline.

Larry was born in New York in 1937 and studied film at New York University. After graduation he worked as assistant editor on various features, such as The Connection *and* The Cool World, *and also spent a year working in Israel in 1963.*

In 1964 he started working for National Educational Television for whom he has edited over eleven hour-long shows, some fifteen half-hour shows, and numerous magazine pieces. He has also worked fairly widely outside NET for various educational and philanthropic organizations, and in 1969 he entered the production field with a half-hour color film entitled With These Children.

Larry talks about the necessity of forming good working relations, and in his own case he has a singularly productive association with Mort Silverstein on more than five films, including Death on the Highway, Banks and the Poor, *and* What Harvest for the Reaper? *for which he received an Emmy nomination.*

Q. What seems to be the most important thing to you, as an editor, in the making of a documentary?

A. The establishment of a good relationship between yourself and the person you're working with most closely. For me, films are made

by combinations of people, and probably the best relationship I've had
in editing terms is with Mort Silverstein. I've known Mort since 1963
and must have done about four or five hour-long documentaries with
him; so we've come to have a very close understanding and appreciation for each other's work and approach to film.

Q. Mort mentioned to me that he took you out on location several
times during the shooting of *What Harvest.* This is a bit unusual for
an editor, isn't it?

A. I quite often get involved with Mort's shooting, because, as an
editor, I see a lot of things from my particular point of view which
might otherwise escape Mort or the cameraman. I'm not just talking
about editing links, but would include finding fresh ways to promote
the idea we are trying to convey.

Q. Can you give me an example from *Harvest?*

A. We'd shot about three-quarters of the film, and then went to
Arkansas to shoot the migrants being recruited. This sequence was
intended for the start of the film. We shot a lot of Anderson, the crew
chief, lining up the men, and also went to his home and shot about
1,200 feet of him and his family.

While we were shooting at Anderson's I heard a lot of noises of
chickens and dogs which interested me very much. Somehow the
noises conveyed the very essence of what it was to be down south. I
then took a walk around the house and saw the chickens and a dog
lying asleep. The whole scene was very evocative, so I told Mort,
"This may be a possibility for something, let's just take it." We got
the shot, and it wound up being the opening shot of the film, because
it sets the mood immediately for a rather slow, somnolent South.
That's an example of myself, as an editor, looking at the scene strictly
from an editing point of view. There were many other situations like
that.

Towards the end of the season we found that we needed more
shots of conditions at the camp. We'd been afraid to get these at the
beginning of the season in case the motives and objectives for making
the film became suspect. So I just walked around with the cameraman
trying to focus on things that would be useful in the editing, things
like cats walking around the camp, beds on cinder blocks, and so on.
At that point I knew how much footage we needed to make the
scenes work. I also knew we needed a certain kind of shot to convey
the terrible feeling of the despair of the migrants, and I could see
these shots very clearly in relation to what we already had.

Q. I understand that you and Mort had to restructure the whole end
sequence. What went wrong?

A. Mort wanted to end the film with the migrants leaving the camp by bus, and the scene was in fact shot that way. However, the most important film magazine, the one taken of the men leaving the camp, somehow got ruined. We were all tremendously upset because we'd waited for at least three or four months for the migrants to depart. This was supposed to be the dramatic closing sequence of the film, and what did we have—a bus starting to pull away, and that was it! You didn't see anybody getting on the bus, and you didn't see anybody inside the bus. It was a disaster, and we were left without an end. So when we went out to the camp for the last time we tried to think of ways in which we could get over this loss of film and still convey the idea of their leaving.

After long discussions what we decided to do was film it all subjectively. We got into a car and filmed through the windows to capture the last view of the camp as it would be seen by the migrants on leaving. Eventually we edited the sequence with voices over, which you had heard earlier in the film, and I think in the end it really came out much better than the original concept. It is a good example of seeming disaster forcing us into doing something which we would never otherwise have done.

Q. The film extended over six months shooting. How did you organize your editing?

A. It wasn't an easy project, but it was a very comfortable one because it was shot in sections depending on the times of the year, so we could edit a section at a time. What we did was assemble all the film in chronological order, look at everything, and then Mort and I would choose the best part to illustrate the point we wanted to convey, which was that the migrants were men who had gone through life, had reached a particular stage in their lives, and now there was nothing left for them—they were men without hope. We had three elements to interrelate—the migrants, the farmers, and the crew chief—and had to weave all three into various sets of contrasts, like seeing the farmers in their luxury church and the migrants in their dilapidated prayer hall. We also had to establish the attitudes of one group for the other, like following the Reverend Arthur Bryant's plea for better conditions with the farmer's comment that Bryant was "a very sick man."

Q. How does Mort work with you? Does he give you notes? Does he view the rushes alone or with you?

A. We look at the film together, and he tells me what he wants to get out of a particular segment and how long he reckons it should last, whether thirty seconds, a minute, or something like that. The way I work with Mort is that he will tell me what he specifically wants put in from an interview in terms of actual dialogue, but will then usually leave illustrative or related footage up to me. If I'm trying to get an idea across with montage, I am usually left to myself. I build the whole thing up, possibly with music and sound; and after I have done it, Mort takes a look and then gives me suggestions for improvements or alterations. He sees it in a fresh light and tells me what he thinks, but that doesn't necessarily mean I'll go along with him all the way. If I disagree, I'll argue pretty emphatically for what I want; but the final decision is, of course, Mort's. He is the producer, and it's his show; but he will always put me in a situation where I have to create the sequence and will then tell me his critique of it.

Q. You build a very good free, imaginative montage over the song "Just another day." How did the idea for that montage arise?

A. We were about forty minutes into the show and felt at this point that everything which was seen before should suddenly be summed up, so that the audience would be outraged to the point where it would say, "Why is the government quiet? Why isn't it doing something for the plight of the migrants?" There's a very good sequence concerning payday where one migrant who owes money to the crew chief has all his money cut off. The man is intimidated and the crew chief tells his wife, who runs the dining room, to cut off his credit. That leads into another segment where we see a migrant, singing "Just Another Day," while around him are sitting a few other migrants and the crew chief.

What we did was start on the song. It was shot very well; you were close in tight, and really got into the man himself; you saw him sweating and really singing his heart out. What I then did was cut to various shots from sequences that had previously been seen in the film, even though the shots themselves may not have been used in the edited sequence—shots of migrants working, a shot of a confused old man looking sadly out of a cracked window of the bus taking him to the fields for the hundredth time. This was a summing up, which I hoped would build to a crescendo of outrage.

At the end of the film, I had an idea for "voice overs," but I wanted these voices only to be ones which the migrants themselves had heard. This, of course, excluded the farmers—but then the migrants are not like real people for the farmers. They see them; they know they exist. But all the contacts are through the crew chief, so I felt that the main voice we should hear should be that of Anderson, the crew chief and intermediary.

Mort said maybe we should use some of the farmers, and in fact, at one point we even had some in; but I argued the point and we took the farmers out. A lot of people told me that they felt this was unfair, because it let the farmers off the hook; but I felt that at that stage we were using a subjective camera to capture the migrants' feelings, and the voice that obviously dominated their time in the camp was that of Anderson.

Q. There's a lot of music in the background to the work sequences. Many people object to the addition of evocative music in a documentary, but you obviously disagree with them.

A. Music was very important in this film to add certain levels of meaning or to deepen a mood. Sometimes a song is used which everybody knows, and it helps illustrate a point you want to get across. For instance, we have the men going to work and, as they drive away, you hear the radio playing "Let the Good Times Roll." Now this is a very fast, upbeat song played against shots of guys just sitting around at the camp, and I think it really got across the sense of irony. We also had music which was specifically recorded for the film to set the mood for the various things. Besides giving the mood it also gave me an opportunity to cut according to the music and enhance the mood.

Q. How long was the rough cut? Did you make many changes subsequent to it?

A. It was about an hour and fifteen or twenty minutes, and contained one sequence which we finally cut out. We had done a sequence with the children in the day-care center, but it wasn't strong enough for the rest of the film without amplification. We couldn't get any more footage because the camp was closed, and it was also a little away from the main point of the migrants and their plight; so we dropped it.

Q. At what point did Mort give you the narration script?

A. As I said, Mort gives me the order of the sequences and tells me what he hopes each section will prove. Then I go ahead and get the rough cut. Narration is never written until the film is about 95 percent locked up. Obviously Mort has a number of things in his mind as he views the film time and time again, but he doesn't give me anything till I let him have the absolute timing of the various shots and sections. He then writes according to the timings, and I see the script for the first time when the editing is almost complete.

Q. I've got one final question. What is the main problem you have to face in editing vérité footage?

A. The cameraman is normally so involved in shooting vérité that he cannot think in terms of cutaways and so on. Therefore, in a certain way this type of shooting becomes quite difficult for you to handle because you are already locked in; much of what you are doing has already been cut for you by the cameraman and his spur-of-the-moment decisions. The shooting really becomes an editing disaster if the cameraman hasn't followed through on everything. The worst part of vérité shooting is that very often the cameraman will stop the camera at the wrong point without any logical reason, and the coverage is insufficient for the editor to work with. When I get the footage all I see is what is on the film. I have to make a logic out of just these thirty or fifty feet; and if the story is incomplete, for whatever reason, it makes the job twice as hard.

There is a very good scene in this film where we shot the migrants eating lunch while the foreman talks to them in a patronizing way. Unfortunately, the camera was nowhere near the foreman; it was on the other side of the shed, but the soundman had picked up the discussion and had readied the cameraman. Now the ideal thing to have done, which was certainly possible, would have been for the cameraman to zoom in on the foreman while he was talking. Well he went in but not all the way, which made things very awkward. I tried to blow up the scene and move closer in optically, but it just became too impractical, and we had to stay with the scene as it was. That's why it's so important that the cameraman stays with the action, gets into the main situation, covers it from various angles, and follows it through even though he feels everything is becoming repetitive. That way he gives me a few editing alternatives; if he doesn't stay with the action, I lose all my options and that's murder.

6

Hard Times in the Country
Jack Willis

Jack Willis graduated from the University of California, Los Angeles, Law School in 1960, and has spent the last ten years working as writer-producer-director both in film and television. His output includes over fifty "Open End" discussion shows for David Susskind and the directing and writing of three films for the CBC between 1963 and 1965.

Willis sits in an armchair, feet on the desk, looking like a healthy advertisement for "Drink X's soda, and stay young." The conversation ranges over sports, skin diving (he suffered a severe swimming accident subsequent to this interview), politics, and economics. "A few years ago," says Willis, "we felt that only blacks and poor whites were being hurt by the economic system. In Hard Times *I wanted to show how the failures of the system also cut into the great middle class."*

In Hard Times in the Country *Willis takes the American food industry and subjects it to a cold, surgical analysis. The body is found to be diseased throughout. What Willis reveals is a situation which enables four supermarket chains to control half the American food production, one soup company to control 80 percent of the market, and three cereal manufacturers to make double the average national yield on their investments.*

A very curious situation results from all this: while food prices rise to astronomic levels, 30 percent of American small farmers have been forced off the land in the last decade because they have been unable to make a decent living.

Hard Times is quite clearly a thesis film, yet its abstract ideas and arguments are supported by strong visual images. Some of the more complex economic issues dealt with are represented through animation, while hard facts are given alongside human interest situations. One sees shots of dried out, depopulated farming towns and old homesteaders set against cellophane wrapped images of cold supermarkets. One hears old ballads contrasted with mechanical computer sounds. And one listens to the sad statements of the small farmers which recall the bitterness and anguish of The Grapes of Wrath.

Willis is no neutral observer. What he provides is a bitter indict-

ment of monopolistic food practices and their consumer and social effects. Most critics accepted Willis' charges and praised his punches, but there were also some bitterly hostile reactions. One critic called the film "a frontal attack on the free enterprise system." Willis himself talks about the film showing "the social consequences of our uncontrolled free-enterprise system." The reviews also produced two other opposition arguments. One attack called the conclusions "arbitrary and unlearned," while another newspaper took Willis to task for not giving the retailers a chance to answer back, notwithstanding the fact that the "fairness doctrine" does not require this. Both these attacks are answered by Willis in the interview.

In retrospect one can see that Hard Times *is no isolated, crusading film of Willis', but is in keeping with a highly developed and moral approach to the use and purposes of film making. This approach sees film as one of the main twentieth-century tools for social investigation and attitude change, whether in the field of race, poverty, or minority rights.*

Willis' varied interest in social issues can be seen in Some of My Best Friends *(1969) and* Lay My Burden Down *(1965). Friends was a television show produced by Willis as an experiment in group relations. For the experiment he took five blacks and five Jews and taped them in a twelve-hour T-Group session, which was later condensed into a two-hour show. Burden was an hour documentary on the life of a southern rural Negro and won the documentary gold medal at the 1968 American Educational Film Festival.*

Other recent films by Willis include Crime in the Streets *(1966),* Every Seventh Child *(1967), and* Appalachia *(1968). The main part of* Hard Times *was filmed in 1969, while the film itself was first broadcast on NET's "Journal" in April 1970.*

Q. I believe you were trained as a lawyer? That seems a far cry from filming.

A. I did law at UCLA, but when I finished I knew I wanted to get into media and so I became a desk assistant at CBS News. Later on I went to work for David Susskind on "Open End" for a year and then quit to join the Peace Corps. When I returned to the United States, I worked as executive producer on a film about NATO with Douglas Leiterman and then went down to Mississippi with two friends to make *Streets of Greenwood* with our own money.

When I came back to New York I needed a job and called Doug. He seemed fairly keen and asked me to come up and produce films for him. I made two films for him and, with the money I made there, came back to finish *Streets of Greenwood,* which went on to win all sorts of festivals. From there, I reckoned I was a film maker.

I made a film for Doug called *The Quiet Takeover,* which was on the invasion of privacy by computer technology, and did a spoof on public relations called *The Image Makers.* I then worked for a while as a free-lancer doing films on science and Catholic education. The Catholic film was called *The Seventh Child;* it was fairly controversial and the Church campaigned to have it taken off the air. That was followed by a film on Appalachia for NET, which really involved me and, I suppose, provided the original inspiration for *Hard Times in the Country.*

Q. *Hard Times* deals with the effects of the concentration into a few hands of economic power in the food industry in the United States. What was your original premise?

A. We started from a paradox in American economics: the price the farmer gets for his goods has not risen in the last twenty years, and yet the price of food has risen dramatically for the consumer. So what has happened to supply and demand and free enterprise? Now the food industry is the largest industry in the United States and is also the last large industry to become concentrated in the hands of a few companies; I felt that what had happened in the food industry was indicative of the entire economy. What I wanted to do was show the social effects of the food-industry monopolization on both the farmer who is being forced off the land and on the consumer who is forced to pay a high price for food. Again I wanted to show how, in the end, the large corporations are taking over the land itself once the farmer has been pushed off, forcing us back to some kind of a feudal system.

Q. Do you think such a film could have been made by a network other than NET?

A. No, specifically because the food industry is the largest advertiser on commercial networks. The cereal industry alone spends over $90 million a year on network advertising, so no one is going to turn around and criticize. But I also think generally that the commercial networks wouldn't dare examine the economic system.

Q. In what way did your film on Appalachia provide the inspiration for *Hard Times?*

A. Appalachia represented for me the worst of capitalism. Large companies were moving into an area, taking the wealth of the locality, making huge profits, and leaving nothing but deprivation. Then the government came in and put the local people on welfare, but it never gave them enough to make a decent living and never showed them a way to expand or grow as individuals. Later, it seemed to me that the effects of the monopolization of the food industry on rural depopulation were very similar.

Q. So did you suggest the original idea of examining the food industry?

A. No. It was suggested by a researcher at NET who came to me with a graph showing the tremendous difference between the rise of farm prices and food prices over the last twenty years. And it was a good moment. I'd just finished the film on Appalachia and in a sense was turned on about the rottten state of economics in this country. At first I was interested in doing a show on broad economic aspects of the United States, but then that began to narrow down and I saw how the food industry might provide a very specific focus. I got very interested in the idea, and proposed to NET that we devote an entire evening of programming to the subject or do three one-hour shows with some live follow-ups. NET said to go ahead, and I then tried to find out what the whole subject was about.

Q. Can we get into the question of research as it's one of the least discussed elements of film making?

A. In this type of film, it's the most important thing. In most actuality films, you cover an event which is occurring or you place yourself in a situation which then becomes the film. In *Appalachia* I studied one particular family and watched what became of them. They, of course, became symbols of ideas, but at a different level they were filmed for themselves. But a film like *Hard Times* is almost totally a film of ideas. It's highly constructed, and one has many options for a framework. So the research became very important.

We spent six months researching the film, studying among other things the complete congressional committee reports on the 1966 Food Marketing Commission. My associate producer was Penny Bernstein, and we spent another three or four weeks traveling around the country—California, Iowa, Colorado, Washington—just talking to farmers, congressmen, and anybody else who had some knowledge of the situation. Finally, we had an outline for two shows—one on the consumers' situation and one on the farmers'.

Then NET said they didn't have enough money and could we do it in one show. I said, "No," thought about it a bit, and said we would take a crack at doing it all in one show. This meant we had to make a new outline of the ideas and things we wanted to cover. We also started direct researching with the camera as in cinéma vèrité. However, this film is different from cinéma vérité film in that everybody and every situation is a symbol for an idea.

Q. Do you recall the main points you jotted down in your outline?

A. Penny made a fifteen-page outline on the consumers' problems, and I typed up something similar on the farmers' end of it. I started from the historical fact that this is basically a rural country, and from the Jeffersonian idea that it was a land of small landowners and shop keepers and artisans. From there I wanted to show how we had grown into an industrial economy in which 207 giant corporations control almost two-thirds of all manufacturing assets. I was curious about how this affects us materially, and how this affects our life style. From there, I went into what had happened to the farmer, how he couldn't get reasonable prices for his goods, and how the corporations controlled his prices and in the end forced him off his land.

Q. Did you have any ideas in the outline which you found eventually just wouldn't work in the finished film?

A. The major section dropped was a section on the effect of absentee landlordship of the land. We filmed a number of situations, especially in the West, where corporations had moved in and were farming; what we tried to get was the effect on the community, on natural resources, and on the ecology. This worked out quite well, but we then dropped it because it was like another whole film.

Q. You've mentioned the lack of a natural framework as opposed to *Appalachia*. Did you foresee many problems in making ideas come alive on film?

A. Sure, that was the major problem. We had to take an abstraction like the economic situation and reduce it to film. In *Appalachia* I tried to cover both the economic and the political situations, and succeeded with the economics but failed with the politics. Yet I feel documentary—especially television documentary—in order to be relevant today, must be able to deal with abstract ideas and economic and political situations, and must be able to analyze institutions. It's no use just describing conditions; you also have to explain them, and it has to be done interestingly. That's what documentary is all about. So the challenge in *Hard Times* was how to take the abstraction of the economic situation and make it visual.

I felt this was relatively easy to do with the farmers' section. The farmers were being driven off the land. You filmed farmers being driven off the land; and you got your typical man who is being pushed down by the system. You can interview him or do his family life or anything else, and you can sympathize with him. I found it much more difficult to show the consumer side because we'd decided to film middle-class whites, and they are more difficult to get on film. There was very little visually that you could catch to show the problem of the middle-class white family who is paying a great deal more than it should for food, and yet the film was designed to show the experience of white middle-class America.

q. Did you find, as the film proceeded, that the balance changed between the farmers' section and the consumers' section?

a. The consumers' section was originally very long, but we ended up spending most of our time with the farmers' section because that was far more visual. It usually happens that a film takes on a life of its own and you go with your most interesting footage. This is especially true of documentary—you go with the footage you think most people can empathize with, which is an emotional experience more than anything else, and so the farmers' section took over. The consumer stuff, which was planned to last forty-five minutes of a one-and-a-half-hour film, eventually only lasted twenty minutes of a one-hour film. However, coming where it did, between the farmers being driven off the land and the corporation taking the land over, it helped tie the film together considerably.

q. You have some interesting visual footage on the slaughtering of animals. It's great to look at but struck me as a little irrelevant. Can you say why you put it in, because I'm not quite sure that section of the film works.

a. We were dealing with a situation where the retail chains control the price of meat and everybody else down the line gets very little, including the packer. Now the packer is the guy who slaughters the beef and then cuts it up. His profits are limited by what the retail chain will give; as a consequence the guy underneath tries to become more efficient and cut his costs, so as to make a good profit even though the retail price is low. In so doing, he steps on everybody beneath him. So the whole idea of that sequence was to show the packer—in this case Iowa Beef—trying to take over the entire process from the raising to the retailing of the cattle. This drive to become more efficient necessitated slaughter on assembly lines and very low wages for the workers. In other words, yet another part of the industry was growing into a monopoly because of pressure from above; and yet the individuals concerned, although they helped increase corporate profits, got very little in the way of decent wages. This monopoly business is like a weed—it grows like a living organism.

q. You said a little earlier that three weeks before air time, you had to cut the film down from an hour and a half to an hour. What changes did you make?

a. Everything was just tightened up. It wasn't that we left out any section; it was just that we shortened everything. We had a longer section in there about the chicken industry. It was virtually the first industry to be totally integrated and taken over by a number of large corporations, and we tried to show what happens to people in that situation. We showed farmers being black listed by companies because they were asking more money for their chickens, and we tried to draw a comparison between the chicken industry and the cattle industry. We took that out and just tightened everything else up. In the end it became slightly less of a visual film experience, but it became sharper and more hard hitting.

Q. In *Hard Times* you take a search light to a number of industries and have analyzed them very carefully and very critically. What were your difficulties in doing this, in trying to get into the thing, and what reaction did you get from the industries concerned when they learned of your research?

A. The main difficulty was trying to understand a very complex economic situation and look at it realistically. Most economists are interested in rationalizing a situation. We weren't. We were interested in showing why the situation wasn't working and what were the human and price effects caused by monopoly. Nobody cooperated with us. It was a very touchy situation. Food prices are very high, but the image of the companies is protected by very high-powered publicity people.

Q. But you had to approach some of the companies for cooperation, didn't you?

A. Yes. The first one I approached was Gates Rubber Company in Colorado. They make wheels and rubber implements for farmers and they had gone into broilers—chickens—in a very big way. They had also bought up an enormous amount of land in eastern Colorado for raising sugar beets and were using up the natural water resource in the plains very quickly. I called them and said I wanted to film them. I told them I wanted to go through their plant, and I wanted to talk to them about their use of the water resources. However, the PR man told me that, since it had become known that besides making farm implements they had actually taken up farming, the farmers had stopped buying their implements. Because of this they had decided as a matter of policy not to talk to anybody at all. That was my first set-to.

The next run-in was with the cereal industry, which is controlled by three major companies. None of them would talk to us. They had something that is called the Cereal Institute which is a lobby which they pay for, and I suppose they tack it onto the price of the cereal. I wanted to do interviews with some of the top executives and talk to them about the high cost of cereal. So we sent them a letter, which was handed over to the head of the Cereal Institute. He wasn't very happy about it and came to me, and together we drafted a set of questions. Two weeks later he called me back and said that because of the MSG and the cyclamate controversy, the cereal companies had decided they just didn't want to go on television about anything. So they didn't appear.

When we did our meat story about the high price of meat, we wrote the four major chains. Three of them said they just couldn't find a way to make anybody available to us, while the fourth one said that, because of the high cost of meat, he'd appear in the wrong whatever he said, and they decided not to come. So, with the exception of the Iowa Beef Packers, we got no cooperation and no company appearances. If the companies come back now and say they want equal time, we can do another program on it. I hope they do. That's what it's all about!

Q. In England, there is a certain tradition of equal time for both sides, and another concept of always balancing an attack by a defense. In *Hard Times* it's all attack.

A. Sometimes there aren't two sides to an argument. They're cheating on us. They are charging us too much money for food. There's no two sides to that; there's no two sides to hunger; there's no two sides to poverty. You can question why it is, which I think we do. We do question why it happens and try to show it in the film, but there aren't two sides to it. Food costs a helluva lot, and the farmers are being driven off the land; it's the economic set-up that is doing it. The other side?—I don't know what the other side is.

Q. Was there any one thing you were very cautious about in making the film?

A. One of my main worries was the need to be factually correct, even though other people might take the same facts and, depending on their philosophy, come up with different conclusions. They might think it was great that we have 200 companies running the country. They might be able to say, "Look at what a wealthy country we are, and look at the great things that are going for us." But I'm interested in looking at the conventional wisdom and presenting a different point of view; in doing that, all I care about is that we are factually correct and that the conclusions are reasonable given the facts.

If you are talking about whether I was worried about censorship, NET's position has always been merely to check that we are factually correct. There will be stations that probably won't run the show, but my point is that you make the film for yourself and you fight those fights later.* Public television and Congress may well be very upset with the film. We attacked people in Congress, which gives money for public television and to which we still go annually for funds. The only thing about that is that when you start to compromise you might as well not make your program.

Q. What was your biggest problem on the film, outside of shooting difficulties?

A. The biggest problem we had was the fantastic amount of research. There was just so much to digest, and we then had to boil it all down so that it could be translated into film. Because of that this film took twice as long as any other film I've made.

Q. How long did it take from the beginning of the research?

A. One year.

Q. How long do you think the film will last, and what do you think will be its main use?

A. I don't think it's going to be very long. I think it is more journalistic than filmic. There are films you look at many times, because you see so many different things working on different levels. But I don't think this film is like that. It makes very clear, sharp, intellectual, journalistic points, and once you get them there is no reason to see the film again. As for use, the film may be of some benefit in helping to organize consumers and farmers. I guess it's the clearest case the farmers have to illustrate their situation, and they'll probably turn to it quite a lot.

* This interview was recorded after the final mix, but before the actual broadcast of the film.

7

Sixteen In Webster Groves
and
The Berkeley Rebels
Arthur Barron

Most of Arthur Barron's film career has been spent within network television, especially CBS. Yet he looks and talks like the complete antinetwork personality; he is too individualistic and too iconoclastic to fit into the disciplined network formula. And he doesn't. Questioned about his reputation in the networks, he replies, "I'm known as their lunatic fringe."

Barron was born in Boston in 1929 and has a PhD in sociology from Columbia University. Like Jack Willis (p. 122) his entry into film came through the good office of David Susskind for whom he researched and wrote a script on Eva Peron.

From 1960 to 1963 Barron worked on a series of taped television shows such as "Behind the News" and "The Nation's Future." His first solo was the film The Rebirth of Jonny *(1963) which deals with the improvement in the condition of an autistic child under the guidance of an understanding therapist. Barron then wrote, produced, and sometimes directed another six documentaries including* My Childhood *and* The Rise of Labor, *before starting to work for "CBS Reports" in 1965, where he in turn produced* The Berkeley Rebels *(1965) and* Sixteen in Webster Groves *(1966).*

The Berkeley Rebels *dealt with four students on the Berkeley campus of the University of California, all of whom were deeply involved in the resurgent campus political activity of the mid-sixties. Although the film received much vilification for glorifying "untypical communistic students," the most curious aspect of the film is the attitude taken by CBS in "straightening it up," which Barron comments on in his interview.*

Two versions are said to exist of the film: (1) the original version, cut prior to the editorial interference of CBS, and (2) the doctored version as broadcast by the network. I have only seen the latter; and while I found it a basically intriguing and faithful picture of university tensions as I remembered them from California, I also experienced myself getting continually irritated by the insertion of too many balanced, neutralizing statements.

In Webster Groves *Barron set out to analyze the attitudes of all the sixteen-year-olds in a wealthy St. Louis suburb towards marriage, education, their future, and the like. After considerable research Barron finally made a film that illustrates a town locked into smugness, complacency, and self-satisfaction. One sees a community where demonstrations are frowned upon, where conformity is the norm, where the girl of sixteen has already picked out the place she wants to live, and where the child's main ideal is to emulate the parents.*

Barron is probably correct in saying that the film accurately portrays the value structure of Webster Groves, and I have no quarrel with his editorial point of view. However, for a program that purports to be based on serious scientific research, the resultant picture seems to provide a mere surface description rather than any serious sociological analysis. A description of a situation is given, with the blame being laid at the door of the parents; but there is little discussion of other possibilities, of ways out, of the capacity for change within the situation. This may be asking too much of a fifty-minute film, but I felt the omission of such questions marred an otherwise excellent program.

Since Webster Groves *Barron has made* Birth and Death *(1968),* Johnny Cash *(1969), a vérité profile of the country and western singer, and an interesting trilogy for CBS called* The Great American Novel. *He has also become head of the film program at Columbia University.*

As of 1970 Barron seems to be moving away from the networks and in the direction of features. Thus he is currently at work on a feature called The Turk Comes for McGarrity, *and is also considering doing* Prince Valiant *as a kind of James Dean character, with background music supplied by rock and roll.*

Q. At the 1967 American Film Festival *Sixteen in Webster Groves* was awarded the prize for the best social documentary of the year. Was this study of middle-class American youth your idea, or did it come from CBS?

A. A little while earlier I had made a film for CBS called *The Berkeley Rebels*; and because that was a film about youth, I sort of became typecast at the network as a youth expert and was called in one day and was told that I would be making my next film about teen-agers.

Q. Do you have any idea why CBS was particularly interested in the subject?

A. Evidently, CBS considered that the problem of where the teen-agers were going was about to become an important, newsworthy, and topical issue, and therefore they wanted to do a film about it.

That's how projects usually get started on the networks—out of a sense of what will be in the news, what will be topical, and what will be important. What is beautiful or what is interesting for its own sake, or what is timeless, or ageless, or universal about the human condition doesn't seem to matter. What is important is what will be on the front pages of the newspaper tomorrow. So I was given the topic of teen-agers—and that's all the direction I received. From there on it was up to me to come up with some kind of concept. But I was also given a warning. I was told that my film had better be more objective and balanced, and more journalistically accurate than *The Berkeley Rebels,* because *The Berkeley Rebels* had created enormous controversy within CBS of a rather unprecedented kind, not in quality but in terms of the people it affected and so forth. So I was put on warning that this film about teen-agers would be watched very carefully.

Q. How free was CBS in terms of time and budgets?

A. The networks are very generous about time. Generally speaking, you have as much time as you need to finish a film of this nature—six months, eight months, whatever. Budget is another matter. There are innumerable discussions with the business affairs people of the network, who go over every penny in a kind of adversary proceeding with the producer, till you finally arrive at a figure on which you both agree. And it's important that you stay within that figure. I had a reputation of going way over budget all the time, and when I was doing *The Berkeley Rebels* I was told that if the picture did not come in according to the budget, I would be fired.

Q. What led you from the broad topic of teen-agers to the specific investigation of the school children of Webster Groves?

A. What interested me was not teen-agers en masse, but the suburban upper-middle-class teenager, the representative—so to speak—of the American dream. I wanted to look at the communities where the American dream of affluence and education is being realized, and I wanted to find out what was the quality and meaning of life among young people in such a community. And it seemed best to do it by filming one particular community that might typify a great number. I then decided one other thing. I thought it might be very interesting —both from the sociological standpoint but also from a kind of defensive, protective feeling since I had been burnt so badly on *The Berkeley Rebels*—to make a scientific study of all of the teen-agers of sixteen years of age in one community, and base the film entirely on those findings.

Q. Why did you settle for the sixteen-year-olds?

A. I decided on the age of sixteen for various reasons. It's the age at which kids get their automobile licenses, it's the age in which they are in the middle of the high school system, it's the age when kids begin to think seriously about themselves, and so forth.

Q. Did you have to check back with CBS after you'd defined the line of the film?

A. Once you've agreed with them ahead of time on the budget, and on the general theory of the film, they pretty much leave you alone until the rough-cut stage if you are an established producer.

Q. What happened after you'd decided on the survey idea?

A. CBS thought this was a kind of nice idea, because such a thing had never been done; and then I went out to the research center at the University of Chicago and designed a survey with them. We went to the census bureau, and asked for a list of six or seven very typical, upper-middle-class communities that would most clearly represent the suburban, upper-middle-class American community in terms of education, home ownership, income, and so forth. They came back with a list of seven places, and after a little bit of exploration I finally chose Webster Groves. I went to Webster Groves, saw the principal of the high school, and told him I wanted to give a very detailed questionnaire to every sixteen-year-old student in the school. I also told him I wanted to do a few sample interviews of two or three hours in length with some of the sixteen-year-olds, and that eventually I wanted to make a film about it all.

Q. Was the principal cooperative, or was he suspicious of your intentions?

A. I had to get permission both from the principal and also from the school board. My explanation was that the mass media had not portrayed the teen-ager very accurately. Films and television had shown the teen-ager as either a leather-jacketed, rough, tough, delinquent kind of kid or as an empty-headed, silly kind of person. I said that CBS wanted to correct these myths. We believed that out there somewhere there must be a kid who differed from these two extremes, and for once we wanted to depict the life of the real teen-ager on the basis of an objective scientific study. I also said that Webster Groves was a fine community, that most of its kids went to college, that it had a very good school system and that we thought we could find here an affirmative and positive demonstration of what the teen-ager was really like. They warmed very much to this idea, thought it was terrific, and gave me their permission. This, by the way, was before the study was designed, and before I did three or four weeks of research in the community to get a sense of the people, of the kids and their parents.

Q. When you talked to the board did you already have a shrewd idea that your film might indict the community and its values rather than praise them?

A. I must say that I wasn't totally honest in persuading the school board to let me do the film. There was, as in many films, a certain amount of conning and manipulating involved. I think it is fair to say that I left the impression that my feeling was that an honest study would reveal something affirmative and positive, which had not been said in the mass media before, about the seriousness of students, their devotion to studies, the solidity of their home life, and the like. That impression was a kind of background to all of the discussions in the community. I agree that I never said to the community or CBS that what we would find was a highly materialistic society whose individuality was crushed, and whose values were absolutely deplorable, but then these were things I didn't know myself at the time.

Q. Do you remember some of the questions you asked in the survey?

A. Yes. What is your major goal in life? What do you think it takes to be successful as an adult? Do you respect your parents? Have you ever played hookey from school? Do you drink beer or liquor? Can you identify the following people: Dick Van Dyke, Richard Nixon, etc.? Do you have a driver's license? Do you have a private bank account? How much allowance do you receive? Do you want to go to college? Why do you want to go to college? It was a very deep and probing assessment of the behavior and attitudes of teen-agers. After I got the answers, I met with the National Opinion Research Center people and made a presentation of the results. They were amazed and horrified.

Q. What did the results show you?

A. The people involved at the University of Chicago said to me the film shouldn't be called *Sixteen in Webster Groves* but *Forty in Webster Groves*. The picture revealed by the survey was not one of youth experiencing a beautiful freedom and undergoing a period of extreme idealism and self-expression, but a picture of children who were robotized, narrow, prejudiced—dupes of the values which produced their parents and which produced an American capitalist, middle-class, bureaucratic society. It was a picture of children who were perfectly designed replacement parts for suburban, placid America. That's what the results indicated.

Q. How did you develop the film after the results? How did you plan sequences to illustrate visually points you knew were psychologically and sociologically true?

A. I have basically worked in two styles of film making. The first style is represented by *Webster Groves*, which is a highly directed kind of style. In such a film you have a specific message or a specific point of view that you want to communicate; and then you shape and bend everything to that kind of expression. You create scenes, you design scenes, you set scenes, indeed you stage scenes, to evoke that particular method and point of view. The other style I've worked in is cinéma vérité, with nothing staged at all.

Q. The kids driving their cars was obviously a "created sequence." How did that arise from your survey results.

A. I took the results and found in the results that the car driving thing was very important. It was a kind of metaphor for the freedom of the youngsters, for getting away from parents and for experiencing self. I decided that there had to be a scene in the film which reflected that survey finding, so I designed a scene to evoke that feeling. What I did was send out the word to twenty kids that I wanted them to assemble with their cars at a particular hour on a particular day at a particular spot. I told them we would rendezvous with them at a particular time to film them, and some we would meet later; I told them that the cameraman would be on this street, with the camera down in the sewer, and would do the filming, and that there would be a helicopter section of filming, and so on. It was designed and shaped almost as though one were making a feature film.

By the way, I took a calendar, and I planned a shooting schedule. For example, Monday from ten to one we will shoot cooking class. Now in some cases, I was just shooting on a hunch that the scene would be useful. I didn't really know where the cooking class would fit into the film. Eventually the sequence with the turkey and the pie and the music became a symbol for American TV commercials, *Good Housekeeping* magazine, clean kitchens—that kind of thing.

Q. After the survey you shaped the film to illustrate a certain thesis based on the survey. But did you obtain material that didn't conform to that point of view? and if so, what did you do with it? For example, you have a group of parents who are sitting talking, who are all very uptight. Did you, however, find a group of parents oppositely inclined whom you excluded from the film?

A. That's a very good point. One of the criticisms I got after the film was, "You picked a group of narrow conservative parents, but you might just as well have picked another set of parents who would have disagreed with what the first group said, because such parents do exist in Webster Groves." The thing is, I wanted it that way. You remember that while the parents talk you can see a red convertible car just outside the window. That wasn't accidental. We went out in the streets and put lights on that car, because I wanted people to see this sleek red, rich car, behind the people. That detail indicates my feelings about the scene.

I thought very seriously about making the group more dynamic, in the sense of having parents who disagree, but rejected it for the following reasons. It is not my job as a film maker to be an encyclopedia, to show what is the total reality of a situation. I'm not omniscient. In *Webster Groves* I was out to evoke the essential truth about the community. I wanted to show the nature of it and the currents in which it was flowing. I wasn't out to show that there were eddies of dissent. I was out to capture the overwhelming feeling of the community, and I wanted to do that in the strongest, most cinematic, most devasting way possible. I feel that the parents in that room are the perfect embodiment of the dominant value system of that society, and that was my justification. My feeling about film is that there has to be an intensification of reality—it is not just a recording. It is an intensification and dramatization, reflecting the passionate point of view of the film maker; and as long as one does not betray the essential truth, everything is fine. I must say that I was out to get those people, pure and simple; and I sat down and I designed a shooting schedule which would enable me to present in visual and emotional terms the findings of the survey.

Q. One sees a lot of a boy wearing a carnation. Did you make him wear the carnation? Is he to be taken as a symbol of the mass?

A. He was a quarterback in the football team, and on the day before a very important game all the ball team were wearing carnations. He is a symbol, and I used him as a symbol. I kept coming back to him because he seemed to me to be an important figure in the film.

Q. The film comes out as an indictment of a certain dream. Did you have problems with CBS, when they saw the way the film was going?

A. Not really. There was no question of censorship or difficulties regarding the truthfulness of the film or the political consequences of the film. As a matter of fact most of the executives at CBS were delighted, and said, "Yes, that's the way it is." But then everything I had was backed up by the survey data. If I hadn't done the survey it might have been different. What difficulties there were seemed to center around cinematic decisions. For example, there was a scene that I had filmed for the opening of the film which was censored, which we were not permitted to use.

Q. Could you specify?

A. The opening scene was one of the most ambitious kind of scenes I have ever attempted to film in my life. We had five camera crews, and had placed Charles Kuralt, the commentator, in a helicopter. The idea was that the film would open with Kuralt flying over *Webster Groves* in the helicopter and saying, "It has so many people, it has so many churches, it has no bars." He would then fly over the high school and he would land in front of the high school. At the very moment of his landing, the doors of the high school would burst open, and 3,000 screaming, shrieking students would run across the field, and surround him, and in the midst of all their confusion he would start asking them questions like, "How old are you? What kind of community is this? What do you like here? Do you date?" We did this with five crews, including one in the helicopter and one on the roof of the school, and got the clouds of dirt from the helicopter, the wind, the noise, the confusion, and the kids running madly from the school. It was an incredible gas of a scene. We cut it to a rock and roll score, and it was wild! It's one of the most exciting openings of a film I have ever seen. Then the vice-president in charge of documentaries sat down, looked at that scene, and said, "I never want to see that again. Out! That will not be in this picture."

Q. Did you ask why?

A. He said, "A CBS newsman doesn't descend like Batman into a community; a CBS newsman is a dignified, serious person. If there was a flood or disaster, I could see him landing with a helicopter."

Q. You've got a rather nice slow-motion sequence near the end. Did they raise any objections to that?

A. The president of CBS news at the time looked at the scene and said, "There's something wrong with that footage; people don't run that way. What's the matter, is there a mistake?" I said, "It's slow motion," and he said, "But you can't use that, that's not journalism; that's like for an art picture." When the picture was all over and got a lot of favorable attention, the president of CBS news called me in and said, "I want you to know I like your work a lot; I think you are one of our most gifted film makers; but, in the future, we don't want scenes like the car scene or the makeup scene."

Q. What did he oppose in the girls' makeup scene?

A. The way it was shot like a television commercial. It lasts for maybe a minute and a half or two mintes, and it shows girls putting on makeup, lipstick, eye shadow—all in close up. Then, to add to the scene, we took vaseline and smeared it on the lens to give it a kind of cloudy effect. I was told that in the future I was not to do scenes like that because they weren't true. It was shaped journalism. This brings in the whole problem of objectivity, truth, and journalism on the networks. For the networks the truth has to be recorded, not shaped.

The newsman is a kind of unfeeling, objective, analytic, recorder and capturer of reality; he's not a person who shapes and intensifies reality to evoke a particular kind of response. That's what I'd done, and that's the sin I had to avoid in the future.

Q. What was the reaction of the Webster Groves community?

A. A howl of rage. It was tremendously angry. I was charged with betraying the community. The charges were very specific and were sent to the Federal Communications Commission and to the president of CBS. I was accused of exaggeration, distorting scenes, line bending, and so on. However, the criticism that most worried CBS was that expressed by its local affiliate station before the broadcast. The affiliate said to the CBS network people something like, "You'll ruin us. We won't be able to function in this community. What are you going to do about it?"

As a result, the president of CBS news called me into his office and said, "How would you like to make a film in which you go back to Webster Groves on the night of the broadcast and film the responses of the people as it is being broadcast, and then hang around the next day and get further reactions? Do you think that would be a good film?" And I said, "No. I think that would be an atrocious film." He said, "All right," and then a day later called me in and said, "I know you think it's a bad idea, but I am ordering you to go and make this film." The reason he gave me for doing this was that it would provide a unique opportunity for CBS to contribute understanding and insight into the communication process, and would show how a film was received and perceived by interested viewers. It would be an innovative contribution to the understanding of television's impact on society. However, I got the feeling that the return shooting in Webster Groves was also motivated by the desire to let all the people who were angry blow off some steam, and have the last word.*

Q. You mentioned before that various problems had arisen with the network over *The Berkeley Rebels.* Can we go back to that film and discuss some of its problems. I gather the topic was specifically proposed to you by CBS?

A. Yes. They wanted a film about youth for the "CBS Reports." They told me that there was a lot of trouble out at Berkeley, and the situation was becoming difficult and controversial. They then suggested that I explore the situation in terms of the goals of the youth of today,

* A second film was in fact made by Barron a month after the first broadcast, called *Webster Groves Revisited* (1966); it examined the impact of the first film on the community.

THE BERKELEY REBELS
Preparatory Notes of Arthur Barron

1. *Focus*. This film is *not* about the University of California; it is *not* about the class of 1965; it is *not* about mass education; it is *not* about the demonstrations which have taken place at California. These are all elements in our story, but the film is basically about something else. It is about a selected group of students. Call them "activists," "the new radicals," "FSM'ers," or "green baggers." This picture is about *them*. It seeks to explore their world. It seeks to answer these questions: Who are they? What do they want? Why are they important? It seeks to reveal the mood, posture, and attitudes of a new and different generation of committed student.

2. *Point of View*. We do not state a point of view directly, but we do have an attitude toward these kids, and (hopefully) it comes through. It is this: despite their faults (intolerance, a tendency to see things in "black-and-white," immaturity, rebellion for its own sake, a certain disrespect for law and order), these kids are a positive and admirable force in American society. They are idealistic, committed, vocal, brilliant. They are *alive*. They are willing to say "the emperor wears no clothes." They are generous, compassionate, and moral. They take America's promises seriously (so seriously it will probably break them). They are, in short, our conscience.

3. *Style*. This is a highly personal film. It is intimate. It is emotional. Its style is human revelation rather than reportage. It is told subjectively, rather than objectively. It is told from the inside out, rather than from the outside in. It is more a diary than as essay, more an autobiography than a report, more a drama than journalism. Its model is Salinger's *Catcher in the Rye* and Nick Webster's *Walk in my Shoes*. Its goal is to *enter* the world of these kids, rather than to observe and report on it.

4. *Narration*. The rule here is: *as little as possible*. Ideally, the story will be told completely in the words and voices of our kids. First person all the way. This includes exposition (where required), as well as "inner thoughts" and "attitudes." We intend to use a CBS reporter merely to set the scene, to indicate that (distorted or not) this is the way these kids see the world, and to conclude. The twenty-odd hours or so we have on quarter inch tape of these kids *is* our narration.

5. *Format*. The film is in three acts. Each act corresponds to an underlying cause of agitation and disaffection among the activists. Act I is "Kate and the Multiversity." It follows Kate Coleman, a senior who will graduate in June. On a personal level it is the story of her satisfactions and dissatisfactions with California. On a broader level, it is the story of the achievement and failures of mass education. Act II

and see what kind of a picture I could make. I said, "Fine," and went out to Berkeley for three or four weeks to interview kids and get a feel for the place. I then returned to CBS and told them I wanted to do the film around four people whose lives and habits would illustrate the three themes or problem areas out of which the troubles come.

is "Ron and Sal: Love and All That Jazz." It follows Ron Anastasi and Sally Leary, two unmarried students who live together. In this act we reveal these kids' attitudes toward authority, responsibility, their parents, the older generation, and individual morality. The message of this act is this: our kids feel the adult world is corrupt and morally bankrupt; they believe they must decide what is moral for *themselves*. Act III is "Mike: The New Politics." Mike Rossman is a grad student. He teaches math. As we follow him, we gain insight into the political mood and stance of his generation. Mike's politics are different in important ways from any generation which has preceeded him. We show how and why this is so, and we reveal what this means to youth today and to America.

6. *Film Technique.* There are three kinds of scenes in this show. (*a*) *Actuality Scenes.* These comprise the bulk of our shooting. They are scenes of events which were shot as they happened with a minimum of intrusion by us (e.g., the picketing of "lily-white" restaurants by 2,000 Berkeley students). (*b*) *Fantasy Scenes.* These scenes are designed to reveal intensely personal "inner states" in an unusually imaginative and dramatic way. (*c*) *Staged Scenes.* There are a few scenes where we directed students, told them to do something, and filmed it (e.g. to show loneliness and alienation filmically, we had Kate walk down a long Pentagon-like corridor in the University. As she walks towards us, we dolly toward her until she walks into black into the lens. We hear nothing but the echo of her clicking heels as she takes this walk, which plays for about 30 seconds). To put it another way, most of our scenes are genuinely documentary, but some are created. This is because we rely in good part on the beauty and originality of *visual* images to tell our story.

Q. What were these themes?

A. One of them was the political theme, dealing with the new breed of kid who is very antiestablishment and involved with the new left. I'd found a kid called Mike Rossman who embodied this kind of thing, and I wanted to follow him. Another area of trouble was the disenchantment with the large university, in which the educational system becomes too impersonal and too removed. Here I wanted to follow a graduating girl called Kate Coleman. Finally I wanted to follow a young unmarried couple who had rebelled against their parents and were living together, and represented a kind of new search for values.

Q. The style of the film is rather different from the usual "CBS Reports"?

A. Yes. I told CBS I didn't want to do an analytical investigation. I didn't want to do a piece of objective reporting, and I didn't want to use the factual approach. What I wanted to do was evoke the world of these kids as they saw it themselves, in their own words. What I thought we could do was have a CBS spokesman come on at the beginning of the program and give a short introduction, something like,

"There's been a lot of trouble at Berkeley. There's been a lot of trouble around the nation. There's a new breed of kid, and tonight we're going to let them speak for themselves. You might think they're crazy, you might think they have a very warped outlook; but in order for you to understand what is going on, you have to get a sense of their world. Tonight, we are going to present that world in their words. Here it is! We are not saying we approve; we are not saying their answers to problems are accurate. But for a while let's see their world, see through their eyes, hear with their ears, and reject or accept. Thank you very much. And now, the Berkeley Rebels." That's what I wanted to do. I didn't want analyses or objective reporting. I wanted to evoke the world of the students with as much dynamism and strength as I could. And, after a bit of discussion, CBS agreed to go along with that approach.

Q. How did you shape the film?

A. The film was a mixture of things. On the one hand there was the simple diary-like following of people; but then, like in *Webster Groves,* I tried deliberately shaping scenes to evoke a particular mood. For example, I tried a sequence which I called "Facts, facts, facts." One of the criticisms of the university was that the kids were being fed information and facts but were not being taught wisdom or how to think. So I designed a sequence called "Facts, facts, facts" to illustrate the point.

We had a bathtub filled with soap bubbles, and suddenly out of this bathtub emerges a huge bearded student with water dripping off him. He looks at the camera and says, "The square root of the hypotenuse is so and so," and then he sinks back into the water. You remember those skating boards people used to have? In another shot I had a guy racing down a hill on one of these skate boards and as he goes past the camera he'd scream, "The Athenian Wars began in. . . ." For another evocation sequence I took a dog and gave him molasses candy to eat. As he chewed it looked as if he was talking, and we put a voice under the dog with a german accent. It was a very funny sequence, but it drove CBS completely up the wall, and they threw it out. Do you want another example?

Q. Yes.

A. I originally began the picture with four Berkeley Rebels riding motorcycles across the campus with a kind of beautiful music behind them and had them take the motorbikes through an outside terrace where kids were having lunch. People were screaming. Dishes were flying. It was incredible. Anyway, those were the evocative sequences. There was a lot of cinéma vérité, where I just followed events as they occurred.

Q. What was your relationship with the university authorities in all this?

A. I got permission from the university at the highest level to make this film. Then as the word began to get back that we were filming people in bathtubs, that we were filming people on motorcycles going through terraces, that we were not filming any experts or professors, in other words that we were not behaving like the typical CBS news documentary crew, I began to sense a kind of problem, a kind of tension and difficulty. Yet nobody from CBS told me to stop. Nobody flew out there. They let me go on, but I could tell there would be difficulties. As a matter of fact, one day there was a demonstration against CBS. The conservative students who felt we were acting in a very prejudiced way ran a demonstration with signs like, "CBS Go Home" and "CBS Unfair." But we went on with the film, and I brought it back and made a rough cut.

Q. You mentioned that CBS took out the talking dog sequence, but were there any sequences which you yourself dropped before the rough cut and which aren't in the final film?

A. There were a number of sequences which worked, but which were aesthetically unpleasing. We had decided to begin the film at Sproul Hall, which was the central administration building where all the trouble had taken place. At one time the kids had occupied the building, and the police had come with night sticks and tear gas and dragged them out. So it was a kind of symbol. I decided that we would open the film at night, and shot Mike Rossman wandering through Sproul Hall at midnight kind of remembering the events. I also wanted to have Kate Coleman standing on the spot where she had been arrested in front of Sproul Hall, and Ron and Sal standing on the spots where they had been arrested. The atmosphere would be quiet and mysterious. Then, in this otherwise deserted place with just Mike wandering around, we would begin hearing the yelling of the police and the screams of the students. I thought that it would look fine on film, so we shot it, and it didn't work. It was lousy; it was wooden and stagey and terrible, and we threw it out.

Q. That sequence didn't work aesthetically. Were there any other sequences you left out because they seemed too extreme, or too unfair to individuals, or too biased?

A. One of the students was very critical of his parents, and particularly of his father; we filmed a very moving interview with him, in which he spoke about his parents and about the meaning of their lives. However, I felt the interview was just too brutal to be used. I felt I could not take the responsibility for those parents seeing their son talking about them in that way before millions of people. I left it out with some regret because the boy was weeping, and the whole scene was very strong and powerful.

Q. Who had to see the rough cut at CBS?

A. Generally the vice-president in charge of news documentaries would screen a film several times and then suggest a few changes. Sometimes the suggestions for changes were couched in terms of persuasion; sometimes they were direct orders. After these changes had been made the film would then be screened for the president of CBS.

Q. What changes were suggested in this case, by your network superiors?

A. There were a lot, and what the changes added up to in effect was a winnowing out of the picture of those evocative elements which had been shaped and staged and had not developed spontaneously out of a given situation. For example, the "Facts, facts, facts" sequence was taken out as was that of the talking dog. I had also placed motor-cycles all over campus for the beginning, and all of the motorcycle scenes which were shot in places where motorcycles don't ordinarily go were thrown out. There were deletions like that all the way through. I'll give you another example.

One day I went to this young couple who were living together and said, "I just want to film you all today," and they said, "Okay," and we stayed there eleven hours. At one point when they were very tired of us, they both got on top of the bed and began to tickle each other. Then they began to have a good time and began to kiss and cuddle, and we filmed it and cut a sequence which was very natural and beautiful. CBS, however, felt it was too bold. What right did we have to pry into their private lives and feelings? That kind of comment was terribly revealing to me about the attitudes and approach of the networks. According to the networks, it is not part of their job to penetrate into the soul of the person. Their job is to deal with that part of a person that is controllable. They want to deal with the issues. The notion of really going after a person and getting some real naked insight, that's terrifying to them. They don't want to do that —it's not news. So the scene on the bed was thrown out.

In contrast to these exclusions CBS insisted that certain factual explanations had to be added. For instance, very early in the film we find Mike Rossman in his room. He's walking around and talking to the camera, and in the background you can hear the music of the Swingle Singers, which I felt created the right mood. But one of the executives reviewing the picture said, "Did you shoot the phonograph?" When I said, "Yes," he said, "I insist that it be in the film." That literally realistic attitude is revealing, isn't it. So I had to go and look through our footage, find the phonograph, and insert it—just to show we weren't adding the music for mood and that it was a factual part of the scene.

I must say in these screenings with the president and vice-president of CBS news, the executives bought the general line of the picture. They understood that it wasn't CBS news objectively reporting and weighing and balancing, but that it was an attempt to enter the world of the students and that the kids were their own narrators. So they approved the picture; then, a very strange thing happened. One day I got a call from the vice-president in charge of documentaries, who said, "Arthur, we want you to stand by for a special screening of the film with William Paley and Frank Stanton, and there may be some changes made." This was maybe three weeks before broadcast, after the picture had already been approved. I said, "Okay."

Q. Wasn't Fred Friendly in charge of news then?

A. Pretty much. Fred is a very gutsy guy. He finally quit CBS over this kind of thing. He had approved the picture, with the changes I indicated, and I remember him calling me during this period and saying, "Arthur, I've approved the picture, and I'm prepared to defend it, but I want you to assure me that there is nothing now in the picture that is not honest, that did not happen on its own. I don't want anything that you paid people to do because I am putting myself on the line for the picture, and I'm doing it out of confidence and respect for you; so if there is anything not right in this picture, now is the time to let me know." I assured him, got this call to stand by, and about three hours later my boss called me into his office and said, "They've seen your picture, and there are going to be some changes." He was very sympathetic and as unhappy about what was happening as I was. I didn't know at the time that there had been a tremendous fight, and that Fred had said, "I have approved this film, and there won't be any changes," and that his superiors had said, "That picture is not going on the air in that form, and these are the changes you are going to make."

Q. Do you have any idea of the reasons for this sudden interest and concern for your film?

A. I was told later that what had happened was that Clark Kerr, the president of the University of California, had written a letter to Frank

Stanton saying in effect that he hadn't seen the picture but had been told that it was very dangerous and unfair; that it was distorted and full of lies; that I had paid people to say things; and that there were various erotic scenes in the film—in short, that the whole thing was going to be a disaster and would be very embarrassing to the university and to CBS. As far as I understand, Stanton didn't interview Kerr and got no expert testimony. He just bought the story, hook, line, and sinker. So, I was told to make these changes. I can't really tell you what they were; there were too many.

Q. Can you give me just a few examples of scenes they forced out?

A. There was a wonderful thing called "the spaghetti scene." One of the criticisms the Berkeley Rebels made of the other kids at university was that they were careerists and materialists, and that all they wanted out of life was a decent salary and a nice home in the suburbs. The fraternities embodied all these things that the Rebels criticized, and so I decided to film inside a fraternity house on an evening they were having a Tom Jones party. Tom Jones parties were the rage among the fraternity kids that year, and what the Tom Jones parties meant to the kids was to dump a lot of food on the floor and eat it with their bare hands, with no silverware or napkins or anything, and smear it on the girls' faces and bodies.

Anyway, we came to the fraternity house, and saw that a sailcloth had been spread over, and that apart from a juke box, the room was empty. Then the kids turned on rock and roll music on the juke box, and people came in and dumped huge tubs of spaghetti and meat balls on the floor. Someone gave a signal and the guys and their dates rushed into this room, began eating the spaghetti with their bare hands, smearing it on the girls' breasts, soul kissing each other with meatballs, and throwing food at each other. It was a scene that even Buñuel could not have invented. Our cameraman, Walter Dombrow, who had been to Vietnam, was shaking like a leaf when this was over. He said, "I've filmed in combat, but I've never seen anything like this. I have to rest up." It was unbelievable. Fred Friendly loved the scene, but it went out of the picture, the reason being that it was a slander against nice kids. Everyone agreed that this kind of behavior went on, but since we were not showing the other side of these kids— the fact that they studied hard and were really decent kids—the scene had to go. Do you want any more examples?

Q. Just give me one more.

A. The classes are really huge at Berkeley. In history, for example, they have something like 800 kids in an auditorium with the lecturer. Then upstairs, they have the same lecture on television for other classes. We started filming the lecture downstairs and then continued with a dolly shot down the corridor, so that as we went by each classroom, we saw the kids watching the same lecture on five television sets in five classrooms. Then, in a continuous movement, we dollied into a room where a kid wearing sunglasses was watching this lecture, and you could see the television lecture reflected on his glasses. When we edited the film we cut back and forth from screen to sunglasses and sunglasses to screen and had Kate Coleman say, voice over, "It's so weird. Education here is like two movies watching each other." So they threw out the sunglass scene. They said it was too extreme, too manipulated.

Q. How would you characterize the nature of the changes CBS wanted?

A. The first thing that happened was that the really eloquent and strongest scenes were thrown out of the film. The second thing was that they decided there had to be more balance in the film. This meant I had to fly out to Berkeley and interview professors analyzing the revolt and saying things like, "The kids are immature and impatient. It will all blow over," that kind of thing. The third thing was they made me put in two or three minutes from a speech Clark Kerr made in the Greek Theatre in Berkeley. It was again the idea of balance.

Q. What would you consider was the most damaging thing you had to do?

A. I had to insert a CBS correspondent, Harry Reasoner, at the beginning and end of the film and write dialogue for him, which put a kind of stamp on the film and toned down everything. You know, "These are young people, it will blow over, it's not very important." I also had to put restraining commentary in the film itself. For example, we filmed a bull session of the kids where they are rapping about the condition of America and saying things like, "They're crazy. They give us things like the Declaration of Independence to read. Don't they understand that kids are going to read this, and are going to take it seriously? If those ladies in tennis shoes who believe there is going to be a Red Chinese invasion from Mexico ever really dug what they were doing giving us the Declaration of Independence to read, they'd freak out." Or they'd say, "Mass education is going to dig the grave for this society." Things like that .This was no good, so CBS had me write something like the following for Harry Reasoner to say at the beginning of the sequence, "The bull session—an old and true ritual of young people, wherein much heat but little light is shed." Do you understand? And every single scene had that kind of narration, that's just one example of what happened to the picture.

The picture that went out had very little relationship to the picture I made and had intended to make.

Q. Is that the way the networks still behave, from what you can see of America now, in 1970?

A. I think so. I think it's even worse than that now, because in those days under the leadership of men like Fred Friendly, they were at least tackling a few hot subjects and today they're not. There are very few serious hours on television.

Q. Where are you at now?

A. I am not happy with the relationship of the documentary film maker to the networks. I'm into a very different kind of film now, what I call "documentary of human revelation" as opposed to documentary films like *Birth and Death* and *Factory*. I have found a way to make films which are outside the mainstream of network television ideas, but which are very satisfying to me. I'm not fighting the old battles anymore. I'm just trying to make beautiful films.

A Married Couple: *Antoinette and Billy Edwards*
(*Aquarius Film Ltd.*)

High School: *The Dean of Discipline and student*
(*OSTI, Inc.*).

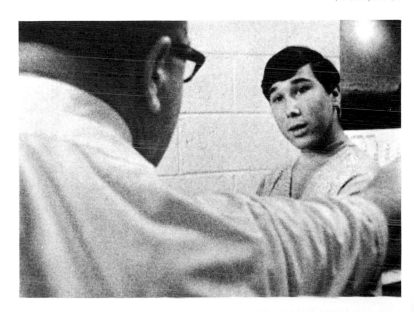

SALESMAN: *Paul Brennan (Bob Adelman).*

WHAT HARVEST FOR THE REAPER? *One of the migrant workers who followed the dream of "Santa Claus is coming" (National Educational Television).*

THE WAR GAME: *Fire fighters attempt to save a man trapped in a burning car (British Film Institute).*

THE DREAM DIVIDED: *Lelia Goldoni as Zelda and Edward Woodward as Scott Fitzgerald (British Broadcasting Corporation).*

CATHY COME HOME:
*Author Jeremy Sandford
(extreme right) and director
Kenneth Loach (middle)
on location during filming
(Birmingham Post and Mail).*

CATHY COME HOME: *Sean King as Sean, Ray Brooks as Reg, Stephen King as Stephen, and Carol White as Cathy (British Broadcasting Corporation).*

MONTEREY POP: *Janis Joplin and friends (Leacock-Pennebaker Inc.—Jill Gibson).*

DON'T LOOK BACK:
Bob Dylan (Leacock-Pennebaker Inc.).

THE ROYAL FAMILY: *The Queen is filmed by Cawston's crew while holding an informal audience (ITC—Incorporated Television Co., Ltd.).*

SIXTEEN IN WEBSTER GROVES: *The key car sequence (Walter Dombrow).*

The Berkeley Rebels: *Sally Leary and Kate Coleman at
the scene of the Free Speech Movement
(CBS Television).*

A Cry for Help: *The motorcycle cop and his
son (George Stoney Associates and Louisiana State Medical Board).*

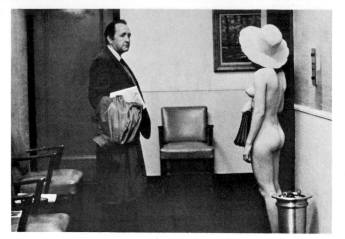

WHAT DO YOU SAY
TO A NAKED LADY?
*The nude coming out
of the elevator
(United Artists).*

PAS DE DEUX: *Multiple superimpositions created by shooting
"staggered" images with an optical printer
(National Film Board of Canada).*

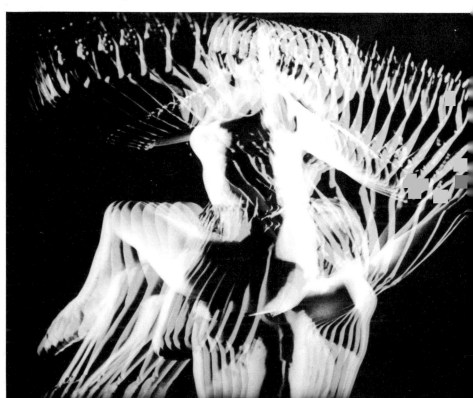

Reconstructions and Reenactments

8
The War Game
Peter Watkins

It may be the most important film ever made.

KENNETH TYNAN, "THE OBSERVER"

The War Game *was produced and directed by Peter Watkins in 1965 and was denied a television screening by the BBC in 1966 as a result of a directive by the then director general of the BBC, Sir Hugh Greene. In spite of Sir Hugh Greene's restrictive policy, the BBC finally bowed to pressure and ultimately released the film for theatrical but not television screening.*

The War Game *starts with a series of maps showing the vulnerability of England to nuclear attack. It then suggests an international crisis which culminates in a Berlin confrontation between the Russians and the Americans. As a result of the crisis the allies use tactical nuclear weapons in Europe, which in turn provokes the Russians to drop atomic bombs on England.*

What follows is a hellish evocation of disaster. Carefully prepared civil defense plans prove futile and useless; children are blinded, firestorms rage, and the dead lie in the streets. After a while there are hunger riots; police are assaulted and food thieves are shot by execution squads. It seems, in fact, as if civilization is disintegrating.

The style of the film is highly composite. Live interviews are mixed with carefully staged vignettes; the beginning of a story line is broken by comments quoted from religious and scientific personalities; grainy newsreel camera work suddenly gives way to the smoothest of Hollywood set lighting. In theory it shouldn't work; in practice it all blends together as a unified piece of art.

Although defenders of the film saw it as an authentic vision of catastrophe, it was damned by many British dailies and written off as a grossly distorted message by the British right wing. Watkins was charged with failing to show hope and the resilience of the human spirit. He was also accused of being too harshly realistic, and (worst of all) propagandizing for nuclear disarmament in the crudest possible way.

All art, however, is propaganda in one form or another, and to seek "objectivity" in a film about the atom bomb seems to me to be a red

*herring. Watkins was presenting a personal vision based on well-re-
searched facts which few critics bothered to challenge. Secondly, a
great deal of the criticism very definitely exhibited an ostrich-like
approach to life, which Bertrand Russell commented on as follows in
his autobiography: "Those who try to make you uneasy by talk about
atom bombs are regarded as troublemakers, . . . as people who spoil
the pleasure of a fine day by foolish prospects of improbable rain."*

In reviewing the whole situation it seems a pity that The War
Game *led to Watkins's resignation from the BBC. It was unfortunate,
because the BBC in the past has been relatively open to the dissenting
voice and the individual opinion (certainly far more so than the commercial networks in the United States) and would have seemed to
be the ideal place for Watkins to work out his own personal and
committed brand of film making.*

*Since 1966 Watkins has trod a varyingly successful path in fea-
tures, with the direction of* Privilege *and* The Gladiators *to his credit.
At the time of writing (November 1970), he was engaged on a series
of films dealing with key events in American history, such as the Civil
War, and their relevance today.*

*This interview took place on a freezing Sunday morning in Tor-
onto. Time was very limited, and because James Blue had already
covered a lot of the shooting details of the film in an excellent interview with Watkins published in* Film Comment,* *I decided to concentrate my questions on the preliminary research rather than on the
film making itself.*

Q. What was your background prior to entering the BBC?

A. I wanted to be an actor, but my drama training stopped when I
did my national service. I came out of the army in 1956 and, for no
reason at all, suddenly decided to become a film maker. I saw somebody using an 8 mm camera, and I guess it excited me; I can't remember why. It all happened in about a week, and I stopped trying
to become an actor and began the long dreary uphill trail of getting
into the film business. First, I became an assistant producer in an advertising agency doing commercials. I then became an assistant editor
and finally a director about seven years later in a London sponsored
documentary unit. That was the professional side of it. However,
about once a year I spent all my money and made an antiwar film. A
couple of them won amateur film awards and were shown on television.

By that time I was getting a little fed up with England, and as my
wife is French I decided to try and get some work in France. I bashed

* *Film Comment* (vol. 3, no. 4, 1965).

away with nothing happening for five months, then decided to apply to the BBC. Luckily, I was saved from some of the hapless formalities that you have to go through in joining the BBC, as Huw Wheldon had seen an amateur film of mine called *The Forgotten Faces*. This was a reconstruction of the Hungarian uprising of 1956 which had been shown on television, and Wheldon had liked it. So I became one of the first of the new wave of people who were taken into the opening of Channel 2. As it happened I never worked in Channel 2; I stayed in Channel 1, was a production assistant for a year, and then I said I would like to make a film about the battle of Culloden.

Q. Was much supervision given on what was, after all, your first film for the BBC?

A. They let me do it completely on trust and on my record of amateur film making. I had read a very interesting book on the battle, thought the scope of the subject tremendous, and Huw Wheldon said, "Well, just do it." I don't think he had time or particularly wanted to read the script; he just let me do it. It was completely subjective, of course, as those were the golden days of documentaries; I am not sure that the freedom I had exists any more. But it was marvelous at that time. Unfortunately, Huw Wheldon went up to his high position, and the situation has changed.

Q. Your history of antiwar films seems to indicate that *The War Game* wasn't a sudden inspiration, but was the result of a development over a number of years.

A. Well, way back in 1961 or 1962, like most people in England, I was an observer of the Campaign for Nuclear Disarmament. I felt very strongly about the issue but didn't join the campaign because, although I agreed with their objectives, I disagreed with their strategy. Those were the days before I joined the BBC and I had an idea for an amateur film about a group of atom-bomb survivors in a cellar. I wanted to do face-to-face interviews of what they had been through, and that sort of thing. Anyway, it sort of lay there ticking for a number of years; but as soon as I had done *Culloden* I raised the subject with my boss.

At that time I was a good boy in the eyes of the BBC. *Culloden* had been well received and I had a certain amount of rope given to me. By that stage I suppose I must have abandoned the cellar idea and broadened the whole to include the wider effects of a nuclear attack on England. Wheldon was a bit worried about it, but said, "Okay, I'll have to put this to the higher-up people, and they'll probably want to see a script." So it went through to this upper echelon, but they really didn't approve of the thing until five days after I had started shooting, when their reaction was, "Well, we'll wait and see it, and then evaluate it afterwards, because it may be difficult." It was left on a very vague basis.

Q. One of the striking things about *The War Game* is the amount of research it must have involved. Was the information on which you based your script readily obtainable?

A. The more films I do, the more I research. It's a growing pattern. I tend to put more and more emphasis onto the solid basis of research. With *The War Game*, I had to do a great deal of original research, because nobody had ever collated all the information into an easily accessible published form. Quite a lot of books had been written on the effects of thermonuclear bombs, but very few of these had ever been seen by the public.

You must realize that there are an infinite number of books published, which the public can get at, on a normal historical subject like the American Civil War. In contrast, there is an extreme dearth of literature available to the public about the Third World War. What literature there is, is stacked up on the shelves of the American Institute of Strategic Studies and those sorts of places, and is never read by the public. So it was an extremely esoteric subject for a film maker to delve into and quite hard to find basic facts.

Q. Did you employ a research team?

A. No, not really. I did it all myself and mounted the research in several different areas, such as technical and sociological. On the technical side I went to Germany and tried to get the essence of Berlin, the Berlin Wall, and the situation there; because even before I started writing, I had an intuitive sense that I would need a hypothetical "bust-up" place, and in 1965 Berlin was a little warmer than it is now. But as I always say to people, the flash point is really immaterial. The point is, what happens when the war comes. After Berlin, I met professors, biologists, physicians, and radiologists from London University. I also met with people from the London Institute of Strategic Studies, and did research into the payload of rockets, the effects of fallout on white and red blood corpuscles, the effect of radioactivity, and the like.

It was all immensely complicated—the amount of force required to fling a brick 300 yards in how many seconds, the amount of thermal heat required to melt an eyeball at this and that distance. I read reports from Hiroshima, Nagasaki, and Dresden and found that, though there is plenty of technical material, the emotional effect of an atom bomb on people has been much less thoroughly investigated.

Q. When the various places supplied you with pamphlets, did they want to know your motives or anything like that?

A. You have to differentiate here between people in general and governmental bodies. The experts, the professors and so on, were extremely cooperative and very interested. A few were a little skeptical of an amateur blundering into their little domain, but they freely supplied what little information they had. The governmental bodies were different. In general they said "No."

I made formal approaches, realizing that I was rather putting my head in the lion's mouth; but I thought, what the hell, I've got to try it all ways round. So I went to the Home Office, I think the A.G. 4 branch was the department in charge within the Ministry of Civil Defense, and I said, "I would please like to know . . ." and I gave them a long, long list of questions about civil defense preparation in Britain. I said, "I want to know your placings and the amounts of your stockpiles; I want to know your withdrawal policies; I want to know who are going to be regional senior government officers." It was a long, long list of questions. A few may have touched on semi-secret data, but I am sure that 80 percent of the answers came within the realm of information that should be available to the public.

The BBC sort of gingerly supported this request for this information, but the Home Office was rather taken aback. Then there was silence for three weeks before I was called into a BBC office and told, "We're afraid you are not going to get this information, and we believe it's best for you not to push the point." In other words, something appeared to have happened between the BBC and the Home Office. I can't be sure of this, but I think the BBC was told to cooperate in persuading me not to obtain this information. But then what happened later was worse, because the Home Office withdrew all official help.

At that juncture I was in the process of asking for help from the various branches of the Kent Auxiliary Fire Service, the main fire service, the civil defense, and the police. This went right down to the sort of nitty-grits of technical help in supplying the radioactive meters, civil defense uniforms, rescue packs, ambulances, police information, and so forth. The Home Office put the clamp down on that immediately and told everyone to have absolutely nothing to do with me and to give me no help whatever, of any shape, size, or form. So, in most of the places I went people said to me, "Sorry, we've been told not to touch you."

The only group that helped me voluntarily after that was the Fire Service, which appeared to me to be the only group or agency in England that had and has a realistic approach to the effects of a nuclear attack. They were the only people willing to talk to me and willing to supply me with the needed bits and pieces of equipment. They said, "We've been told not to, but we realize this is an important subject." They didn't say, "Look, if a nuclear attack comes, we'll mop it up easily in England." They took the reverse approach, because they had had to deal with the small scale fire storms in Kent during the Second World War. They had seen the ravages of a mass incendiary raid, and they knew that a nuclear attack would be infinitely worse. They knew of the terrible toll in the fire storms in Dresden. These practicing technicians were the weak link in the official "happiness bureau." They knew what it would be like, and they helped me. And they did it unofficially. Officially, there was a complete clamp down.

Q. How much time did you put into the research?

A. I suppose the amount of actual pure research, of bashing around and talking to these radiologists—rushing out to Oxford to meet a man who knew about the "Honest John Rocket" in Germany and meeting people doing strategic studies here and there—probably ranged from November 1964 until January or February 1965. It took about three months. I shot the film in April 1965, but I kept on researching up to the end, so you could say solid research was about two to three months, while there was some polishing during the period I was writing the commentary.

Q. You mentioned doing sociological research as well as technical probing. Would you mind going into that a little more?

A. The sociological background to a third world war was just as important to me as the technical research, but here the research was more in terms of people than books. I went to see from thirty to fifty people, ranging from poets and sculptors to conductors, composers, writers, producers, and so on. I wanted to hear what they felt about the silence on the whole subject of the effects of nuclear war, and what they felt about their part as intellectuals in contributing to the silence. I just wanted to feel the response, which was quite an experience. In fact one day I'd like to write a book about it. These meetings were the most interesting and moving part of the research, and the responses I obtained were continually fed back into the film.

Q. At what stage did you begin trying to formulate a script?

A. Script is something I can't be very tidy with you about, as I am not very tidy about it myself. I wrote a document which was about half the size of the London telephone directory. It was tremendously detailed; I believe it was quite authoritative and, apart from anything else, presented a complete indictment of British civil defense by showing the futility of their planning and methods.

Q. Did the script go through many versions before you were satisfied with it?

A. Yes. Originally it was much more padded and there were many more incidents. I wanted to follow many more individuals. I seem to remember I had a man in Kent, who was working in a factory, but I can't remember what he did. There were also various other individuals, like the doctor, who are now in the film not really as characters, but just as human beings caught up in the holocaust. I hadn't developed their characters much more in the original script, but I had placed them with much more regularity throughout the film. We kept going back to them, characters like the police inspector, and they provided a continuing thread.

Q. How close did you work to your final shooting script? Was it a guide or a bible?

A. The script was overly long and immensely complicated. It had everything in it, almost too much. It certainly had all the logistics of the attack and why the English civil defense couldn't pick up the pieces. It had all this, but was far too long, and was in the back of my mind rather than in the forefront during the shooting. In this kind of a situation you have three or four weeks to make the film, and you just try to extract the essence of what you're doing while facing the daily problems.

Q. What kind of problems—artistic, logistic . . . ?

A. You are constantly having to grapple with, "Has Mrs. Brown got up this morning?" "Who's going to come and be the warden for this street?" "Has Mr. Baker got his train for Tunbridge?" "Are the police going to let us use this street?" "That guy over there, knocking down that house, is he going to stop acting half mad?" "Is it going to stop raining?" "Is the hotel going to supply lunch for the cast?" All these things were part of the film making. It was just a hard, bloody fight, going on for weeks, with a lot of the niceties of the script just going down the drain. When you've got a long document like I had, even more goes down the drain. What you are continually trying to do is hold on to the essence of the whole thing. You are having to deal with a myriad of contingencies while you're filming, while at the same time you're doing a stripped-down précis of the script and praying to God that you're retaining a structure, even if it's changed from your original concept.

Q. How limited were you in your budget?

A. That's an interesting question. No one ever stated precisely how much I could have. I seem to remember that they sort of drew the line at about £12,000, but you must remember that BBC costing is extremely complicated. They have an "above" and "below the line" system, which means in fact that nobody ever knows what you're spending. Quite a lot of overheads are charged to the BBC. I think that they said that the above-the-line costs would be £12,000. It was said that I spent £20,000, but nobody ever told me whether the extra £8,000 was above-the-line or whether it was an expression of the BBC's overheads.

Q. One is struck and overwhelmed by the sense of factual reality in *The War Game*, the veracity and truth of the actors which makes part of the film look like a newsreel. This realism was also one of the most brilliant things about *Culloden*. How do you achieve these results?

A. It doesn't happen by accident. My drama training helped somewhat, but I really think that a large proportion of the realism is due to the fact I try to make my films provide a common experience for the people in them. Both *Culloden* and *The War Game* are films made in unusually adverse conditions. For me, they are practically pure conditions, as I think this is what film making is about. When you do a film like *Culloden* or *The War Game*, people have literally to stand in the gutters, in the howling wind for hours on end, fed probably on beans and a hamburger.

In *Culloden*, people were standing in fairly good reproduction Highland costume, which meant a plaid, probably a pair of jockey shorts underneath, and something on their feet—and that was it. They then walked for the best part of two weeks in the biting wind, in the rain, over moors more than a foot deep in water. And something built up between them. A similar kind of thing happened in *The War Game*. And all this is done out of enthusiasm. The people aren't paid, or paid only token amounts.

Q. How do you approach these people? How do you get your participants?

A. There are various ways. A bad way, which still works, is to advertise in local papers that you're making a film and are going to have a mass meeting for people who are interested. The other way is to approach local cine and dramatic groups, of which we have a lot in England, or to go to the schools and universities.

I usually start the ball rolling by having a mass meeting in town, at which there might be 200 or 300 people from different drama groups and the like. I then get up on the platform and talk for two or three hours. I tell them why I'm making the film. I try to get them involved in the subject and to understand its importance. I try to get them to understand its connection with them as human beings, and what might be the worth of the collective experiences of making a film on the subject. I then usually terminate the meeting and try to meet every single one of these people individually.

I have an idea of the sort of people I am trying to cast but it has to be immensely flexible. If I see a guy who I think might be a good policeman, I make a note of that; I talk to each person for about ten minutes or quarter of an hour; it depends on the number of people there and on the time pressures. Then the thing narrows down a little. People drop out; other people stay with you. In *The War Game*, I built up an aggregate of about 400 people who stuck with me the whole time. Not one was a professional actor, and fewer than 50 percent had ever played in front of a camera before.

Q. How do these people get this realism? How does somebody just simply cry?

A. You cannot just pull a man in from a job, and say, "Okay fellow, I want you to suddenly become involved in a nuclear war, and I want you to give me a very stark realism which has to come smacking across as if you were actually caught in those circumstances." That doesn't just happen in five minutes. You have to get to know the chap, you have to pull him into the communal thing of making films.

Filming is the most God-awful boring thing for people who are in it, at least in this sort of film where they have to stand around for hours on end watching you grapple with the problems, waiting to do their little bit as a policeman. Maybe you've told Mr. Brown, "Now you've gotta be here at half-past nine on Monday," but at half-past two on Wednesday you still haven't filmed him. You have to pull people through all that; and what holds them might possibly be my personality, but it certainly has to do with what you have impressed on them as the meaning of the subject.

What also comes through is their desire as a person to express themselves; and when you make my sort of film, you find yourself unexpectedly tapping this. It's a collective "thing," plus what you say to them just before you start running the camera, or you talk to them the night before—something like, "You're going to be a nurse and I want you to think about holding a child, and it's dying." And you go through this, and you maybe act it for them, maybe you don't —but I try essentially to let them come out with it themselves, which they usually do on the first or second take.

I must emphasize that there's no pat answer to this; it's part of a collective experience. It may have come from something generated for them over a couple of meetings or the collective thing of two or three weeks of filming. What matters is getting people involved in a human experience or emotion, and letting it develop and flower in the particular way you need. I have also found that using nonprofessionals in this sort of film is usually a little better, because professionals often bring in a tremendous art and craft and technique which spoils the naturalism. But it's a difficult problem. There are no rules.

Q. You've got a number of comments in the film about what people think of carbon 14, or whether we should bomb Russia in retaliation for them dropping a bomb on us. Were these comments written into the script, or are they real off-the-street reactions?

A. That's one of the main questions that's been asked over the past few years and I can understand why. People know that the film is a reconstruction; therefore, they probably say, "Ah, he's reconstructed this." Yet the carbon 14 sections and the "retaliation against Russia" section are the only ones that *aren't* reconstructed. In other sections I've got people playing churchmen or strategists; what they say is what I heard and learnt talking to churchmen and strategists during the research. But the statements of the women in the street talking about carbon 14 and retaliation are completely genuine from members of the cast.

One morning I got the cast around and said, "I want to do something a little bit different for the next couple of hours, but I'm not going to tell you what exactly it is." My cast were housewives from Gravesend, and they looked at each other thinking, "Oh God, what's he going to do with us now"—this was after they had been thrown out of windows and trapped in fires for the sake of the film in the last two weeks. Then I took them aside, one by one, and said, "Okay, now I'm going to ask you questions, and I want you to answer me whatever way you feel. Just say whatever you think." And for a moment they became what they really were—ordinary lay members of the British public. I asked these questions about fifty feet away from the main group; no one could hear what I was saying. And those questions and responses—particularly the responses—are perhaps the biggest single indictment in the entire film of the way we are conducting our present society and of the lack of common public knowledge of the things which effect humanity.

Q. Could we move into the technical area and directorial decisions?

A. Technically, the film was very difficult to make and was shot at a ratio of about twenty to one. I think if we discuss the fire storm sequence that will sum up for you many of the difficulties of the film and the problem of obtaining a kind of documentary authenticity.

A fire storm is very different from an ordinary fire; it's an all-consuming tornado, and it was very difficult to create that effect.

THE WAR GAME
The Fire Storm

Vision	*Sound*
Fire storm sequence Buildings on fire	COMMENTATOR: Rochester in Kent. Now 2 square miles of fire resulting from the heat of a thermonuclear missile which exploded "off-course" from London Airport, 3½ miles from this position.
Firemen	This is the unknown phenomenon which could perhaps happen in Britain following a nuclear strike against certain of our cities. This happened after the bombing of Hamburg, at Dresden, at Tokyo and at Hiroshima. This is what is technically known as a fire storm.
Fire alley	Within its center the rising heat from multiple fires caused by both the heat flash and the blast wave upsetting stoves and open furnaces is sucking in ground level winds at speeds exceeding 100 mph. This is the wind of a fire storm.
People running/bowled over Woman in fire storm	WOMAN: "I saw a man being caught by great gust of wind, tore the coat right off his head. . . ."
CU man with gasmask	
Caption	NEWSREADER: During a recent meeting of the Ecumenical Council at the Vatican—a bishop told the press that he was sure "our nuclear weapons will be used with wisdom."
People bowled over by wind	
Bishop	"I believe that we live in a system of necessary law and order—and I still believe in the 'war of the just'."
Car burning	COMMENTATOR: Within this car a family is burning alive.
Car explodes	

161

Vision	*Sound*
Brooks	COMMENTATOR: Charles Brooks, Chief Fire Officer of Chatham. Already three of his appliances have been smashed, gutted or overturned.
Firemen — roof explodes	Already 17 of his 60 firemen have been crushed, hurt, or killed by flying debris.
Firemen collapsing	This is a firestorm. Within its center the oxygen is being consumed in every cellar and ground floor room, to be replaced by the gasses of carbon monoxide, carbon dioxide, and methane. Within its center the temperatures are rising to 800°C. These men are dying—both of heat stroke and of gassing.

We were working in an old barracks that was about to be pulled down and that gave us the impression of large buildings which might vaguely be taken for office blocks. We put white magnesium flares in all the windows, and then built up the fire behind. For the sound track we tried a mixture of fire, volcano, and other things, all treated very coarsely. I then brought down a friend of mind, a stunt man, to help me with the management of the people caught in the fire storm.

We put a mattress down, and got the people to sort of run and pick themselves up off the mattress. It's extremely difficult, and it doesn't work completely—but it works. As you are running, you have to suddenly feel yourself caught and turned by an air current. To achieve this we started pulling them with wires, but finally decided not to do that, as we thought it would hurt them. We also thought it would look false. So everything is actually what they do themselves, plus the cutting of the best sort of positions. We also helped the effect by having flares roaring in the background and putting two fans quite close to them to whip bits of shredded paper and flour across, so that you get the visual impression of a sudden whipping across of something. As they ran to a particular spot where their mattress was, the white bits of paper would whip across and catch them, that would be their cue for letting themselves be caught in it and turned. That's just a small example of the solution to a technical problem; it really has nothing to do with film making, but it's what that nutty film is about.

As far as camera techniques are concerned, well, obviously we were letting people shout, letting them distort the microphone, and letting them deliberately butt into the camera. What we were trying to do was create a sort of a total emotion, or total involvement, which affected us as well as the actors. I would give the cameraman specific directions, but obviously things would often be happening very suddenly and he'd be on his own.

Q. Did you use any stock shots?

A. Every single frame in that film is us. We put the film through a particular process to try and get it to look as if it had been grabbed out of archives of twenty years ago. I forget how we did it; it was a case of getting a dupe negative, then getting a particular harsh grain positive, and reprinting from the positive—that accounts for that extreme contrast in look in a lot of the film. That was obviously deliberately sought after and finally achieved by us, and by the laboratory which did very well.

Q. There was one scene where a rocket goes off. Was that your rocket?

A. Yes. My art director went out and built a bit of a rocket. He was able to wheel the thing up the ramp just about three feet, and at that point I'd bring the camera up so that it was near the top of it. The rocket and every other single inch in that film is us. Some of it, I must admit, is not done as well as I would have liked, but it's all us, with all its faults. It's all us, every foot of it.

9

Cathy Come Home
Jeremy Sandford

In 1956 there were over 12,000 people in England living in temporary shelters provided by local authorities. It was also estimated that over three million people were living in appalling slum conditions. And there were uncounted others searching for a roof over their heads for a day, a week, a month. Such is the background to Jeremy Sandford's Cathy Come Home *(1966).*

Cathy *has been screened three times on BBC television, and may be the most effective drama on contemporary social and living conditions ever shown on the BBC. It caught the public interest and imagination in an unprecedented way, and it is necessary to ask why.*

The form is that of a documentary drama, and at first reading the script seems very dull. Cathy marries a driver, Reg. There is an accident. He loses his job, and with cash now tight they have to leave their apartment. Slowly, they begin to move down the social ladder, living in rooms, slums, camp sites, and ruins. Finally, Cathy and her two children are forced into an institution for the homeless, while Reg vanishes, looking for work.

There is little in the way of conventional conflict and drama, and the continual occurrence of so many disasters would seemingly become very boring—but doesn't. This is partly due to the excellent acting and to the superb directing of Ken Loach, who later made Poor Cow *and* Kes. *It is also due to the accuracy of the dialogue and situation, and to the high degree of involvement that Sandford is able to create on the part of the viewer.*

But besides all this there seem to me to be three other reasons for the success of Cathy. *First, it was fairly unique in being a play that felt no need for British balance. It condemned unequivocally and without pulling punches. Second, the need for a secure home environment is one of the necessities of our civilization. So among the viewers there was probably a strong element of "there but for the grace of God . . . " Finally,* Cathy *attacked a target which could leave most viewers' consciences clear. Instead of "us," the target was the impersonal "them,"—feelingless bureaucracy, the local authorities, the grey men.*

Critical reaction to Cathy *among most newspapers was tremend-*

ously enthusiastic. But there were also other voices, like that of the Birmingham city councillor who said of the characters, "They are just puppets strutting across the screen, poisoning the minds of the people watching."

Author Jeremy Sandford could well pass for a rather tall, shy, unkempt undergraduate. Born in 1930, Sandford read English at Oxford where he produced among other things a musical poetry show called Flagrant Flowers.

After serving as a clarinetist in the German contingent of the Royal Air Force band stationed near Hanover, Sandford worked fairly extensively for the BBC radio, directing about forty documentaries on various aspects of British life and writing three radio plays for the BBC's Third Program. Sandford also wrote a play called Dreaming Bandsmen *which was produced at Coventry Theatre, and which was described by a local reporter as giving the feeling "of being drugged through a sewer backwards." In between times Sandford has traveled to Mexico and Ethiopia, and has written up his impressions for various London newspapers.*

Though Sandford is best known as the author of Cathy, *his television work predates* Cathy *by several years and includes his controversial film on the Savoy Hotel which became the subject of a noted court injunction. Since* Cathy, *he has written three linked social plays for BBC television, a travel book on Mexico, and a book on social conditions called* Down and Out in Britain.

Q. How did you first become interested in the subject of the homeless?

A. In the early sixties, I was living in Battersea in a poor district, and one day a neighbor of mine was evicted. The family's furniture was thrown into the street, and they disappeared, apparently without trace. They had nowhere else to go, and I wondered what had become of them. A few nights later, a friend came to tell me that this neighbor had arrived in a place which was more disgusting and more frightful than one could possibly imagine. What I found when I went to visit my former neighbor angered and saddened me. It was a scene of horror, all the worse for the fact that no one knew about it.

Stacked into an old workhouse were hundreds of families, consisting of mothers and children who had been separated from their husbands and fathers. Some families were in single rooms. In other cases four, five, or more families had all been shoved into the same room. The toilet facilities were completely inadequate, and dysentery was rife. Ambulances called every day, often more than once a day.

There was a feeling of complete demoralization. Husbands were allowed to visit their wives and children only for a couple of hours each night. In the afternoons, even when it was raining, mothers and children were forced out into the streets. The reason given for this was that they were meant to be finding accommodation, but this was almost impossible. Obviously, they would hardly be in these horrible conditions if they hadn't tried to the end of their ability to find accommodation before they ever arrived here.

Feeding was communal; and some of the mothers, fearing that their children too would catch dysentery, forbade their children to eat. Ultimately, however, hunger would prevail. They would eat and become diseased. For the privilege of living here these families in fact paid quite a high rent, which further aggravated their difficulties. Since the money of the husband's wages was being used up in this way and also used up in travel by the husbands coming to see their families, there was no money to pay for outside accommodation, even if they were able to find it.

At that time, there were a few thousand British people in this situation. The heartbreak of mothers and children unwillingly separated from their husbands and fathers was a terrible thing to see. Added to the heartbreak of disease, and the shame of being in these places, was a yet further humiliation. On arrival, all families were made to sign a document in which they stated that they clearly understood that the accommodation was only emergency accommodation for three months. In practice, this rule was not strictly adhered to. Many people were still in the accommodation after a year or even two years, but at the end of the time there still came the moment when homeless families were told, "You can't stay here any longer."

At this point, the mother, knowing what lay ahead, would become very frantic. Often by now the husbands, ashamed, humiliated, and unable to cope with the situation, would have abandoned their families anyway. This is no slur, I think, on the husbands, but it is a slur on the situation which society had provided for them. The women would redouble their efforts to find accommodation; but in their demoralized state, they were in no fit condition of mind to find it even if it were available.

I remember being with one mother when she received a rather brutal letter telling her she had to leave the home. This was an incredible building, in which thirty homeless families were housed in a vast chamber, along whose sides were stable-like stalls with wooden walls about five feet high, flimsy curtains across the front, and no roof on them. She knew what this letter meant. She knew that when she was evicted, the children would be taken away from her and put into care. I learned that at this time it was happening to something like twenty-one children per week in the London area alone.

I felt that conditions so vile should immediately be brought to the attention of the public. To my surprise, I was told that a large number had in fact written letters to newspapers, but these had been ignored or sent back with polite but evasive replies. The homeless were not news! My immediate reaction was to ask whether I might do a program on the BBC sound radio about these homeless families. The BBC agreed, and I did it with a neighbor of mine, Heather Sutton, who had first brought my attention to the situation. The program consisted of recordings of homeless people interspersed with what struck me as the somewhat bland and heartless explanations of those who had the job of looking after them. The place where we went to record was called Durham Buildings. It was an unpleasant place but not nearly so nasty as Newington Lodge, the place I had visited right at the start. However, all the families in Durham Buildings had passed through Newington Lodge, and the experience had clearly had a terrible effect on them. Even in Durham Buildings, everybody still felt desperately insecure. The men here were allowed back with their families, but there was still a lingering sense of shame. One man said, "I was a prisoner of war and I spent five years behind the wire fighting for this country, and I still feel I'm a prisoner. I've never had a place of my own where I could do what I like."

We went also to Newington Lodge, and made some illegal recordings there and also to the place with the stable-like stalls. Here the pressure, indeed sheer bloody-mindedness of the staff, seemed to have created a different picture. People were terrified of talking to us for fear that the authorities might hear about this, and it would go against them, and they would be evicted. The fear of these pathetic women was a horrible thing to see; and realizing that we were an embarrassment to them, we didn't choose to stay very long.

Q. What was the public response to your broadcast?

A. The reaction to the radio program *Homeless Families* was absolutely nil. One had the impression, as one has so often when working for radio, of shouting something very important down a deep well.

Q. When was the specific idea of *Cathy* conceived?

A. After the radio broadcasts I was commissioned by the BBC to script a film on life in a luxury hotel. Treading the flashy corridors of the Savoy, then passing through the green beige doors, and entering the squalor of the stark quarters inhabited by the staff gave me the opportunity to think a little about our society, which provides so much for some and so little for others. This stately, cynical, somewhat irreverent film was brilliantly directed by Tony de Lotbinière. Later he went on to make films about the royal palaces, and somehow I don't think his feelings about the Savoy were the same as mine.

I was immensely pleased with the finished film and its public reception. I realized what a wonderful medium a television film is, and —disturbed by the fact that my friend in Newington Lodge was about to be evicted and lose her children—I resolved to try to write a film about this. The film would use many of the techniques of the documentary, but would nonetheless have a story line and be done by actors.

Q. Why did you resolve to use actors?

A. Real people are often inarticulate, especially when disaster hits them. There can be flashes of emotion in a true-life documentary, but these flashes cannot be sustained through a film. An actor with an actual script avoids that problem. Also, at this time, cameras were not allowed in the homes for the homeless. Even had I been able to get in and make a television documentary, as I had done with the radio program, I wouldn't have been able to do justice to the emotional reality of the condition of these human beings who were in there. Instead I saw it all in the form of a play. I had written plays both for radio and for the stage and had always been intrigued by Shelley's line about writers as, "the unacknowledged legislators of the world." Any writer worth his salt seems to me to have a social responsibility, and the situation of the homeless was exactly the kind of situation one had to write about.

Therefore, enthused with the success of the Savoy Hotel film, I decided to try to write a full length story film about a girl called Cathy. Ted Kodcheff, who had previously directed a play of mine at Coventry, was anxious to do it with me and to direct it as a film, either on television or for commercial cinema.

Q. Did you find the idea easy to sell?

A. I had done the writing on speculation, as I do most of my work; but as it shaped up I believed there would be no problem in selling it. I was wrong. Ted and I tried to raise cash from many areas—including various charities, foundations, film companies, and television companies—but were unable to do so. "The television play should not be a political forum" was the sort of reason given. One producer referred to it, even after its first showing, as "patronizing the proles."

What I had conceived was, I think, something new. It was a new idea, halfway between drama and documentary; and its newness may have alarmed people. The general feeling of film companies we approached seemed to be that the subject was too gloomy. The charities we approached also reacted negatively, although since then many have grasped the possibility of using film in order to popularize their causes. Some have since approached me to do films for them, including Christian Action, which didn't even bother to reply when I wrote to them about *Cathy*.

q. I take it you used a lot of material from your previous programs?

a. The research for *Cathy* was nearly all done for other media. The caravan section, where Cathy goes to live on a rundown caravan site, was basically researched in a radio interview program called *Living on Wheels*. The tapes that I used in this radio documentary in fact formed the wild track for the equivalent part of the *Cathy* film, of course supplemented with others I made on the actual location while the film was being shot.

It was while doing research for a series in *The People* newspaper that I learned of the appalling number of deaths in caravans which caught fire with children in them. I asked how often this occurred and discovered that you could reckon on one major fire involving children every month. It was while working on the newspaper series that I came upon the actual case on which the fatal fire in *Cathy* was based. I followed the proceedings in the coroner's court, and then I more or less transferred what occurred to the sound track of *Cathy*. For instance, there's the scene where the girl describes how the caravan was filled with smoke, and how she escaped with little Gary in her arms. "And what happened to the others?" the coroner asks. "They all got burned up," she says. The dialogue is verbatim from the court report.

The research for the section in which Cathy lives in a slum and then camps out in a derelict building was done while compiling another newspaper series. Most of the articles were written out of Liverpool, where I found whole families living in basements and houses without windows, electric lights, gas, beds, or any conceivable amenities except a few sodden mattresses on the floor. I remember water dripping down the walls, from which the women would fill kettles and boil up a cup of tea. Later, I did further research in the Birmingham slums, and also drew on a radio documentary I had done called, *The Old Backyard*.

However, the most important influence of all in the writing of *Cathy* was my involvement with a particular girl, seeing the situation through her eyes and feeling it through her heart. It was through knowing her well that I was able to experience the human tragedy and suffering behind this, and the destruction of the human creature. If I had not been able to indicate this, the writing of the play would have been pointless.

Meanwhile, I was also researching into the larger questions concerned. I read Audrey Harvey's excellent pamphlet, *Casualties of the Welfare State,* and this had a great deal of influence on me. A careful reading of the Registrar General's Annual Report also made me realize that the number of children separated from their parents each year for no reason other than homelessness was in the thousands.

After my experience in Newington Lodge, I didn't go to those in authority for information. Instead, I spoke to those directly involved. When I met a woman in Liverpool or Birmingham who had been many years on the housing list, with no chance of getting a house, I didn't need to consult statistics to know that her situation was a grave one. Later, I got the figures which were used in wild track in *Cathy*. I also had some good friends in official positions in the bureaucracy —childcare officers, other social workers, people working for the Social Security—and under a cover of secrecy, they were prepared to tell me everything that they knew.

Q. How did you structure things after your research?

A. I started by writing *Cathy* as a short story of three quarto pages, single spaced. It was the story of a girl who came down to London full of hope, built up a family, and then lost that family—husband, kids, the lot—through a complex chain of events. I realized it was essential from the point of view of audience identification that Cathy should be blameless, and one of the things which had struck me in Newington Lodge was the blamelessness of most of the people. It would have been a different sort of film if I had presented, in *Cathy*, the story of a girl of whom people could say, "Well, she was inadequate and a hopeless sort of person. It's a pity, but it could never happen to me." In the girl Cathy, there is a certain feckless quality, which is good because I was anxious that she not be too perfect. For instance, she and Reg take on an expensive flat without working out how much it's going to cost. They then start a family without working out how they are going to be able to continue to pay for the flat when Cathy has to stop work because of the pregnancy. This sort of thing was intentional, because it is a sort of fecklessness I have myself and yet I don't think of myself as basically inadequate. Cathy's dreamy-eyed decision to have kids, without ever having considered where she was going to live with them, might also be thought of as feckless; but in my experience this is a common habit of the majority of womankind in England and every country. They tend to have the children first and worry afterwards. I don't personally blame them for this. I feel that a civilized society should be able to take this into account and not punish many of them as ours does.

So, although Cathy was to be feckless, I also wanted her to be basically blameless. She was to be a girl that any girl could identify with and any boy accept as a possible girl friend.

I scripted Cathy coming down from the country to London, courting and winning her dream boy friend, and setting up home with him to be almost like a commercial. I intended that as far as possible it should correspond to the perfect dream romance and marriage as envisioned by a great number of people. I didn't want Cathy to have too strong a character; I wanted her to be the kind of person that the maximum number of people could identify with. Having created the situation—the very typical situation of a young girl in a beautiful flat, married and in love, and starting her first kid—I got to the point where the story got interesting for me, and from then on, the structure fell into an unusual pattern of an unending series of disasters.

There were five sections, each ending in a worse disaster than the previous one. Cathy is turned out from her luxury flat because children aren't allowed, and anyway it is too expensive for them. She and her husband Reg run into debt and are shocked to find that it is so difficult, on a low income, to find accommodation that will accept children. Then Reg has an accident, so that his earning power is now a fraction of what it was. After trying many places and meeting many rebuttals, Cathy at last finds an extremely unhygienic couple of rooms in a Birmingham slum. They and the children are happy in this slum, but are finally evicted from it by a trick carried out by the new landlord who takes over when the existing landlady dies. Again a hopeless search, till they sink another rung, when Reg finds a place for them on a caravan site.

Although the conditions here are terrible, they achieve more happiness than perhaps at any other time in their lives. They get in with a group of people who are free, happy-go-lucky, and don't care too much about anything. But then a fire in which children die awakens public interest in the site. The local authorities move in, the caravans are towed away, and the odyssey continues. But Cathy has suffered too many moves and is demoralized. She tries to sleep out in a ruined building and makes a few more discouraging attempts to find accommodation; finally she, Reg, and the children arrive at the doors of the home for the homeless. So the story continues. Reg disappears, and Cathy is eventually evicted from the house and her kids taken from her.

Q. What kind of considerations guided your drawing of the characterization of Reg?

A. I designed Cathy's husband Reg to be an attractive man, who is ultimately not strong enough to keep the family together. I wanted viewers to identify with his dilemma, where, after a certain point, he is too ashamed to continue with his family. I didn't want to show him as a thoughtless bastard, because then again, this would have given viewers a case of special pleading, special inadequacy, and the tragedy would become a particular one rather than a general one, which was what I wanted to show.

Nearly everything in the film was founded on something which had actually happened. An incident, like the fight in the home for the homeless where Cathy strikes one of the staff, was an amalgamation of two real incidents. One concerned the principal of one of the homes who alleged that an inmate had talked to the press, and in consequence they threw her out. The other incident involved the death of a baby—something which I'm sorry to say happened more than once in homes for the homeless—and the belief of the inmates that this was due to dysentery. The staff claimed that it was due to the mother's neglect. I combined these cases into a cameo where an inmate writes to a paper about a baby's death.

Q. Did the television script change much as it progressed?

A. In earlier versions of the script, I had myself in as journalist who appears at various intervals in the script. The journalist watches over Cathy's plight, grieves at her deterioration, and tries in vain to do something to help her. Later, I realized that to have myself in the script was purely self-indulgence, and that it detracted from the simplicity which I wanted to achieve in the story.

When we first discussed the script, the director, Ken Loach, felt that we should cut out the caravan sequence. He thought it would seem too way out for viewers to be able to identify with. However, a stay in a caravan is so frequent an occurrence in the story of the average homeless person. The incident also provides a moment of lightness in an otherwise grim story, so we decided to leave it in.

The actual process of writing was as follows: I filled a hard-backed spring binder with bits of quarto paper which had the headings of the various sections of the film on them, such as caravan, slum, luxury flat, courting, mothers-in-law, the first home for the homeless, the second home for the homeless, and so on. I then worked from a very large number of newspaper clippings that I had accumulated through the years, transcripts of tape recordings, actual tape recordings, notes of people I had met, and places I had been to. I went through all this material, picking facts and incidents out at random, seeing if they fitted what I wanted to do or not. Most of the selection I ultimately rejected; but those incidents which seemed to fit, I would put in, sometimes in an altered form, sometimes almost verbatim. This all went on for a couple of months.

Having written a large number of little scenes like this for each section, I juggled them around into the best order; then I had the whole thing typed. The story went to the typist two or three times after that. Each time I would work it through, trying to see the development with objective eyes, excluding some scenes, altering the position of others, amplifying incidents, and writing in a few new scenes out of my head. I'd add touches to Cathy's character, and so on. It was the general drudge which I expect many writers go through till they consider the script is right.

Q. How long did all this take?

A. About three or four months. I try to avoid working at home; and I had found a delightful, very small attic room, very high up at the back of a house in Oakley Street, Chelsea, with white walls and ceiling and a little fireplace. It was a bit tatty but rather delightful and very pleasant. I was able to scatter papers everywhere in deep piles like snow, and I was going to enjoy myself. But, in fact, writing *Cathy* was a very grueling experience; and although I had a feeling of immense satisfaction and fulfillment, I often finished the day feeling more dead than alive, since I had never tackled so large or serious a subject before. And sometimes, especially when writing the final sections, I would find myself weeping uncontrollably.

Q. How did it happen that the BBC finally picked up the story?

A. I had thought there would be buyers for *Cathy*, but there were none. I had a first-rate director wanting to do it. I thought it was a powerful script, but there were no buyers. So, for a year and a half I worked at other things, periodically pushing *Cathy* in all sorts of directions. In the end, I became so doubtful whether anybody would buy it that I decided to turn the script into a book, so that *Cathy* could have some kind of a life. About halfway through the transformation into a novel, a BBC producer named Tony Garnett, whom I had never met, rang me to say that he had found my synopsis at the bottom of the BBC Wednesday TV play filing cabinets, was very enthusiastic about it, and wanted Ken Loach to direct it.

We met for lunch in the BBC canteen, and I explained to Garnett about the play's previous history of refusals, thinking that this would put him off. But it didn't. We did resolve, however, to keep the subject of the play a secret and for the moment to give it a different title. We also agreed that if anybody asked us about the play we would refer to it as a knock-about family comedy, which it was in a way, except for the comedy bit.

Q. Did the director, Ken Loach, make any suggestions concerning alterations or the like?

A. Ken has a wonderful gift for simplification and made many suggestions at this point, the effect of which was to give the story a more simplified or "classical" shape. The major suggestions which he made and I agreed to were in the opening section of the film, where I had gone at great length into Cathy's arrival in London. I had shown Cathy getting a room on her own. I showed her relationship with the people who were living in the street and her reactions as a country girl finding herself in town. I had also gone into more detail about her courtship. Ken suggested we prune these scenes, and also pointed out that Reg veered a little towards being "wet" and that it would help things if we could make him stronger. He was certainly right about the second thing, although I'm not sure about the first. I think there's a danger that the beginning is too glossy, and a little more time getting to know Cathy before the commercial-type love scene might have been better. But I don't know.

Q. Were you satisfied with the way the script was finally translated to the screen?

A. I couldn't have been happier. I don't think that any writer could feel that his ideas had been translated more accurately or with more compassion. Ken and I worked together on choosing the locations; but all of them were actually found by me, mainly because I knew the right areas from my research. But it was the production assistant, John McKenzie, who had the unheard of audacity to ring Newington Lodge, the most infamous of all homes for the homeless, and ask whether we could shoot a film there. To our amazement we were allowed to, so that when the team moved in it was amidst the situation of children still being carried off with dysentery and husbands still having battles with the staff owing to being separated from their wives.

This atmosphere of hopelessness and helplessness which hung around the home for the homeless had an immense effect on the cast and enabled them to live out the scenes with conviction. We shot nearly all of the film on location, which enabled Carol White, who played Cathy, to identify very closely with, for instance, the caravan site. Ken shot very freely; often, vision and words run separately, so that while the camera is exploring one thing the words continue to carry the sense along.

The film is fantastically closely packed. This was my original intention, and Ken adhered to it. One gets the feeling often that there are three or four strands going contrapuntally. An official voice quotes statistics. In the background we hear somebody else talking about the inadequacies of the toilet. And on the screen we see, perhaps, the face of one of the protagonists talking, against a background of life in the homes. I think the compactness is important, and I find that different people often remember different things about some specific sequence in the film. The reason for this is that often much more is happening at any given moment than the average person can take in, so that, like existence itself, one subconsciously makes a selection.

The film was shot in three weeks. Given all these locations and something like a hundred speaking parts, it was a miracle of organization. I can never speak too highly of Ken's direction. I feel that he gave life to something that in the hands of another director could perhaps have not lived so vibrantly. His craftsmanship was consummate, and without him *Cathy* could not have been the film it was.

Q. What are your main feelings looking back on the film?

A. I feel some regret at the success *Cathy* has had, because it's so much better known than anything else I have done, thus labeling me the "Cathy author." But as regards its effect on the country and the housing situation, I can only be glad. It is good to know that I have altered, if only slightly for the better, the condition of life in my own society.

As a result of the film and certain meetings which we held afterwards, Birmingham and various other towns ceased their practice of separating three or four hundred husbands per year from their wives and children. The husbands were allowed to return to their families in a great gushing stream. It was intensely moving. I was lucky enough to be present on this jubilant occasion; and that moment, if no other, justified not only my writing of *Cathy*, but also my own existence.

10

The Dream Divided
Fred Burnley

In The Dream Divided *(1969) Fred Burnley and co-writer Barbara Barkham use the letters and novels of Scott Fitzgerald to build up a dramatic portrait of the writer and to show in particular the flowering and progress of his relationship with Zelda Sayre.*

The main structural device used by Burnley to organize the film is to have Fitzgerald interviewed in an unidentified house by an unidentified writer. As Scott reminisces in each room, the scene cuts to dramatized sections of his novels that are sufficiently autobiographic to reveal the nature of his marriage to Zelda, his affair with Sheilah Graham, and his eventual decline into alcoholism and obscurity.

The film is fascinating as an experiment in biography that manages to get away from the normal interview method or reconstruction by newsreel pictures. It compels and holds in the same way as Dante's Inferno, Ken Russell's *essay on Rossetti, but doesn't suffer from Russell's stylistic indulgences. Though the choice of an unknown reporter and flashbacks strike one as a bit cumbersome, the film still manages to provide a remarkable insight into the character and style of Fitzgerald.*

Scott and Zelda are played by Edward Woodward and Lelia Goldoni, and both give convincing performances. There is also some sensitive directing and camera work which, in combination, provide an accurate picture of the jazz age.

Fred Burnley is one of the younger BBC producer-directors who, like Jack Gold and Ken Loach, is equally at home in both documentary and drama. However, his background is in editing, which he took up after getting a first in politics and economics at Oxford.

After university Burnley joined Ealing studios in 1955, starting work as an assistant on The Ladykillers *at six pounds a week. He left "because the studio belief at that time was that it took fifteen years to train an assistant as an editor. That seemed a bit too much. Anyway I quit after six months because there was a strong prejudice against anyone who was educated or ambitious."*

Burnley then started editing TV commercials, sponsored documentaries, and the occasional feature. He worked for Michael Cacoyannis on Our Last Spring *which he calls "a total disaster," cut* The

System *for Michael Winner, and went on location to Thailand to participate in a Tarzan film.*

In 1965 Burnley was invited to join the BBC as director-producer on the recommendation of Richard Cawston. Since that time he has directed eight of the well-known "Whicker's World" series and produced a film for "One Pair of Eyes" featuring Kenneth Tynan in Oxford. Burnley also did the first color film for Intertel on the working of the Voluntary Service Organization in Malawi, before joining "Omnibus" under the executive control of Norman Swallow. The Dream Divided was Burnley's first film for "Omnibus," and has been followed by a film biography of Modigliani.

Q. I believe your early work for the BBC was primarily in the field of documentaries, including a lot of shooting for "Whicker's World." Fairly recently you moved into an entirely different section of the BBC. Was that your choice or a decision from above?

A. I left documentaries because I felt that I had reached the end of all that I could do in this field. I wanted more control. It is almost impossible to direct the kind of documentaries I was doing, and a director wants to direct. I simply got tired of crossing my fingers and hoping something would happen, and instead moved into arts features, with the intention of working for "Omnibus," which is a BBC Sunday night program about the arts. I spoke to Norman Swallow, who is executive producer of this series, and he said, "Yes, fine."

At that time Norman was toying with a program about Raymond Chandler, the American mystery writer, and asked me to go ahead with it. I met the scriptwriter, John Foster, and together we worked out an approach. We were going to reconstruct parts of Chandler's life, but were determined to use original material only. We wanted to use his letters and his prose to create a part for an actor who would play Chandler and who would talk to the camera about himself and about his attitudes, as if Chandler were alive and were being interviewed for a documentary. We then planned to intersperse this material with dramatized scenes from his short stories and his novels, to illustrate the kind of writer he was. We also intended using clips from the Hollywood films that had been made of his novels. It was also agreed that I would go to Hollywood and film Los Angeles from one end to the other, since one of the most interesting things about Chandler was his evocation of California. We made that, and I also prepared to do a similar kind of film with Scott Fitzgerald for which I would shoot some material while I was in Hollywood.

Q. Who suggested the Fitzgerald idea?

A. Actually the idea of a film on Fitzgerald had been lurking in my mind for fifteen years, ever since reading Budd Schulberg's novel *The Disenchanted*, which is based on Scott's life. I thought Fitzgerald's life was far more interesting than Chandler's ever was. My original concept was solely to deal with Fitzgerald's last three or four years in Hollywood when he lived with Sheilah Graham. By a strange coincidence, Sheilah Graham was in London at this time, so I contacted her and said, "I want to do a program about you and Fitzgerald. Can we write it together?" We discussed the project at some length and decided that she would talk into a tape recorder for several days telling me everything she knew about Fitzgerald (most of which had already been published in her books *Beloved Infidel* and *College of One*).

In the end she wanted far more money than the BBC could afford, so I dropped the idea of her collaboration. The other reasons for dropping the Graham idea was that I discovered that it had all been covered in the film *Beloved Infidel*. It also seemed to me, as I researched further into Fitzgerald's background, that there was much more interesting material than those years with Graham, and it would be doing Fitzgerald a disservice to concentrate on that period of his life. So I then proceeded to read everything that Fitzgerald wrote, trying to hunt for a new approach.

Q. Did anyone help you in this reading or analysis of Fitzgerald's past?

A. I had a researcher working with me at the time, Barbara Barkham, and together we roughed out a general approach to the film. What we did was pinch an idea from Fitzgerald which seemed to provide the ideal structure. The idea was based on a Fitzgerald story called *Author's House*, which was written after the period of his crack-up. In the story Fitzgerald does a mini-biography of himself, using as a narrative foil the device of an imaginary reporter who comes to visit him in a quasi-symbolic house that represents various phases of Fitzgerald's life. The reporter is never identified, but is shown around the house while Fitzgerald tells little anecdotes about himself, starting in the cellar for his childhood and ending up in the attic for his last period—that is in 1936, when the piece was written.

It seemed to us an excellent way to structure a television program. An English reporter would come to visit Fitzgerald in a large, Victorian-type gothic mansion in which he lived all alone. The reporter would be well informed and would ask key questions. Fitzgerald would answer those questions about his life and each answer would be from his own prose, from his letters and articles. It would be, in fact, Fitzgerald's autobiography recreated at the end of his life.

In each room of the house Fitzgerald would talk about a particular phase of his life, each room representing such a phase. He would talk about himself when young, or married to Zelda, or one of his rows with Zelda, or what have you. Fitzgerald and the reporter would enter really bare rooms, which we would suddenly furnish and fill with people, in a flashback to a dramatized scene from a short story or novel.

Q. I take it your selections were from autobiographically inclined novels?

A. Yes. We carefully selected the stories on that basis. What I was aiming at was a kind of autobiographic fiction. Norman Swallow agreed to this framework, so Barbara and I then proceeded to reread all the stories and novels that we thought could help us in this approach. I then went to America to shoot the Raymond Chandler program, leaving Barbara to dramatize the relevant short stories, novels, and letters simply by editing down, but with no rewriting.

Q. What was that first draft screenplay of Barbara's like?

A. It was on the right kind of lines, but wasn't feasible because it was too literary and not filmic enough. It didn't quite hold together dramatically, structurally, and visually. So we then had an extremely intensive two weeks working together in which I scrapped half the sequences, reread all the material, and found new stories which I felt we should have used.

Q. How did consideration of budget or more general matters affect the shaping of the script?

A. Working at the BBC, you end up doing what the budget dictates rather than doing what you want to do. For instance, Fitzgerald and the French Riviera are very closely associated. He spent a lot of time there and it was a very important phase of his life, which I simply could not do because it was too expensive to take actors and entire crews to the French coast—even though I had a pretty hefty budget.

The second problem was with Fitzgerald's estate. We couldn't do anything at all without permission from his daughter, Scottie, who controlled the rights to practically everything he wrote, except *The Great Gatsby* and *Tender Is the Night*, both of which had been sold to Hollywood movie companies, who don't usually allow extracts to be filmed of their copyrighted works. So, we completed the script omitting *Tender Is the Night* which is the key work for the Riviera, and not allowing ourselves to film on the Riviera. Instead,

I thought we might be able to use film clips from the Twentieth Century Fox movie of *Tender Is the Night,* which would give us a few Riviera scenes. As far as *The Great Gatsby* was concerned, we intended just to let Fitzgerald talk about it, but we weren't able to include any dramatized excerpts.

The third limitation was that I couldn't shoot the thing in America. While I was in America the script was still being written by Barbara in England, and I had no idea what would be necessary for the film. So I thought; I'll cover myself. I'll shoot where he lived in Hollywood; I'll shoot Princeton where he studied; I'll shoot the Staten Island Ferry which was very crucial symbolically to *The Great Gatsby* and I'll do some interviews.

In the end I only found two interviews that were worth doing. One was with a lady named Frances Kroll, who was Fitzgerald's secretary in his last years in Hollywood; and the other was with Lois Moran, who may have been the young girl Rosemary in *Tender Is the Night.* They were very interesting interviews; but when I came back from America, I discovered they didn't really have a place in the kind of reconstructed dramatized film we were doing. At first I did try to script them in but soon dropped that.

Q. What was your preliminary budget figure?

A. Well, after the script was written we budgeted it at about £6,300 above the line and about £6,200 below—about £12,500 altogether. I think the below-the-line costing was a bit unrealistic, and in reality it was more like £10,000—adding up to £16,300 for a fifty-minute program in black and white. I wanted to do it in color, but the BBC decided it was too expensive and so it had to be in black and white.

Q. Your budget was based on your second screenplay. Did it go through any more drafts?

A. Yes. I rewrote the screenplay once more without Barbara Barkham because she had left to go on some other project; that, in fact, was the fourth rewrite. When it was settled the big problem was who was going to play Fitzgerald. I *had* to have someone who looked like him. The BBC demands that kind of authenticity. This wasn't a drama; it wasn't a play. It was a reconstructed and authentic account of what Fitzgerald was like, in his own words; and that was its strength. The only actor I thought was good enough and looked like him was Edward Woodward, who played Callan in a very popular private-eye series. I sent him a script and he liked it. So that was Fitzgerald settled.

Q. You mentioned that the rights to most of Fitzgerald's work were held by his daughter. At what stage did she give her permission?

A. I had met the daughter's agent in New York; I subsequently sent him the script, and he gave me permission to go ahead. It was the first time that the agent had ever given permission for a television program about Fitzgerald. I think that he and Scottie were influenced by the fact that it was all totally authentic, that we hadn't made Fitzgerald into a drug addict (which he wasn't, of course) and hadn't over emphasized his drinking. They saw that we were interested in a serious portrait of Fitzgerald as seen by himself, and they gave me the copyright permission almost for nothing.

Q. Did you have to do much casting about for Zelda, which is a terribly important part?

A. I'd always admired Lelia Goldoni, who was in John Cassavetes' film *Shadows*, and asked to see her. When she came along she said playing Zelda was one of the ambitions of her life and had wanted to play it for twenty years. She seemed absolutely right and American, and I thought I'd found the ideal cast.

Q. You've mentioned the budget restrictions on shooting in America and on the Riviera; but how did you set about your English preproduction planning?

A. My production assistant was instructed to find a Gothic mansion with enough rooms to suit every part of the script. That's three living rooms, a ballroom, a cellar, an attic, a kitchen, bathrooms, and several bedrooms. And we needed rooms large enough to shoot in and owners who would stand for us practically living there for three weeks! It also had to be within the London area, because we couldn't afford to take the unit away on location and pay hotel bills. We advertised and investigated everywhere, but in the end we couldn't find any one house that would do the trick and had to settle on three houses. One for the exterior of Fitzgerald's house, plus a number of rooms; another for a few more rooms that we couldn't find in the first house; and a third house for the Paris interiors of a bedroom and living room. They were decorated in French Empire style and seemed appropriate. So my original plan of a nice, simple, three-week schedule all in the same place never worked out.

Q. The sense of style and atmosphere seemed to me, when I saw it, absolutely crucial to the film. This is obviously a matter of understanding between you and the cameraman. Were you allowed to choose your cameraman, or were you just allocated one from a list?

A. In the BBC you can't normally choose your cameraman. BBC technicians belong to the Film Department, and the Film Department is a law unto itself. They allocate people as they are available to producers who are available. If you loathe each other, they try to help; but normally, if there's no positive dislike you have no choice. However, by dint of special pleading I managed to get the cameraman I most wanted. This was Brian Tufano, a young man about twenty-eight with a very good reputation. I knew he was particularly good both in black and white and with a hand-held camera, and he seemed ideal for me. I had no choice about the sound recordist or editor, but they both were recommended so I said "that's fine."

Brian was hard at work on a million other productions, but I sent him the script and he seemed to like it. About three days before shooting we finally met to discuss the general style of the film. I wanted a rather harsh black and white, and I suggested doing the sequences of Fitzgerald and the reporter on Kodak XX. I thought we could do the flashback sequences on a softer stock, and Brian said that sounded like a good idea.

Q. Did you survey the locations with Brian before shooting?

A. We had a quick flick round through one house so that he could get a general idea of lighting problems and he said, "O my God, all the rooms are too small," but they always say that. We agreed we would have two electricians and the normal number of lights that come with two electricians, which is a full set of eight colortrans if it's color. In this case it was one 5 K, a couple of 2 K's and pups, and some odd quartz lights.

Q. What did you decide to shoot on?

A. I personally prefer an Arriflex BL, because I find the Eclair quite hopeless. It's too unreliable and the focus is often soft on the zoom lens. Brian had also come around to that view, and so we settled on the BL. The unit itself consisted of Brian Tufano who was lighting cameraman and operator, his assistant, a camera grip, a sound recordist, a sound assistant who held the mike, two electricians, my own secretary, and a trainee production assistant who learned very quickly. Besides costume and makeup girls we also had an art director (who is called a designer at the BBC). His main job was to convert several rooms into the right period and find the appropriate furniture and curtains and stuff.

Q. You'd mainly directed documentaries before. How did you handle the action? Did you talk much together? Did you go through many rehearsals?

A. I asked Woodward whether he wanted to rehearse before we started shooting, and he said, "Quite frankly, no. For one thing I'm far too busy, and secondly I don't think it's a good idea anyway." Lelia Goldoni wasn't working at the time and, being more used to American methods, was very anxious to rehearse, particularly with Woodward; but that just didn't work out. Instead she did a great deal of research on Zelda's character, by reading biographies, by reading Zelda's own novel, and by talking to me about the script at great length. I tried to give her a very solid idea of what I wanted her to do. She then told me that she was going to work out what she was going to do, wouldn't tell me in advance what it was, but would show me on the set. If I liked it, fine; if not, we would work out something else.

We began shooting and were behind schedule within a day. The biggest nightmare of all is getting behind schedule, because an extra day's shooting for the BBC, where the cost is moderately low, is almost worse than going over budget in a major feature. I was in agony for the first week trying to catch up that lost day. But I learned one thing: always make the first day as easy as possible, because if you get behind the eight-ball your morale is gone.

Q. What had you planned for the first day?

A. I'd thought the first day's shooting was relatively simple. All it consisted of was several scenes of Fitzgerald talking to the narrator. But I hadn't reckoned on the fact that these long speeches were from essays and letters, and were written in a very literary kind of prose. It certainly wasn't dialogue. And Woodward soon realized that it was absolutely impossible for him to learn all this the night before, and in any case he would have preferred to have winged it—you know, come in on the day and say, "What are we doing today? Can I learn it while you're lighting?" and that kind of thing. That was all very well for short dialogue sequences, but it was murder for two paragraphs of very complicated Fitzgerald prose. And I was determined not to let him alter the dialogue. Fitzgerald wrote the stuff, and Woodward was going to say it. As he couldn't learn it letter perfect so quickly, we decided to cheat.

We made idiot cards with the words written on, and held them up behind the cameras for these prose sequences. It worked quite well, because Woodward was such a consummate actor. He would half know it and would just take an odd glance at the words on the wall, and then know it perfectly, and he would feel better about it. These relatively uncomplicated scenes between Fitzgerald and the narrator were shot in the house in a few days. Lelia Goldoni then joined us, and I slackened the schedule a bit because I reckoned the dramatic scenes were much more difficult and would take longer.

Q. Did you go through a very precise story boarding for the film, or did you work out your camera and dramatic solutions on the spot?

A. I told the cameraman exactly what I wanted for each shot. I decided on rather complex, long set-ups because I didn't have enough time to shoot a series of short covering shots and because the dialogue in most scenes between Woodward and Goldoni seemed to flow better without the interruptions of intercutting.

As to a story-board, I never actually worked one out; but two weeks before we began shooting, I went through every single scene and planned in my mind the moves and the set-ups. I then drew simple elementary diagrams of where the camera was and where the actors were in relation to the room. I then decided where the actors would move, what sections of the scenes I would cover with what shots, where I would need a master two-shot, where I would need a tracking shot, and so on. I reckoned that I had better not shoot too many shots and planned on about seven or eight set-ups a day. A sort of feature average. My working rule was an hour a set-up, and I more or less stuck to that no matter how complicated the shot.

So I knew exactly what I was going to shoot, how I was going to break up the scene, and what moves I wanted the actors to make. In the case of the more simple stuff with Fitzgerald talking to the narrator, we did it just like that. The first day or two I said to Woodward, "You do this" or "You do that," and we'd do a quick runthrough. He'd then go away for makeup while we lit the set. After a while, when we got used to each other, we didn't even bother to do that. I just told the cameraman what we were going to do while Woodward was being made up. He would then come down, and we'd do a quick walk through and shoot it.

For the more complicated dramatic scenes with Zelda I allowed one day per three-minute scene as compared to the five minutes a day on the other scenes with the reporter. In the scenes with Zelda I reduced the amount of shooting and increased the amount of cover, because I thought it was more important. Usually, we rehearsed the whole scene the way I had thought it ought to go, and in most instances the actors agreed with me. Occasionally, when I said, "Right, you'll be standing and he'll be sitting there," they would say, "No, that's not right," would think about it for a few minutes, and then say, "Look, if we're both standing and if we're both over in this section of the room, it'll be better." They would then explain why. If the suggestion was good I would then hastily reconstruct my method of shooting the sequence according to their suggestions, and play it their way.

Q. Were you content with the performances you got?

A. I couldn't believe how good they both were. Both of the principals were staggering. Woodward looked completely like Fitzgerald; and although he's English, his American accent was absolutely impeccable. The style in which he was playing was so remarkable that I couldn't believe my good luck.

The moment shooting finished, I started work with the editor. We were allowed six weeks for editing, which was meant to take us up to the fine cut but not the negative cut. I saw all the rushes with the editor every night of shooting, and I made my selection of takes every night. The first week of editing, I said to the editor, "You know my selection of takes; here are a few pointers but not many. This is how; go ahead and cut it." This first rough cut turned out to be eighty-three minutes for a 50-minute program. I then went over it very carefully to get the reactions which weren't quite right. We then went through it again, and I took out several shortish scenes at the beginning of the film which I thought were boring, and lost about five minutes like that.

Q. What were the scenes you cut?

A. You remember the film starts with Fitzgerald taking the reporter chap around his house and with his childhood. I had gotten a boy of fifteen to play Fitzgerald as a young man. I didn't like it when I shot it, and I hated it when I saw it in rushes. I didn't like Fitzgerald walking through the cellar and walking across the hall and into the first scene in the living room. I felt the beginning of the film had a very slow start; I still think so. Anyway, I took out several bits there and made the cutting rather forced by doing this; it never quite works because of that. The film had a dreary opening, which I always knew; but I felt we needed it because it was necessary to show his childhood. I realize now it should have had a much stronger start.

I also dropped an entire three-minute sequence which cost me a day's shooting. It was also at the beginning of the film and showed Fitzgerald's first girl friend, Genevra King. I didn't like the performance of the actress, and I didn't like the way the scene was written, so out it went. Apart from that I did some more trimming and reshaping here and there—dropped out some library film, dropped the interviews which the editor had put in, and dropped out the stuff from *Tender Is the Night*—and ended up with about seventy-six minutes for what was supposed to be a 50-minute program.

I went back to the cutting room once more and finally got it down to seventy-one minutes which I liked. I showed the cut film at seventy-one minutes to Norman Swallow, the executive producer, who liked it very much and said, "Right, I'll ask for seventy-one minutes for you and you're in." We then did the music—which was mostly of jazz records of the twenties—had the credits drawn and photographed, did the opticals and the dub, and two months later it was transmitted on the air.

185

Specials

11

Don't Look Back
and
Monterey Pop
Don Alan Pennebaker

The film *Don't Look Back* is the most effective presentation of the reality of contemporary youth attitudes that I've ever seen.

RALPH J. GLEASON,
"SAN FRANCISCO CHRONICLE," 1967

Pennebaker's Don't Look Back *was shot in 1965 and covered that
year's triumphant tour of England by Bob Dylan.* Monterey Pop *was
shot two years later. Both films give vivid insights into the youth
generation of the mid-sixties, the one by concentrating on the folk
idol, the other by looking at the generation en masse at a pop festival.*

In Don't Look Back *Pennebaker uses cinéma vérité techniques to
get into the flesh of Dylan just when, as one critic put it, "he was
feeling around the edge of fame." One sees Dylan confronting audiences, blasting out "Hattie Carroll," putting down interviewers and
matching his style against that of Donovan. Occasionally, however,
Pennebaker's camera leaves Dylan to capture the lyricism of Joan
Baez or to record Dylan's manager Grossman making a deal with the
BBC.*

*But at the center there is always Dylan, looking at the camera, com-
menting, pacing up and down, and working at a song. What emerges
is a brilliant portrait of a nervous, talented, and sensitive artist. The
portrait may be a shade too flattering, but I suspect it's fairly near the
truth.*

Monterey Pop *covers the international pop festival held in 1967 in
Monterey, California. The performances of the late Janis Joplin, the
Mamas and the Papas, the Who, and nine other groups or individuals
are well shot, but the depth of penetration varies. Thus, the earlier
performances seem to be two dimensional, with the real spirit of the
artists as individuals only being captured in the performances of Otis
Redding and Ravi Shankar. However, the real achievement of the film
is that it breaks down the barriers between audience and artist, to
reveal the flow between the two.*

Monterey Pop *inevitably suffers comparison with Mike Wad-
leigh's* Woodstock *(1970). The latter is more of a technical tour-de-
force, but becomes weak at the edges when it attempts to become a*

documentary of ideas. Monterey Pop *hardly goes into documentary coverage; yet I find it much more subtle in conveying the mood and feelings of the masses of beautiful youth, intellectuals, Hell's Angels, and hippies who wander around with flowers and decorate the festival.*

Along with the Maysles, Leacock, Terry Filgate, and a few others, Pennebaker can be considered one of the founding fathers of American cinéma vérité; he has constructed a style and approach to film which has influenced a whole generation of film makers. According to Pennebaker, film must show something that no one ever doubts. The audience must believe what it sees, even if this conflicts with the ability of a film maker to express his own point of view. Truth is all important.

Pennebaker was trained as an engineer; he got his first film experience with Francis Thompson making reenacted documentaries. In the late fifties he teamed up with Ricky Leacock, then a young cameraman who had shot Flaherty's Louisiana Story.

A few years later Leacock and Pennebaker, sometimes individually and sometimes together, were responsible for shooting a large number of films for Time Inc's "Living Camera" series. The aim of most of the films was to follow an individual or a number of individuals for a few months through the resolution of a crisis or critical situation, varying from a Broadway debut (Jane) *to John Kennedy fighting an election primary. My own choice among these films is* On the Pole, *a film about racing driver Eddie Sachs, and* The Chair, *a study of Paul Crump waiting for commutation of his death sentence. Since* Don't Look Back, *Pennebaker has worked with Norman Mailer on* Wild 90 *and has also done some shooting for Godard. As to the future, he sees himself being pushed more and more into fictional films.*

Q. Who first suggested the idea of a film about Bob Dylan?

A. Dylan's manager, Albert Grossman, came to see us and said he wanted to make a film about Dylan's trip to England. Dylan also wanted to get into film making himself and wanted somebody to show him the ropes and give him a sense of the thing.

Q. Were you required to present an outline? How did you settle on the budget?

A. We just shook hands; there was no formal contract. There was no outline, no script—in fact I've never ever used a script on any of the films I've done so far. As for money, I was paying for the film, so the money was my problem.

Q. What attracted you about doing a film on Dylan?

190

A. Dylan was important—that was the first thing I was convinced of. I wanted to find out more about him, and I didn't know any other way. Asking questions was no good; I wanted to watch Dylan in as intimate a way as possible. Of course, there were limitations to this. I knew I wasn't going to find out everything about him and nobody could expect me to. What was important in this case was that the pictures themselves were secondary. What really concerned me was the ongoingness of the mood. To me films are like dreams.

Q. Did Dylan put any restrictions on you?

A. No. No more than I would impose.

Q. Was there any discussion about the audience for whom the film was intended?

A. I always assume that there is a wide audience for a good film. I believe that, if a film is any good, people will want to see it, and you charge the best fee you can get.

Q. In approaching this, were you conscious of any sort of influence from other films like *Lonely Boy?*

A. No. Frankly I think that *Lonely Boy* wasn't a very good film. Certainly Paul Anka didn't seem to me to be a very interesting guy; but on the other hand, I think he was more interesting than was shown by the people filming him.

Q. You've said or written somewhere that in many ways the Dylan film presented some of the most difficult problems you've ever come across. Can you outline some of these problems?

A. Dylan wanted to make a movie alright, but he wasn't particularly interested in having people understand *him*. Sometimes a guy wants a film, but he's not going to help you at all. You can't even state the rules. So you're three-quarters through the film and it's marvelous, and then suddenly for some reason you breach unspoken or understood rules, and he says, "I don't want you to film any more." It's a game in which no rules are ever stated, but you must understand what are rules of nature.

Q. What were these unspoken rules which you say were gradually developed between you and Dylan?

A. They are hard to put into words because, as I say, they are not word rules. You don't violate certain things. You don't oppose the standards of the person you're filming, or if you do you must suffer the consequences. You also have to listen the whole time—and let the person being filmed know that you're listening and giving him your 100 percent undivided attention. At the same time you have to realize that he is not necessarily interested in what you have to go through. If you have to bring in a lot of lights and have him go through things twice, he's likely to say, "This is a drag. I don't have time, and I'm not interested."

Q. Could you be more specific about breaching unspoken rules?

A. Well, at one point, Joan Baez was with us when we were driving near Liverpool. We stopped at a gasoline station, and a bunch of gypsies drove up. Joan then began talking to the gypsies, and I just happened to be filming, for no particular reason; I wasn't particularly interested in what was going on. Joan then went over and got a couple of little kids, and when one of them recognized Dylan she asked if they wanted to go and meet him. They said "Yes," and she brought the kids over to the car. Dylan was mad at Joan; he said, "You just don't treat kids like that; they're not toys. I lived in a truck like that once, and I know what it's like. You just don't do that kind of thing." He was furious with her, and he was mad at me for filming it because he assumed somehow that my filming it had made it happen. He thought Joan had fallen into the trap of the camera. He saw it all as a kind of camera game, and it annoyed him because it was neither true nor real. That got him so mad at me that I knew in his mind the whole of my filming had become slightly suspect.

Q. You mention "falling into the trap of the camera." This brings up the old question of the camera itself altering or creating the situation. Were you aware of people playing the camera game? Did you ever stop shooting because of people's acting?

A. It happened very seldom, because all the people involved had a very good understanding of what the camera was doing. They knew that the camera was recording them in a way in which they elected to be recorded. They were enacting their roles—Dylan as well as anybody else—but they were enacting them very accurately. In this instance, I don't think I ever elected to decide whether or not I thought they were acting well or not well. If Dylan wanted to come in and look solemnly at the camera, I had no business telling him not to do that. He understood what a camera was. What determined my turning on and turning off, in most instances, was whether I thought the situation was interesting or not. What you are kind of asking is, did I ever knowingly censor? and I don't think so.

Q. How do you sense an interesting situation developing? Can you give me any instances of beginning to shoot and then cutting off, or others where you suddenly realized that you were onto great material?

A. Once Johnny Mayol came in and sang some of his Irish folk music. I knew it didn't really interest Dylan and it didn't interest me much, yet it would have been impolite to stop shooting. So I continued but I knew that I would never use it. Now, when Donovan walked in the place and began to sing, it didn't matter whether he sang well or not. Dylan was so interested in Donovan, and in finding out what was going on in Donovan's head, that every instant was interesting; I just kept shooting because I had no idea what was going to happen.

q. What was your biggest actual technical problem?

a. By and large, the calisthenics involved and keeping up with a story in rain or snow; carrying the equipment; not having any crew. The crew was just myself and a girl—Jones Alk—who did the sound.

q. What were the difficulties in editing?

a. It was just a matter of timing. You start at one end and you go through to the other end. It's like writing a book. You try to disabuse yourself of all your preconceptions of what it should be; and as soon as you get your mind cleared, then it's very easy. It took me three weeks to edit that film. I did it on a viewer—I did not even use a Moviola.

q. Let's move on to *Monterey Pop*. How did you get involved with the film?

a. John Phillips and Lou Adler were going to do the festival and wanted to film it. At the time, there was a lot of nonsense going on which I wasn't fully aware of; they were to sell the film rights to ABC in return for which ABC would underwrite the major part of the festival. I think the sum being talked of was $400,000 of which $100,000 would have paid for the film; the rest was underwriting the festival. In the end ABC chose not to do it, and we had to get a release from them and pay back the $400,000 out of our net. So it started off as a theatrical film with a fairly high chunk on its head as opposed to what it really cost to make.

q. What do you reckon was the total cost of the production?

a. $125,000 to $150,000.

q. With these kinds of big events, festivals and so on, there is quite often a problem of releases. How was that covered?

a. It was quite complicated. I know that initially the foundation that set up the festival was supposed to cover releases. That is to say, the releases were the responsibility of John Phillips and Lou Adler. It later developed that they hadn't gotten complete releases, and some people even contested the ones they had. As a result we had to spend maybe nine months hunting for releases, and it became a big hassle. If you have the money up front to pay for a release from a guy at the time, that's the best, because that is when everybody is most anxious to settle. If you don't do it then, you might as well leave it until the film is complete and you can see who exactly you have in.

I don't think in the end it really matters. I don't think anybody is going to hold you up in the end because of the lack of a release. For instance, we had Ravi Shankar running much longer in the film than was permitted by his verbal commitment; but when he saw the film, and the way he was used, it was alright. We had to pay, but he wasn't unreasonable. I have never had anybody be unreasonable, either in releases in general or in terms of money. Of course, you have to pay performers, but people in general you don't.

Q. You were producer-director of this. How did you put together your crew?

A. This is probably the first film I have made where a lot of other cameramen were involved. Two or three people had worked for us previously, and one guy was a still photographer from California and I had a sense of his being hip to the California scene. Altogether, we had six cameramen. Barry Fienstein was one of them. Then there were Nick Proferes, Jim Desmond, my partner Ricky Leacock, Roger Murphy, and myself. I went out to Monterey a couple of days in advance, got a sense of the place, and as far as the filming went gave each person a certain area to shoot in. I also set up a way of indicating which songs we were going to shoot, so we wouldn't all shoot different songs.

Q. What kind of cameras did you use?

A. They were our own cameras, the cameras that I designed for this kind of thing. They sit on your shoulder and the magazine tilts back. Two cameras front stage had 1,200-foot magazines which I felt was essential; if they both started at roughly the same time, they could carry us through a major hunk of music and the reloading wouldn't be a problem. All the other cameras were running on 400-foot loads.

Q. How did you have your cameras set up?

A. There was no backstage camera—it was onstage and was my camera. We never set up any specific play positions—the cameras could move as they wanted—nor did I indicate types of shots. I let everybody decide what they wanted to do—close ups, wide-angle, what have you. What we did eliminate was the wide-angle covering shot from the back—the old protection shot. It is useless, particularly for television.

Q. In a musical festival such as this, the sound recording setup must have been fairly complex.

A. Yes. What we did was set up the sound on eight tracks. Even though it was for television, I was hoping to go stereo. We just set the volume level on each track and stopped worrying about mixing trumpets with drums or voices with other voices. Everybody had their own track, and as long as they didn't overload the track I could mix them later as I wanted.

Q. You had six cameras working, and with every camera you had crystal control?

A. We had a recorder working with each camera, which was cue-sound, from the position of that camera; but the actual sound of the music was recorded from stage mikes into a big Ampex eight-track recorder. One of the tracks carried a sync signal, which later enabled us to sync it up to the cameras. All the cameras were crystal controlled and in sync with each other, and as I've said also synchronized to the cue track. I could always find where I was on the main track.

Q. You had six cameramen around. There were also cameramen from the various TV stations. Did you get in each other's way at all? Did you try to define areas for shooting color?

A. We weren't worried about that. When we weren't shooting the musical performances, everybody was out shooting anything constructive and interesting, and I made no effort to find out whether people were covering the same thing. It never occurred to me they would. I wasn't after one person covering the main gate and somebody else covering the Hell's Angels. I was after what interested them; and if a guy found himself covering the Hell's Angels and wanted to stay there, that was his business. In the end, I think everybody got into some aspect of the thing that I could never have anticipated; and in a most surprising way, it all pulled together.

Q. Can you say a word about the color stock you used and any problems in processing.

A. I used 7242 reversal Ektachrome, and most of the film was shot with a film speed of 500 ASA. The idea of using the 500 ASA enabled us to have only one type of film in the camera and shoot under very dark conditions, or go out in daylight with either a neutral density filter or stopped way down. This way we managed to get the widest possible latitude for shooting and avoided that ridiculous changing of magazines from one kind of film to another.

Q. Did you play around with the color when it went to the labs?

A. You mean to get special effects? No.

Q. Where artificial lighting is concerned you normally have to be very careful about the color temperature of your film. You were shooting under all sorts of strange lighting conditions. Did this question of color balance worry you at all?

A. Not really. Color balance is something that has come out of the

super-elegance of the Hollywood film concept and is furthered by
industrial and advertising films. If the faces don't match or the colors
don't match, everybody gets offended. They say that if the pictures
don't look real, people will be offended. You know Cézanne put an
end of all that a hundred years ago. I am not particularly offended by
slight excess of blue light or a slight excess of red light. It depends
on how you use it. Color is just like sound—it's like musical sounds
that a band makes. There are no laws that say you can or cannot use
any color, or have to worry about color match in film—that is not
the point of it. One has to understand what a film can do under certain
conditions and use it the way you want it.

Q. What were the main things that went wrong?

A. My camera. At one point I think somebody gave me something
strong. I think Chip Monck gave me something and my legs became
wobbly, and I put my camera down and forgot I was using a battery
belt. As I walked away I pulled the camera off the table, and broke
the lens on the cement floor. This was just before Hendricks. The
camera was a mess, but I managed to put it all together again and to
finish shooting with it. I had no idea whether or not it would work.
Things like this always seemed to happen.

Q. Were there any other mishaps like that?

A. We had camera and focusing problems; batteries would wear out,
and I wondered whether we would have enough equipment to survive. The logistical problem is with you all the time, and the problem
is that the equipment is not that well manufactured and designed. Our
equipment is better than existing standard equipment, but it isn't
good enough for a war.

Q. You couldn't have done the film with an Eclair or a BL?

A. At the time the Eclair wasn't crystal controlled, and you can see
what the problem would have been of going to a master track. If you
wanted to cut from one camera to another, you would have had to do
something with the speed of your sound and nothing would have
been in sync.

Q. What sequences did you drop in editing?

A. Certain long things didn't go in, like the Grateful Dead. It was
the first time I had ever seen them in person, and I was really knocked
out by them; but they ran so long—maybe three-quarters of an hour
—and knocked things off balance. We dropped certain obviously bad
performances, and there were other groups that I just didn't think
were musically interesting. We dropped Mike Blufield's band although they were in the first two-hour version of the film. Then a lot

of people were really turned on by the Electric Flag, so leaving them out was a distortion in a way.

A lot of people perhaps saw the movie as being a kind of an award —all the winning bands—but it wasn't meant to be that because obviously I don't think of Simon and Garfunkel as a winning band; but I think that the song they did and the work it did in the film was essential. I didn't think you could just start off with the Jefferson Airplane. I don't have any rules about it, but it seemed that if you took Simon and Garfunkel out you just didn't have a beginning.

Q. Did you use the sequences chronologically?

A. In a way, yes. The film has a chronology in my head, but I don't think it's the actual chronological sequence of events.

Q. You mentioned the dropping of certain groups. I believe you also cut out Paul Butterfield?

A. Originally the film seemed to me to swing out when it came to Paul's group and that of Mike Blufield. I happened to like those groups, and I wanted them there. But when we played in Paris with those groups, I felt the film came to a stop. The audience survived the stop, and it was okay; but when I did the same thing with a very long sequence with Ravi Shankar, the film became unbalanced. You can ask people to sit and listen to something they are not totally interested in once, but it's very hard to do it twice. My reason for including Ravi Shankar and excluding Paul and Mike was that Ravi was something new. Most of the people who saw that film never imagined that they would have to sit and listen to a raga for twenty minutes; but having done that, they were different people.

Q. When you're shooting vérité style, do you find you are also thinking in editing terms?

A. No. I just can't think that far ahead. Your first problem is to get as much of it onto film. In editing you try to find out what you've finally got, but in the shooting the problem is to try not to miss anything.

Q. How did you handle the distribution?

A. We went to a couple of major companies and asked if they would distribute it, and they said it didn't interest them. They didn't think it would go, or maybe they thought they couldn't make enough money, or they had their own things to hassle. So then we decided to distribute it ourselves, which sounds like a nice, simple, brave answer, but it's really hard. It's hard work because we don't do it very well, we are not very efficient at it—how can we be? We don't have the access to theatres, we don't have the sales, we don't have the muscle

197

that a big major has, we can't put out half a million dollars in advertising. We do very little advertising.

When Allan King came down with *Warrendale* I tried to persuade him to release it theatrically, but also said to him, "You really have to understand you will never make any money out of it, whether we do it or anybody else, but it will give you some access to money, or at least to action, and perhaps your next film you can get the money to do it out front." Well, he finally went with somebody else, but I don't think he made much money out of it. That's the most difficult thing—nobody really wants to distribute a hard film like *Don't Look Back* or *Monterey Pop*. They're too "amateurish," too "unprofessional." In fact, the nicest compliment I ever got on the Dylan film was from a kid in Texas who said, "I didn't even realize it was a movie; I just thought kids went along and shot home movies." That was exactly right.

12

Royal Family
Richard Cawston

*In 1968 Richard Cawston was invited to produce and direct the
BBC-ITV consortium project* Royal Family. *Even before its completion the film had been sold to virtually every country possessing
a television service, and in the end it may rate as the most widely seen
documentary ever made.*

*Cawston appears to have been the ideal man to guide such a project.
Educated at Westminster and Oxford, he joined the BBC television
service in 1947 after serving as a signals officer in the war. His first job
was that of film editor; then from 1950 to 1954 he acted as producer
of the BBC's original television newsreel. In 1954 he moved over to
studio productions and became associated with "Panorama," a weekly
current-affairs magazine; a year later he turned exclusively to documentaries. In 1965 he was appointed head of documentary programs
for BBC television; but, executive commitments notwithstanding, he
has continued to work as film producer and director.*

*Although Cawston's films have covered a variety of subjects, the
ones that stay longest in memory are his studies of the British profes-
sions such as* On Call to a Nation *on the medical profession (1958),*
The Lawyers *(1960), and* The Pilots *(1963). The films are sympathetic human documents, welding top journalism to interesting and
sometimes very exciting styles.*

*One English filmic innovation that is associated with Cawston's
name is the development of the noncommentary direct-cinema documentary. This technique was used to excellent effect in Cawston's
inside study of the 1966 Billy Graham greater London crusade, titled,*
I'm Going To Ask You To Get Up Out Of Your Seat.

*All Cawston's films are balanced, objective, and finely crafted ex-
amples of film making. But occasionally one wonders about the nature
of the man himself, and what are the real opinions and views inside
the urbane and well-groomed exterior. I haven't seen* Television and
the World *(1961), which was a study of the development of television in different countries, but according to Roger Manvell, the
English critic and film historian, the film reveals not only Cawston's
sense of humor but also a deep feeling for the responsibilities of tele-*

vision and his alarm at the betrayal of its powers when they are ne-glected or wrongly used.

Royal Family *(1969) may have been the most difficult film that Cawston has ever made. Not only did the shooting involve huge logistical and technical problems, but it also involved a very delicate relationship with England's Royal Family.*

What emerges is a superb film made under difficult conditions. Cawston's direction is unobtrusive and is well complemented by Antony Jay's compact but effective commentary. Within the limits of courtesy the film provides a unique picture of the Royal Family at both the intimate and the state levels. At the same time it also provides a thorough understanding of the function of a constitutional mon-archy wihin a democratic political system.

Q. How was it decided to make a film about Britain's Royal Family?

A. The making of *Royal Family* was a slightly different operation from any other film. The original concept of the film came from within Buckingham Palace. Applications began to come into the Palace from television and film companies all over the world when they realized that the Investiture of Prince Charles as Prince of Wales was going to take place. These companies wanted facilities to make films about Prince Charles, mainly for showing at the time of his Investiture.

As a solution to the multiplicity of requests, the Palace advisers decided that it might be better to have one fully backed film, which would have their total cooperation, to provide a background to the Investiture. However, it was decided that it would not in fact be a film about Prince Charles, but rather about the job that he was going to have to do; and the only way to show that job was to show the nature of the work being done currently by the Queen.

After a good deal of discussion, which of course I know nothing about because it took place before I came on the scene, the Queen agreed that she would allow a film to be made showing the work of the monarch and all those aspects of the work which normally hap-pen in private and which no one had seen before. It was then that I was recommended and invited to be the producer of this film.

I subsequently met the Queen's Press Secretary, Bill Heseltine, and Prince Philip, and discussed the possibilities of this film. Finally, I said I would make it on the understanding that I would be given the normal editorial freedom which I would expect in any other film, that it would not be made by a committee, and that I would be al-lowed to make it my own way as a film maker. This was all agreed.

A small advisory committee was in fact set up, but it was simply there to give me help about information and assistance in getting things done. At no point was I ever told how to make the film or what should be in it.

Q. What were the main things that struck you in the beginning as being different from other films you had worked on?

A. Where it differed from most films, of course, was that it was about an unknown subject. No one had ever seen the day-to-day workings of the Palace, except members of the Palace Household and the Royal Family themselves. Therefore, I couldn't sit down and write a script, even if I had been the kind of person who made films from a script, which I'm not.

One couldn't do a reconnaissance of what goes on, as one would do with a normal documentary, because this would have meant studying the whole of the Queen's work over a period of a year. This in turn would have delayed the start of shooting to the point where the film could not have been completed by the required deadline. I had only been approached in March 1968, and the film had to be finished and ready for showing by the end of June 1969. It was clear that we would need to shoot the Queen's work over a whole year, as only in that way could one cover all the different things she does. Thus, it was quite evident that I was going to have to do my research to some extent as I went along and let the film evolve in the process of shooting.

It was of course possible to make a few basic plans, because the Queen's schedule is laid out so far in advance. For example, we knew there was going to be a Royal Tour of South America, and it seemed to us that this event should clearly be featured in the film. And this was true of other events of a similar nature. But naturally I didn't know what happened inside the Palace. This information gradually became available to me as we proceeded.

The key person in all this was Bill Heseltine, the Queen's Press Secretary, who not only acted as a vital link between the Palace and myself throughout the whole operation, but was always totally ready to accept without question my decisions as a film maker.

Q. When did you actually start shooting?

A. We started on June 8, 1968, with the scene of the Queen riding back after Trooping the Colour. One of the technical considerations which was very difficult to decide was what gauge to work in. I knew that we were going to be allowed inside places which were going to be very spectacular. There would be ceremonial occasions inside the Palace and elsewhere which have never even been recorded by still photographers, let alone movie; and therefore there was a great temptation to use 35 mm, as this would have been better for such spectacular scenes.

At the same time, it was clear that one would want as much in-formality in the film as possible and would want to use the latest film-making techniques in order to get mobility. These two things seemed to point towards the use of 16 mm as well, so in fact we finally worked in two gauges.

At the outset I was not sure whether we would use more 16 mm than 35 mm, so we decided to shoot the big spectacular sequences on 35 mm, and the ordinary material on 16 mm. My original plan was to blow up the selected material from 16 mm to 35 mm and make the film 35 mm in its final form because we knew it might be required for cinema showings in some countries. As time wore on, the 16 mm material became the dominant element. The informal stuff shot on 16 mm was clearly the most interesting and unusual, and therefore what we did in the end was to make the final film in 16 mm, and reduce the 35 mm components to 16 mm.

Q. Could you tell me a little about the film stock and film equipment you used?

A. We were very fortunate because the new fast 100 ASA Eastman color was just coming in, and we planned to use this for the film as much as we could. Until then we had been working with 50 ASA, and this was a definite handicap with the informal material, because it needed a lot of light and I wanted to work with the minimum possible. We got what I believe was the first batch of 100 ASA Eastman color to arrive in Great Britain from Kodak's Rochester factories. In fact, I think it's fair to say we couldn't have made this kind of film six months earlier for that reason; it arrived just in time.

Our basic camera was a 16 mm Eclair, backed up by an Arriflex BL. We also used an Arriflex for the 35 mm element, but this was always shot mute. On the whole, we worked with a single unit, so that the chief cameraman—Peter Bartlett—operated the Eclair. When the oc-casion called for two cameras, the assistant cameraman would shoot with the Arriflex BL. Later we exchanged the BL for a second Eclair, to make the whole thing more interchangeable.

This duplication acted as insurance in scenes which were extremely valuable and unlikely to be repeated, such as President Nixon's meet-ing with Prince Charles, which was clearly only going to happen once and was not being directed. In this case we had a camera on a tripod in the same room, as insurance and to give us extra cutaways, while the main cameraman worked about three feet away from the principals with a hand-held camera.

One of the most difficult problems was the whole question of sound, because the idea of microphones was totally new for the Royal Family. They had never had live microphones near them before, except for making formal and prepared speeches. This is because the words they utter are so widely reported around the world that everything they say is normally checked very carefully before being recorded. Also, the presence of microphones and recordists can easily spoil the look of any public event. Therefore, and very understandably, they were at first rather reluctant to allow me to have the microphone anywhere near. However, I then put it to Prince Philip that if this was going to be a film suitable for showing in 1969, it would have to be a film with natural dialogue. I therefore made the suggestion that if he would only allow us to record everything both he and the Queen would always be able to recognize our sound recordist, who remain unchanged throughout the film.

I also gave a solemn undertaking that all the sound we recorded would be locked away in a vault in the BBC TV center, and nobody would hear it until the film had been edited. It would then be presented to Prince Philip and the Queen to see and hear. If they found they had said anything at all which they didn't like, they had the complete right of rejection. I gave them this undertaking, and happily it was accepted.

Although the Queen and Prince Philip have probably been more photographed than anybody else in the world, they have always avoided microphones. In order to achieve a more natural and intimate film, this was a barrier I had hoped to overcome. It turned out to be really just a question of getting used to the presence of the mike. As time went on the Queen became so used to it that she came to know not only where the mike was but also where the cameras and lights had to be placed. In the end she became enormously expert at being filmed and seemed very interested in the whole process. She got to know the crew and what each man did, and therefore she always knew, even when we were in a garden in Chile, which was her film crew.

This eventual willingness of the Queen to allow an intrusive microphone near her was a key factor in allowing us to give an informal picture of the Royal Family. For example, the picnic at Balmoral, which I suppose was shot in September, was the first occasion where we had natural dialogue. It wasn't until then that we really got used to the Royal Family—to the idea of working this way—and that is why we did a lot of quite valuable sequences at Balmoral, the shop scene, the picnic scene, the scene with her Private Secretary.

Q. How much time did you have for setting up a scene, such as when the Queen went into the shop at Balmoral?

A. The Queen had told us she was going shopping, and we went down about forty-five minutes before to set up the lights. When she arrived we filmed her from the outside going in. I then stopped her after she had entered the shop and asked her if she would mind coming in again. We then went inside the shop and I filmed her coming in the door. The whole sequence inside the shop was filmed literally in one take. On the whole, it was a one-take film, and this called for very good camera operating and very skilful hand-held work.

Q. Can you give me one or two examples of your lighting problems.

A. The lighting problems increased when we moved into the big interiors at Buckingham Palace. These I had deliberately left until the winter. They were very difficult rooms indeed to light, and their sheer size required a large amount of illumination to get the correct exposure. At the same time, we knew that the members of the Royal Family meet their guests—ambassadors, and so on—in these rooms and might be troubled by a large amount of light. Therefore, the cameraman had to keep the lighting to an absolute minimum and work with a wide open lens. This clearly presented a very big focusing problem, and it was difficult for him when we were in a situation of any depth to hold two people in focus at the same time.

As the film progressed the Queen got used to the quantity of light, and by the time we filmed President Nixon, which was in March of the following year, we had all the light we needed. But again this was a deliberate policy, of introducing these technical annoyances gradually, for we knew that, if we offended towards the beginning with too much light and with too much direction and so forth, then the whole thing might have come to an end then and there. I was greatly helped by the efficiency and teamwork of my lighting crew, who worked so fast that none of the normal activities of the Palace were ever seriously affected.

Q. Were there any scenes which you wanted to shoot but didn't?

A. No, I was allowed to shoot everything I asked for. There was never any kind of veto—or rather the veto was a self-imposed one. I never asked for things which I thought would be in bad taste; therefore, there was never any question of asking for something that would have to be turned down.

On the other hand, I can't think of anything I would have liked to have asked for and didn't. It was a question to some extent of the area in which one asked for something and the timing of the request. The final scene in the film, sitting around the lunch table at Windsor, was a scene which I had conceived in my head as a result of seeing the Queen telling stories at dinner. I waited until we were right at the end of the year's shooting before asking if she would agree to this scene, because it seemed it was a lot to ask for and I didn't want to ask for it earlier. But by that stage the Queen fully understood what we were trying to do. A trust had been established, and she therefore allowed us to shoot.

Q. I would imagine that many difficulties arose because of the large number of locations and the necessity of shooting in foreign countries?

A. The Royal Family work to an extremely tight timetable; every minute of the day is planned, and there is no question of altering it—that's the first point. The second point is that when you are in public with the Royal Family, they are the subject of the most tremendous organization—police, crowds, crash barriers, and other press cameras. We were obviously in the way of the press and to some extent were felt to be in competition with them.

What was most difficult was to get the various officials who were present on these occasions—particularly the police, military, and officials in South America—to understand that we were *required* to be on the scene and to work even more closely than the press. This was an unheard of situation, that cameras and equipment should be allowed to be so close to royalty so much of the time. It took a lot of getting used to.

I mentioned that timing was difficult, as there was a very tight schedule. Other problems arose from the normal hazards of film making, except that even towards the end I was very reluctant to direct the members of the Royal Family quite as much as one would have directed other people. It didn't seem fair to put this added burden on them; and I felt, therefore, that the way to overcome this was to rely on really first-class camera work. To set up situations in which things would happen and to rely on good camera work to record those things.

The Queen was immensely cooperative about this. The visit with President Nixon is a good example. It had been arranged that President Nixon would meet the Queen and Prince Philip in front of the press and television cameras in the grand entrance of Buckingham Palace. This was clearly of no interest to us, as it was a news story and would have been dated by the time our film was ready. The Queen suggested, however, that she should reserve the moment of the meeting of President Nixon with Prince Charles and Princess Anne specially for our film. She thought there might be some interesting conversation, which would be helpful to us in our work. She was, of course, absolutely right; we got some marvelous footage.

Q. You did a scene with the American ambassador. Did you advise him in advance on what you required of him?

A. Not only did we advise him, but he walked over the ground with me in advance and we worked out exactly where we were going to film. This was one of the occasions where we did have to stop the action and sound many times in order to complete it all.

Normally, the Queen has several audiences a day; however, on this particular morning she had only one apart from the one with the ambassador. We arranged that the ambassador would arrive and we would shoot him being briefed by the marshall of the diplomatic corps. They would wait while we went and filmed the briefing of his staff. The ambassador then had to stop until we sent a message to the Queen that we were now ready to shoot the meeting of the two of them. This was one of the few sequences which was deliberately constructed in the film; but the dialogue, of course, was unrehearsed.

Q. Could we get on now to the development of structure and the problems of editing?

A. By October 1968 I had a fairly rough outline of the Queen's year. At this point, I asked Tony Jay to come in and join me with a view to acting as a script consultant. His job was to help decide on the style of commentary we were going to need when the shooting came to an end. At that point, we didn't know whether he would write it, whether we would write it together, or whether we would in fact ask someone else to write it. His role at that juncture was simply to discuss the commentary and the shape of the film in relation to the commentary.

By that time we had shot half the film. Tony and I then roughed out a very broad outline for the main sequence order of the film, which acted as a stimulus for research. This research was intended to uncover all the facts and background information we thought we were going to need. Apart from this very broad outline, I worked constantly on the shape of the film with the editor. Editing in fact started in February 1969; but as we went on filming until May, the editing overlapped with the last three months of the shooting.

I always find the editing phase the most creative part of film making. This is particularly true of the "evolutionary" type of documentary, in which so much of the material is spontaneous. You can make a plan and set up all your locations, but you never know exactly what material you are going to get, what people are going to say, and so on. You end up with a great deal to choose from, and the process of selection offers you innumerable permutations and combinations. The choice of the material and its juxtaposition can make either a sad film or a happy film, an exciting film or a boring one.

I was lucky in having Mike Bradsell as editor on this film. I had worked with him before, so we knew each other's methods. We would view each sequence together on the editing machine; I would make a few notes on how I thought it should run and then leave him to cut it. The sound in particular was the subject of a great deal of selection and shaping in the cutting room. A film like this consists partly of commentary, partly of sound effects, partly of music such as military bands, but mainly of natural sound shot on location—most of it dialogue and disconnected remarks.

Every word of this was transcribed on paper so that it could be edited with a pencil; I picked out the best bits and allowed them to dominate the rest of the sound track. It became clear that, in relation to this, the commentary would largely be a factual and linking one, and it also became clear that Tony Jay would be the right person to do it because he has so many years experience at writing this sort of commentary.

When we had cut all the sequences, Mike Bradsell and I viewed them together and then I made a number of basic changes until we had a rough cut that ran about three hours, which I could look at in the theatre to gauge the overall impact. At this point I asked Tony Jay to come and see it with me. After that the committee saw it.

q. Can you give me some examples of sequences which had to be radically altered?

a. There was, indeed, some major reshaping. We all felt the film was not exciting enough at the start, so I hit on two ideas which are used in the final film but which were not in the first cut. One idea was to have the film open with an imaginary typical day. We didn't have this in the original shape—we simply went through the events of the summer—but I thought it would be a good plan to create an imaginary summer's day right at the beginning.

To build the day I had to pull out sequences which were originally in different positions throughout the film. The garden party was there, but I wanted to add an official audience earlier in the day. We then added the Queen's lunch, which was somewhere else, and placed the Queen choosing her dresses, which I thought would make a nice indoor sequence, after the garden party. That brought us to five o'clock in the afternoon. For an evening sequence I put in the visit to the opera, which struck me as a nice way to round off the imaginary day.

The other idea, which I built up after seeing the film first time round, was the insertion of a montage of summer events. The montage follows the scene on the Royal train and the visit to a provincial town. It's a montage of visits showing oil rigs, cattle shows, and all sorts of things, which—combined as quickly as they are—give an impression of a very busy summer.

Q. How much film did you shoot for the project?

A. The quantity was not all that high when you consider that shooting was spread over a year, and that we didn't know in June or July 1968 whether we would be getting much better material in January, February, or March 1969. Also, we were in every case dealing with totally historic situations, and I was very conscious of the responsibility of being in this situation. Quite frankly, the quantity of film we shot didn't seem an important factor. I think we shot forty-three hours. As the final running time is about one and three-quarters hours, the shooting ratio is about twenty-seven to one. This sounds high but is only about double the shooting ratio of an ordinary film shot in four weeks.

The wastage didn't really produce an enormous amount of material which was of any real value in itself. It was nearly all duplication. For example, when we followed Prince Philip around the cattle show, we simply went on filming him talking to farmers. When we came to edit the montage, we only used the one line, "You're not going to reduce their legs any more, are you? I was getting worried that they were beginning to look like dachshunds." That was typical of many other remarks that he made and happened to be perfect visually as well.

Q. Was the script rewritten for America?

A. Yes, but it was a very minimal rewrite, because in the main it only meant substituting words like *around* for *round* and occasionally putting the words *in Britain* in front of a sentence for greater clarity. However, it was recorded for America in a different style. This was simply because to American ears, the delivery of Michael Flanders was felt to be too cold, and they wanted more warmth. I don't know that I agreed with the Americans, but at any rate we gave them a different rendering, and they were satisfied.

Q. In conclusion would you mind commenting a little further on the whole question of security and privacy in the operation.

A. The tremendous security was, indeed, one of the unusual features which we imposed on the making of this film, because as I explained earlier, I gave an undertaking to Prince Philip and the Queen that nothing we filmed of them would be seen by anybody until they themselves had had a chance to approve it. In order to make this possible, I had to avoid any detailed press stories.

We were frequently asked questions by the press, such as, "Is it true you are filming in such and such a place?" "Is it true that you filmed a picnic at Balmoral?" and so on. We then had to be very solid and answer "no comment" to all these questions, because of the undertaking I had given to the Queen. It certainly paid off, because as the months wore on, the Queen and Prince Philip realized that they were absolutely free to say anything they liked in front of our microphones and wouldn't read a word about it in the newspapers. So they realized we were honoring our promise.

Until the Queen had seen the film and had agreed that everything I wanted to put in the final version would be in, we couldn't reveal any details about what it was going to consist of. Because we were working to such a tight schedule, the Queen didn't see the film until May 18, 1969. Since the press show was due to take place exactly four weeks later, during those four weeks we had to write the final version of the commentary, dub it, and make a negative cut and show print—all this in the four weeks following the Queen's approval. The Queen didn't request any alterations or cuts, and so we went straight ahead and finished it.

Q. Dick Cawston told me that he was first approached about the film in March 1968. When did you enter the picture?

A. I was brought into *Royal Family* by Dick in September or October 1968. He had already worked for quite a while on this remarkable film but felt, about that time, that he needed somebody extra to talk to about the whole project. At that stage he didn't ask me to write it. He knew me as a fellow producer and writer who had also done a lot of script consulting, and thought I might be useful to talk to about the shape of the film.

I saw some of the early footage, such as the Balmoral sequence, and I thought it was some of the most marvelous material I had ever seen. After the viewing, however, I wasn't sure whether there would be much need for commentary, as it didn't seem to be to be a commentator's film.

Q. What were your general feelings about the shape of the film at that stage?

A. After a bit of thinking, I came to two conclusions pointing in different directions. One of them was that people enjoy a story, a story that moves forward in a natural progression. An essay is fine, but it is very hard to sustain in television terms for more than thirty minutes. If you're going over the edge of thirty minutes, you want a story about somebody. In other words, you can talk generally about the Reformation for thirty minutes; but if you have a fifty-minute program, you want to do the story of Luther's life. I could see that to sustain abstract ideas for what was clearly going to be at least a fifty-minute program and to shoot and illustrate those ideas, was going to be very difficult.

There was another factor which made me think of a narrative approach, and that was that there is a logic in film concerning the order in which you shoot things. Very often, the best way to tell a story about something which has happened to you is to tell it as it happened to you and the ideas as they struck you, rather than in a logical sequence. Also, in shooting as Dick was, right through the year, there was a logic to that year. All this made me suggest to Dick that we ought to have a time progression. Dick had, of course, been revolving this in his mind with all the other possibilities, and this crystallized it.

My first idea was to build a week or month in the life of the Queen. But Dick said, "no, let's make it a year." I jumped at the idea of a year, because there is something about the changing seasons which allows you to pace a thing, and you can say, "snow falls, and winter comes on." One of the hardest things in television is to get a sense of time passing. Commentary tends to be so insistent and rapid that you feel that everything happens very quickly. To get a sense of time passing we took season shots, like high summer, daffodils for the spring, and snow for the winter. Dick did all these things very well, and in fact they were all shot in the same area in the grounds of Buckingham Palace.

Q. What other problems did you and Cawston see besides the setting of the basic structure of the film?

A. Well, another problem was that the film was never intended to be nor ever conceived of as a "chatty" film, a sort of "keyhole" on the Queen's life. We very much wanted it to be a "theme" program, but I thought that the themes could be brought in by the way, subservient as it were to the narrative commentary. In other words, you accepted the fact that you were primarily telling a story, but you also knew you were free to weave in the historical background or the theory of monarchy if the points seemed important and suitable openings occurred. The information points arise logically from the simple narrative, chronological story of the Queen and the Queen's year. The alternative, of course, was one I was trying to avoid, the purely thematic essay on the role of the monarch.

It then became a question of what material to include, and this was quite difficult. On the one hand we weren't making a public relations film about the Royal Family, but neither were we doing an analytical or critical study. We were simply making a documentary whose function was to show the role of the Royal Family today and the scope of each person's activities. However, you couldn't get away from the fact that it was not really possible, in this particular film, to make critical remarks about the appearance, or the nature, or the way that the Royal Family did their jobs. And this was particularly true after the immense help and extensive concessions and permissions given to the film team by the Royal Family. Therefore, we had to accept that in this unique situation no judgments could be made, either good or bad by the commentary; it was for the audience to make their own.

I've experienced this kind of situation before, and there is only one answer, interesting facts. If you can't do any sort of appraisal, you can only give opinions on topics which are impersonal; but if you can find a really interesting fact, you can keep the program alive.

Q. Did you have any guiding principles regarding the task and function of the commentary?

A. Obviously a lot of the commentary had to be pure indication, to tell the audience where we were, such as "this is Balmoral" or "this is

Windsor." As much of the commentary was dependent on interesting facts, I insisted early on that we had to find a very good researcher. He had to be someone who would really understand the nature of the Royal Family. He also had to be a person who would not only dig out what you told him, but who could also initiate and originate research himself. Luckily, we found someone at the BBC who was not a researcher but a senior official; his name was Roger Carey. He had a first in history and proved to be excellent.

As the research proceeded it seemed to me that we required some original thought on the whole nature of the monarchy. I therefore asked Roger, off the top of his head, to write me a three-page essay on the monarchy. This turned out to be invaluable; it presented the idea that the strength of the monarchy lies in the power it denies to other people, rather than in the powers it can exercise itself. At first we thought we could inject this idea into the middle of the film, but gradually we saw that this was such a good point that it ought to come at the end, as the culmination of the picture. And that was what we did.

Naturally all sorts of other research was needed besides historical research. Here Dick Cawston's assistant, Barbara Saxon, was quite marvelous in chasing down the most extraordinary facts. I would look at the screen and think, "What would I want to know about that? I would love to know if that gold plate was used by Charles I or George IV; I would love to know how many times the Queen shakes hands in a year," and Barbara would rush out to get the details.

Because of the schedule of the program and the time at our disposal, it was possible in many cases to unearth the most interesting facts, and we asked for stacks of them. Naturally, a tremendous number were not used; but always when there was a gap—where the film itself didn't quite stand up by pictures alone—we nearly always managed to find some special fact that we could insert to keep the film alive and interesting.

Q. How did you actually approach the writing of the commentary?

A. It sort of accumulated over a period of months. We went through the film in stages, writing the commentary bit by bit. Dick and I would talk over and discuss in detail each section of the film. Dick of course knew a great deal himself as he'd been present at all the shooting, and it turned out to be very largely a cooperative commentary. I put the words on paper, but Dick has a good sense of how things should be said and a good idea of what the audience wants, just as I have some idea of direction and production. It was a very interesting cooperative undertaking, one which I enjoyed very much.

We would both look at the rushes and he would tell me things that quite often nobody else knew, for example, about the Palace procedure which he had witnessed. When he didn't have the answer to one of my questions, we'd make a note for the researcher. At each stage we discussed what ought to be said here, what ought to be said there, what do we know about this, and whether it was possible to do that.

Only Dick and the editor saw all the rushes of the film. My own first viewing was after a rough cut had been made, but there was still time to talk about changes or compression of the material. It was almost painful, even at three hours, to start taking bits out. We then went through the film sequence by sequence and started discussing what was wanted for this and that. Dick would tell me that this ought to be in here, and that ought to be in there. I would ask him facts about additional things, and suggest points I would like to make and how it would affect my writing of the commentary if we decided to cut here instead of there. This would all take a number of two-hour sessions before we would get all the things down as we wanted them.

I didn't really draft the commentary until I wrote it. I'm not a drafter and redrafter. I wait until I get the thing, and then I write it out once and for all.

In this case, when I finally wrote the commentary, I think I did part one in one morning and part two in another morning; but in fact the writing is purely an executive thing and isn't frightfully important. Dick was getting together a film with his camera and microphones, capturing all the things he could about the Royal Family and then putting them in order; whereas my job was to get together all the facts I could about the Royal Family, sort them out, and then sprinkle them over the picture so that they fell in more or less the right places.

In the end I wrote the thing out very quickly, because the actual writing wasn't difficult. Far more interesting was the discussion Dick and I had about the tone of the commentary. I was terribly worried that it was going to be too pompous and formal, while Dick was worried that it was going to be too chatty and might trivialize the subject. All this hinged on what voice we should use. After many tests with unknown voices we finally came back to Michael Flanders, whose voice struck exactly the right balance between formality and conversational ease.

Q. You mention that you wrote the commentary in two mornings. Did you prepare any draft line of connecting ideas?

A. Oh yes. I had a shot list or sequence list showing me the length of every sequence one after the other. I put all the notes I'd made against the sequence list and could easily see what points were relevant. The factual connections in this sort of thing weren't very difficult.

The film was also connected by a time logic. There was the flow of the Queen's day in the first bit and then the evolution of the Queen's year. There's still the problem of linking phrases, but after you've done a lot of these kinds of film commentaries they're very easy to make. The main theme was always there and as long as you have a main theme, linking is never difficult because you can always link back to your theme. Linking is only difficult when you have a really disconnected film, and you somehow have to tie it together with a commentary in a way that it isn't tied together in the producer's concept. That's a very different matter; but in this case, it was so easily linked there was no problem.

In considering the writing of this film it might be helpful if you recall that English radio program called "In Parenthesis." It was based on the Great War and had three narratives—a narrative of action, a narrative of thought, and a narrative of memory. Very early on it struck us that we had three narratives in *Royal Family*. We had the narrative of the action of the film, the narrative of the background and historical facts, and we had a narrative that tried to get at what the monarchy is about. It was a three-strand narrative, but the narrative of action was always dominant.

13

Dubrovnik Festival

Jack Kuney

The Dubrovnik Summer Festival was established in 1950 and over the years has become one of the best known international music and arts festivals. The festival usually includes performances of folk dance, opera, ballet, oratorio, and chamber music, which take place on open air stages ranging from old courtyards and palaces to the walls and gardens of the city.

Early in 1969 Jack Kuney of National Educational Television was asked to produce a two-hour film of the festival as a cooperative venture with Radio-Television Zagreb. The film is in essence a rather sumptuous and attractive musical special which blossoms over into fragments of lush descriptive documentary of Dubrovnik, its people, and the festival atmosphere and surrounds.

What interested me, however, was the nature of the difficulties encountered in setting up such an international production. The film was shot by both Yugoslav and Canadian cameramen. How did they interact? How did Kuney maintain continuity of style? How did the Yugoslavs adjust to the authority of a foreigner? What were the contractual difficulties? These, rather than matters of shooting technique, seemed to be the key questions to put to Kuney.

Jack Kuney is a tall, loose man, with almost too boyish a grin considering the number of years he has spent in radio and television. He originally trained as an actor and entered documentary radio in 1946. Two years later he went to Israel to cover the fighting during the Israeli War of Independence.

After six years with NBC Kuney was hired by CBS radio, but later moved back to NBC to become associate producer of a children's television show called "Let's Take a Trip." This was followed by a religious show "Look up and Live," about which Kuney comments: "It should say on my gravestone that I revolutionized the face of religious broadcasting in the States. I used actors and drama; I was the first to use Mahalia Jackson, and was the first to bring jazz and modern dance into religious programs." After "Look up and Live" Kuney produced television's "Play of the Week" for two years, directing six of the plays himself. He also did a number of music programs at the same time for NBC.

Kuney's first real encounter with documentary filming came in "One, Two, Three . . . Go." He did twenty-six of these children's programs before moving on to the Westinghouse Group and then becoming executive director of programming with the New York TV station WNDT. "I tried to turn the place on, but the only thing we agreed about were the terms of my going."

Since WNDT Kuney has worked primarily with NET as drama producer and film music specialist. "They seem to be satisfied. I'm satisfied. It seems to work."

Q. Who first suggested filming the Dubrovnik festival?

A. It came up as a result of a number of conversations that took place in the context of the International Television Federation. Basil Thornton, who heads our international division at NET, had met some people from Radio-Television Zagreb, and they had discussed the possibility of cooperating on a film. Later, the discussions became more specific, till it was agreed there would be a co-production deal to cover the festival.

Q. What is the background of the festival?

A. It's a festival of the arts, including dance, opera, drama, and classical and modern music that runs for forty-five days from July 10 through August 25 and is held in Dubrovnik, about which Bernard Shaw once said, "If you want to see heaven on earth, go to Dubrovnik." It's a glorious, radiant, magnificent, beautiful walled city on the west coast of Yugoslavia. The leading feature of the festival is that the natural settings of the town are used as the locations for the different events. They go all the way from playing *Hamlet* on the walls of a big castle, to putting music in the town squares and using the garden of a lovely Dominican church for chamber music concerts. There is almost an embarrassment of visual riches.

Q. How were the functions distributed between you and the Yugoslavs in this cooperative venture?

A. Originally we thought that NET would supply the producer and the raw stock, and that Radio-Television Zagreb would supply all the technical personnel and cameramen. We also thought money matters would be evenly split, with NET covering the above the line costs and the Yugoslavs the below the line expenses. But it didn't really work out that way, mainly due to my own personal reluctance. I needed a cameraman and an editor who could speak English.

Q. What did you expect to spend?

A. We estimated that the total production would cost about $90,000, of which NET would foot the bill for $55,000. However, there were problems in finding the money, so we weren't sure whether the project would go ahead. Then, out of a clear blue sky, we got a million-dollar grant from the Ford Foundation to do a show called "Sounds of Summer."

"Sounds" was intended to cover a series of thirteen domestic music festivals going on around the country and was to be shot on videotape. The executive producer was to be Craig Gilbert, and each show was budgeted at around $40,000 to $50,000, which was also meant to cover office expenditures and staff. This money rekindled the Dubrovnik idea; and Basil Thornton and another NET producer, Curtis Davis, literally forced the idea on Craig, somewhat to his unhappiness. Curt called me into his office late that day and said, "Jack, it's going to happen. We're going to Dubrovnik and we're going to do the festival." I argued about the need for my own camera-man and editor, and it was agreed I would shoot both with Yugoslavs *and* my own small unit. I then prepared to set off on a preliminary survey.

Q. Did NET have a contract with the Yugoslavs before you went on the survey?

A. No. I just went out on good faith. When I got to Dubrovnik, I was overwhelmed. The town is a masterpiece. It's called "the pearl of the Adriatic." The sea is deep blue, the sky is another unbelievable blue, and the streets are like pearl and limestone and literally glow in the dark. It seemed a fantastic setting for a festival.

The first thing I did was to scout around and find who was coming. The list included Isaac Stern, the American violinist; Rostropovich, the great Soviet cellist; Claudio Arrau, the pianist; Glen Tetley and his dance company; and many symphony and opera companies from all over. It was a fabulous list; but the immediate question was, how do you sign all these people? How do you get all these people under contract?

Luckily, Radio-Television Zagreb had covered the festival for a number of years and had a standard contract which they used to draw up with the artists which included radio, film, and television rights. I needed to know whether the contract also covered world distribution rights, which was vital to us, and was amazed to find it did. In America you would never be able to do that. You go to sign an artist, and he has his manager and his television agent and his concert agent; it just gets too complex.

Q. Besides investigating contractual matters, what other matters concerned you during the survey?

A. There were artistic considerations. What did the town look like;

how could we capture the fantastic beauty; would we be able to shoot at night and from where; and so on. That was all easy. Then there were technical considerations. I discovered that much of the festival was going to be covered by television, which meant that the studios would be bringing extensive lighting and sound gear. This, of course, was going to help us immensely if we could plug into some of the arrangements. Other things that concerned me were the kind of power we would have: would we be able to plug in; did we need synchronous motors; and did we need sync generators.

Those were the main things I covered in Dubrovnik; but on my way back to the United States I stopped off in London to order film stock, and to engage Richard Leiterman and Peter Moseley as cameraman and editor, respectively. I took the crew from London, because it meant a considerable budget saving as opposed to using an American crew in Europe.

Q. What final arrangements did you come to with Radio-Television Zagreb?

A. They agreed to supply a producer, a director, and three complete camera crews. I don't want to get into a long discussion about their competence, but they weren't really as used to handling portable equipment as the Americans and the British. Anyway, they were shooting with Arriflexes, while Richard decided to use an Eclair. The film was basically Kodak 7254 negative stock. This agreement, by the way, was verbal and in a series of letters. We didn't get a real contract signed until after I left.

Q. When you returned to the United States after the survey, did you draft any working outline?

A. I must admit I was wondering how we were going to cover all the work without some kind of unity or system. However, my associate, Lois Bianchi, made me sit down and write a seven-page treatment off the top of my head about the line of the film. I knew we had to get visual impressions of everybody arriving. For example, we could get trains, boats, and the hydroplane arriving from Bari. Then we had to get a very extensive coverage of the opening ceremonies. We knew there was a huge firework display on the night of the opening, and I thought this opening would give some personality to the events. I also wanted to cover some of the rehearsals, so that they would contrast with the final performances; and of course, there were the performances themselves.

Q. Were there any events or happenings that you definitely decided to exclude when doing the treatment?

A. Not really. Curtis Davis had said to me at one point, "Don't be afraid to overshoot; shoot as much as you want, and we'll make two or three shows out of it, if we can. And don't be afraid to shoot complete evenings of concert if you've got the stock." So we did. Stock is always the cheapest item you have on a documentary. In our case I'd say we did well because we finished up with a six- or seven-to-one ratio.

There was one limitation to my shooting, and that was the fact that we had to be finished and on the air by the end of September. And finishing meant not only editing but also doing a videotape mix in California, because there had to be a series structure imposed on it. We were actually the last show of the series, and Steve Allen had to narrate a videotape opening and closing from his house, plus some other copy. So I knew I had to be back in America by September 9 at the latest, with a fairly finished film.

This in turn meant that although the festival ran till August 25 I had to stop my shooting after three or four weeks and start on the editing. As it happened the Yugoslavs got me two prime items while I wasn't even there. They got me a Chopin piece by Claudio Arrau and another piece by Isaac Stern.

Q. You mentioned the problem of imposing a unity on your four camera crews. Can you explain that?

A. Yes. I got there the weekend before we were supposed to start shooting, called all the camera crews together, and said, "Look, rather than getting in each other's hair, let me work out a routine. Leiterman is used to hand holding, so maybe he can shoot all the documentary material and local color, and you (that's to say the Yugoslav crews) can cover the actual performances. OK?" Everyone thought this was fine and agreed without much argument.

Another thing I tried to indicate, but a little more subtly, was the fact that as producer I was responsible for where the film was going. You can't make films by committees; and we agreed that whenever there were conflicts, the overall decision would be mine. That rule stood me in good stead when we came to editing in London. There were a couple of conflicts because the Yugoslavs edit film in a completely different way from us. I had a very creative editor in Peter Moseley, and I wasn't going to breathe over every frame, especially when the film was fairly well set. But my Yugoslav counterpart producer didn't want to give the editor any latitude. He wanted to sit over his shoulder and cut the film frame by frame. But I just couldn't waste that amount of time; so when it came to conflict, I just exercised my rights as overall producer under the contract and went ahead my way.

Q. You indicated that Richard Leiterman had more of a natural documentary touch than the Yugoslavs. Can you give examples?

A. Richard had a kind of artistic touch that the Yugoslavs just did not have; it was like the frosting on the cake. The Yugoslavs would cover a concert from rather static positions, and in the rushes you would see just how static it all was. But Richard would cover the conductor, the hands of the harpist, the back of heads, the backs of manuscripts; he'd just bring everything that much more to life, so that when we got down to edit the film more often than not we'd use Richard's shots as opposed to the Yugoslavs' shots of the same material.

Q. How would your cameras be set up for something like an opera?

A. Very often they would be set out like three television cameras—left, right, and center, getting wide, close, and medium shots for total coverage. Sometimes it was looser. One of the things we discovered was that all the opera rehearsals were held behind screens; but people used to peep through and take a look, and we shot them and caught the backs of their heads against the rehearsal. One little boy was even looking under the screen. We then went inside to see the rehearsal of this very colorful Palermo Opera Company, and shot the very voluble director putting the cast through their paces. Later, in editing, we segued from the middle of the rehearsal to the actual performance that we'd shot later that evening.

Q. I don't remember any shots from the sides.

A. No. Unfortunately, we couldn't. It was played in the courtyard of an actual palace, so we had to stay out in front of the palace in order to shoot because there wasn't really any backstage or back of the flats area.

Q. How did you work with Richard?

A. Well, let's take the opening where we were shooting the crowds in the streets. That was pretty much all Richard. Opening night, we were able to get down in among the actual crowd. Dubrovnik normally holds about 6,000 people, but on that night there must have been about 30,000. The opening ceremony took place in the main street, called the Placa. I was on the platform shooting the crowd with the Yugoslavs, but Richard was actually down there in the middle of the ceremony. He annoyed everybody, but that's the only way to shoot this kind of film, to get on the scene and to be shooting up everybody's ass, or, to put it more subtly, down everybody's nostrils.

He got me the greatest shot in the film—a pair of hands raising a banner that looks pure Eisenstein. And he got it the only way possible, by shooting from three feet away. He also got the orchestra at the back and the final cut off from the conductor as the flag is raised. It's very dramatic and gives a great feeling of the presence of the opening.

Q. How did the language barrier affect your control of the Yugoslavs' shooting?

A. None of the Yugoslavs spoke English; so while I could convey to Richard what I wanted, there was very little I could convey to the Yugoslavs except to say to them, "Look, I'd love you to stay as tight as you can because this is for television." The closeup is all-important in television. It's not like film where your master shot is your all-important shot and you work from your master shot. The main thing I was able to convey to them was to get as close as possible.

Now later on I saw the footage, and unfortunately they were zoom-happy. They had seen Richard zooming in and out with his telephoto, and watched his flexibility, and had thought, oh boy, if he can do that, so can we. As a consequence a lot of their footage was virtually unusable. When Richard zooms, he zooms with a purpose; he has such a fine editorial eye. But when the Yugoslavs zoomed it was often to no point at all.

Q. Did you have any trouble with any of the artists?

A. Only one. Rostropovich. I had great visions of meeting him at the airport, following him out to his home, and doing some stuff on his background; I thought I could get a long sequence out of Rostropovich. As it later turned out, he didn't want to do any of this, not even what was written into his contract, because it turned out he had signed an exclusive contract for French television. To rub my nose in it even more, about the second day after he arrived a whole French television unit turned up, and I was told I couldn't touch Rostropovich.

Well, I yelled! Sometimes a calculated scene can be very helpful. Normally, I'm a very even-tempered guy, but this time I said I'm going to blow my stack because, if we didn't go back with some kind of name value (and up till that point we really hadn't had any name value for America), we were sunk. So I argued with the Yugoslavs, who were my contact men and knew all the subtleties and said, "Look, I'm going to take my camera crew and go home. Screw it! If I can't get Rostropovich, I'm afraid the Berlin Opera Company and the Zagreb Orchestra just don't constitute a show for me. I need some

221

names." Anyway, I pulled a scene and the result was that Rostropovich came and gave us a solo concert late at night, which wasn't as desirable as it could have been because I really wanted a concert with the crowds. But it was something.

Q. Did you have a liaison officer with the Yugoslavs to take care of hotels and things like that?

A. My associate producer did most of that. But I hired an interpreter, a rather smart girl who was also a lawyer. She would argue with traffic cops and get us through the massive red tape which, unfortunately, is part of a socialist state; even better, she was able to get our film back and forth out of customs, although it was a running battle the whole time.

Q. Can we take it from the editing process with Peter Moseley in London. You got 40,000 feet; how do you cut it down? How do you try to maintain a kind of variety when you are seeing show after show for two hours?

A. You must remember that Peter started editing almost immediately, with the first film that came back to London. Everything was slated and numbered and I was trying to keep editorial control of it since I was also the writer. I had seen *Monterey Pop* before I left the States, and I had said that what I would like to achieve was a kind of classical *Monterey Pop*. I wanted a film where the images told the story, and there's very little talk. I didn't want any narrator saying, "The golden sun sinks in the west." I wanted the story to tell itself.

In order to coordinate the ideas of Peter and myself I wrote him seven letters in the three and a half weeks I was in Dubrovnik. In these letters I described sequences which I saw in my mind, and how they related to the shots we were getting, and how we could build the sequence. And I was amazed how closely Peter followed my directions or improved on my basic outline.

Q. Can you give me an example of how Peter would take a suggestion from you and create a unified sequence from it?

A. We were out for a walk one day and I had said to Richard, "Let's get some color." It was very early in the festival and I didn't know what I wanted. Suddenly we heard a band playing Sousa's "The Stars and Stripes Forever." Richard and I both rushed down to the next square and there on the corner was a Yugoslav army band in civilian clothes playing the song. Richard is alert and the sound man is alert, but they caught the march in the middle. Luckily, however, the band repeated the tune. So there we were, with "The Stars and Stripes" being played by this Yugoslav army band in Dubrovnik. Now I hadn't got the faintest idea how this was going to be used and

I told Peter this, but it struck me that somehow or other we would find a place for it, maybe in the opening or in a rehearsal.

When I got back to London they had already edited the sequence. They had cut it together with some opening travel shots and a jet landing. At one point, when the band comes up with a very strong drum and trumpet beat, just after the introduction, they had cut to a long shot of a jet arriving at the Dubrovnik airport, landing exactly on the beat of music. The next shot is of a boat arriving on tempo, then some hikers, and so on, each in the same tempo as the march rhythm. The last part of the sequence is a light shot of the tuba player going boom, boom, and you see his face as he turns around and looks at the camera. It was lovely!

Q. What were the hardest things for you to delete in the editing?

A. We dropped a lot of background color, but I wasn't happy about the deletions. For example, there are a lot of rooms in Dubrovnik and the kids stand outside the town with signs saying "rooms to let." We spent two or three days trying to get this sequence, and then we never used it. I suppose I was just never satisfied that the color which went into the film was as good as the color which we had in the cans. Even when I went back to America, I was never fully satisfied that the look and feel we had of Dubrovnik in our film was as good as the stuff I saw and thought we shot.

Q. You had total control over the picture. What was the reaction of the Yugoslavs to the film you finally presented them with?

A. I think there were ego problems there, unfortunately. The Yugoslav producer was a kind of swinging cat. He didn't care. But the Yugoslav director was a rather strange man who was never really happy with what we were doing. Even though he had read my outline, he didn't understand the freedom we were trying to get in the film; and towards the end of the film he got tighter and tighter. He thought his artistic integrity was being circumvented. At one point he had to go back to Zagreb, and I said, "Look, if you are really unhappy with what I'm doing I'll give you a dupe negative and you can cut it however you want. I've got a deadline I have to make, and I'm just going ahead."

Q. How did the fact that the film was part of a series affect the finished product?

A. The final film was mixed on videotape on the West Coast. Holes had been left in the narration so that music could also be mixed in later and there was going to be some extra dialogue written by Steve Allen. So I really didn't know what final form that narration would take. I think it's terribly important to control your own film right through to the last frame. I was terribly sorry that I never really finished that film. I had 98 percent control of it, but no editorial power over the other 2 percent. Cuts were made in the film so that it could fit in to the series time slot. And when Steve Allen came in I saw that he threw certain portions out of balance. I was quite unhappy with the end result, although the public response was good. I think the original film was better than the version that finally appeared on the air.

Sponsored Films

14

A Cry For Help
George Stoney

A Cry for Help *(1962)* is one of a series of dramatic documentaries intended for use in police training, sponsored by the Louisiana State Mental Health Association. Its subject is the police role in suicide, and it splits up into a series of vignettes that illustrate the variety of problems which confront the police in dealing with the subject. About a third of the way through, the film moves on from providing a general background to suicide or would-be suicide cases to the police role in prevention. This is done by following four fictitious but representational case histories.

There is the college boy afraid to tell his parents about his failure in his exams; a girl waits for an invitation to a date that never comes; a middle-aged woman cashier is suddenly jilted; and a motorcycle cop is forced to give up his bike because of heart trouble. The illustrations show problems that may seem minor to an outsider but which are of sufficient gravity to the person concerned to lead them towards suicide.

The narration is brief. Statistics are given, and the dramatic incidents turn abstract arguments into revelatory human situations. The film persuades and teaches without sermonizing and is a model of what an educational film should be.

George Stoney is one of the most prodigious and successful producer-directors in the field of the sponsored documentary in the United States, with over forty films to his credit since 1950. The sponsored educational and business film is not particularly noted for its standards of cinematic craft, but it would be fair to say that Stoney has contributed a great deal to the raising of levels within that particular field.

One of his main approaches is to develop a fictitious drama to illustrate the way to deal with certain situations. This method was very well shown in All My Babies—*probably the best of Stoney's films*—which deals with the experiences of a Negro midwife in Georgia. This method was also used throughout the police training series.

Stoney was born in 1916 and minored in journalism at the University of North Carolina. On graduating he worked as a freelance *journalist dealing mainly with topics of social relevance, and also contributed to the Gunnar Myrdal study of blacks in America,* The American Dilemma *(1944). This was followed by a short session as information officer for the Farm Security Administration, and then war service as a photo intelligence officer.*

In 1946 Stoney joined the Southern Educational Film Service as a writer-director, and in 1950 branched out to form his own company. Since then he has made films on subjects varying from birth control, insurance, and the mentally ill, to the nature of the Bahai faith and the situation of the Canadian Indians.

Stoney has also been considerably involved in education and has taught at the University of California at Los Angeles, and at Stanford and Columbia universities. From 1968 to 1970 he was executive producer of the Canadian Film Board's "Challenge for Change" series, and in October 1970 became chairman of the Department of Broadcasting at New York University.

Q. How did you get into the field of sponsored films?

A. It wasn't a matter of choice, but happened to be where the opportunities lay. It wasn't a very logical or thoughtful development, but happened to arise naturally out of my work with the Southern Educational Film Service. We were working with government agencies, and every film was directly sponsored.

This whole relationship with sponsors is quite interesting and insufficiently discussed. Over and over again, I get visits from students and young film makers who say, "I don't want to make the ordinary film. I have seen a couple of your sponsored films. They weren't bad, but of course they could have gone a lot further. Anyway, I'd like to make that kind of film." My answer is, "OK, but you have to go out and hunt up that kind of film. You've got to find a sponsor." Then they reply, "But I'm not a businessman."

The problem is that every film begins to be shaped the moment you start talking with the person who has the money. The only reason I produce my own films is that I have found that's the only way to have any control over the end product. The reason I don't have a big office or a large staff and all that sort of foolishness is that I know I have to be in a position where I can stall on the film and argue for things I believe are necessary to it. I don't want to be under the pressure of having to get that next payment just to meet office expenses, and therefore pleasing the sponsor just to get that sustaining check. Every dollar that goes into the film is like a link in a chain around your neck. It's that kind of dirty business finally.

In working with sponsors, I think the first thing to keep in mind is this: Is the film worth making? Once you start, there is so much blood, sweat, and tears that you can spend the next six months getting all the chores done, kid yourself into thinking this is a great film, and then look at the answer print and think, "Oh my God, there goes six months of my life for something that wasn't worth the time."

Q. Do you have to spend much time consciously pursuing sponsors, or do they come to you?

A. At any one time, I have at least a dozen films that I want to make and for which I need a sponsor. I find that when I go to a sponsor with an idea, quite often it isn't the idea he wants, but his mind starts working on other ideas for the two of us. So it's a trick of salesmanship as much as anything else. I would say that I've had to hunt for sponsors for half my films, while the other half have been suggested to me by people who've seen my work and liked it. *A Cry For Help* is a good example of how the initial move was made by the sponsor.

Sometime in 1959 I got a call from Dr. Lloyd Rowland, the executive director of the Louisiana State Mental Health Association. He didn't know me; I hadn't heard of him. He had seen a couple of my films, and he wanted to come by the office and talk to me about making a film for police training. This was not a field that had ever interested me; but he said some flattering things about a couple of my films, as he knew that was the way to get my attention.

A couple of weeks later, Dr. Rowland came by. He was a man in his middle fifties, very mild mannered, very precise, and he sat on the couch in my little office on East 44th Street, not at all disturbed by the unpretentious surroundings. He told me that he had written a pamphlet about the various ways police handle mentally disturbed people, and the National Institute of Mental Health wanted the pamphlet to serve as the basis for a film script. If suitable, the script could be turned into a film to train police in the handling of these situations. Was I interested in such a proposition? I said I would read the pamphlet and see what I thought.

The pamphlet was very well written, very down to earth, simple, direct, and visual. I also saw that the pamphlet covered so many aspects that what was really required was ten or twelve films, not just one. I accordingly wrote out a prospectus for Lloyd saying that this should be not one but a series of films about police and the mentally disturbed. Lloyd said, "Yes, but we have to start with one, because we can't raise money for a series just like that. They'll turn me down, and I don't know how much money we are going to be able to get anyway." So I drew up a preliminary budget. We were told we could get $20,000 for one fiscal year, but that there could be no guarantee that we would have money for the next fiscal year. This meant we could start shooting the first film, but we weren't sure we'd have enough money to finish it.

By that time I was so interested in the subject that I was willing to do it on that basis. This was not just from reading Lloyd's pamphlet, but was also the result of working with some people in New York, people in the police department and mental hospitals. I'd also ridden with an ambulance crew for several days and was beginning to familiarize myself with the problems.

Then came the matter of writing the script. All the ground work had been done in New York, and the film was going to be shot in New Orleans. So here I was being forced into a situation of writing a film without really knowing the area in which I was going to work. Yet without a preliminary script the NIMH wouldn't give us the money. So I had to fake it.

Finally I wrote a fairly elaborate descriptive script, which became the basis for the first film which we called *Booked for Safe Keeping*. The film interwove a series of dramatic cases illustrating the ways in which the police should handle the mentally disturbed. I then went down to New Orleans with this script, got to know the police, and started revising my notes around the people and the cases I found down there. Then I wrote up a new script based on two cases, one in which the police did well and one in which the police didn't do well.

In researching *Booked for Safe Keeping* I had to go into the jails, the courts, and the police headquarters. And naturally, I began to see a hundred films I would prefer to be doing rather than the actual film I was making. This is, of course, a great temptation. Here you are making a small training film for the police when you suddenly see the whole world around you just crawling with film ideas. But you don't have the money. Money is the ruling thing in film making. It's a "kept" art, and you have to decide that right from the beginning.

Booked for Safe Keeping was pretty successful. The sponsors liked it, and money was forthcoming for a second film which we eventually called *A Cry for Help*. This film narrowed in on the problem of the police, and the way they treated the would-be suicide. This time we decided to make it in Chicago, because W. O. Wilson had taken over as chief of police and seemed the right man to help us. The actual head of the Police Academy was George O'Connor, a very brilliant young fellow, who guaranteed us his backing and a place to work. We also had the help of Drs. Norman Farberow and Edwin Shneidman, who ran the Suicide Prevention Center in Los Angeles. These two acted as my guides, and with all their support the film augured well.

Q. How did you immerse yourself in the subject?

A. I worked on this film in my usual way. I read the basic theoretical approach to the subject, then made use of the background I had already accumulated while working with the police in New Orleans. Finally, I spent about two months riding with the Chicago police in the prowl cars and testing out ideas against what I actually saw in practice.

These films were for training, so what we were trying to do was put on the screen a kind of practical ideal. That is, we were trying to show police doing *good* work in real situations. This wasn't necessarily the way the majority of the police worked; but it seemed to me that in a teaching situation this is what one should do and certainly this is the kind of thing which is the most acceptable.

You have to look at these films in relation to the kind of training films which are usually used in a police academy, where emphasis is on the accuracy of the detail in terms of *procedure*. For example, they will show a man going to a shootout; and when he gets out of the car he will turn and close the door of the car very quietly, because this is supposed to be the way you get out of a car. Every policeman knows this is just emotionally ridiculous, but because the training manual says you close the car door quietly that's what the films show. The old films would be accurate to that extent, but would have no reality.

We tried to operate in a different way by creating realistic situations and reactions. And if our films hold up with audiences it's because they sense that, however clumsy my police actors are as actors, they act true to life in given situations, and this is the central thing.

Q. You've mentioned certain problems with the script of *Booked for Safe Keeping*. What was the generating impulse for the script of *A Cry for Help?*

A. The script for *A Cry for Help* developed out of a series of theoretical propositions given to me by Shneidman and Farberow, which outlined the reasons for suicide. They gave me the basic theory and I had to illustrate the theory in practice. We knew we had to get a cross section of types and a cross section of situations, and it was up to me as a dramatist to see how we could make it all into something emotionally satisfying.

I knew that I had to get the ordinary policeman to identify with what was happening. He had to see the situation as relevant to himself and his actions. In *A Cry for Help* the way we did it was not only to show police handling suicides, but actually to set up a policeman as a potential suicide victim. The problem was how to make this acceptable to the audience. What we did was show a number of policemen in the film acting very commendably in difficult situations. This meant that when we showed a policeman attempting suicide, we hadn't alienated our audience. I also tried to work out the motivations of this potential suicide fairly precisely. I wanted the audience to identify with him as a motorcycle cop who was having to give up his wheel, as an athletic fellow who was going to fat, and so on. These problems were to be the reasons for his contemplating suicide.

In our test screenings we found that this didn't work, because so many policemen go into the job for security. So when the man had a choice of "giving up his wheel" and taking a soft desk job, the test audience didn't understand the dilemma. They didn't understand why he didn't immediately jump for the soft desk job, because this is what they would like to do themselves.

Q. But in the film it seems to me there are scenes which do provide a certain identification.

A. Yes, but the identification only came when we added a scene in which the man's wife was cruel to him, and in effect drove him out of bed by denying him intercourse. Then we had the identification. Originally, I'd written the film without this scene, and even after I'd shot it I felt it was such a blunt thing that I left it out of the first test screenings. But then I found that the policemen were not identifying with the man. It was only when we inserted the bedroom scene into the test screening that we got the identification we were after.

Now this script was probably the tightest of all the films I did on police training. Every sequence that was in the film was written almost precisely as shot. I was working with a very precise cameraman and a rather expensive union crew. We shot for eighteen days, and the only material on which we overshot was material which I did not script in advance but which I was attracted to afterwards.

Q. How much did the film cost?

A. It was budgeted at $40,000 which for a half-hour in action with a union crew in Chicago, and using 35 mm, was a low figure at the time. Remember this was when we were shooting with the heavy Mitchell, no hand held stuff. This amount was agreed to in advance and the film came in for that.

We were working with nonactors, and as there were many police roles to be filled I did a lot of my casting in the police department. For this I had to get permission from Wilson and his public relations people. It was another matter getting the individual policeman to participate. You have to sell yourself to the individual guy; he knows that if he gets in trouble—if he doesn't look well on the screen—it's going to be his neck no matter what you say, because you can always leave town. So you have to sell yourself and the product all the way down the line.

Anyway, the first thing I had to do was to clear up the matter of paying the police who were going to appear in the film. Now Chicago, like so many other places, is a place where the police are used to picking up extra money. Until Wilson came on the scene, it was said that you actually bought your corner as a traffic policeman; you paid so much to the precinct captain, and then you made up the money on the weekend stopping people and giving them a ticket or picking up change. This was the background. But Wilson raised the salaries until the fellows were actually making more honestly than they were dishonestly probably; but that took all the fun out of it, because the wife knew how much you were really making, and all the adventure was out of it. Then I came along and was going to be paying these fellows for being in my film, so I had to set a rate and determined it would be the same for the captain and the patrolman. I would pay them all at the sergeant's overtime rate, and would pay them by check so that we would have a record. However, Wilson had been so strong on the business of not taking money that the fellows didn't really believe they were going to get paid.

q. Which scene did you select as your starting point for shooting, taking into consideration all the problems you've just mentioned?

a. We started with the first sequence in the jail. A prisoner hangs himself and the police have to do mouth-to-mouth resuscitation. I deliberately picked that as the first place to shoot because it was in headquarters, above the chief of police's office. I wanted to start in a place where the professional nature of the film would be obvious and news about it would permeate the rest of the department. Very often you have to do this kind of thing when you're using nonactors. You have to convince them at the beginning that you are really serious about it all. You have to show them you're not just play acting, and that you really are professional.

The arrangement was that, if the police were on duty and I was using them as the men in the jail, I would pay them $5 even though they were, in effect, on government time. In other cases they got the off-duty rate which I think was $10 for anything over an hour or $26 for an eight-hour shift. So we did the first scenes and I gave out the checks on the first day. The next morning when I arrived, the place was bedlam, because the order had come from the chief that they had to give back the checks. I knew that the test had come, and I said, "This is ridiculous; we have a promise that the men can be paid." I marched right through the receptionist and all, up to the chief, who was giving dictation, broke right into the thing and said, "This is what's happening up in the jail. There's bedlam, and I can't work this way. You gave me a promise. Your department said that we could pay these men under this arrangement, and we have to go ahead on it." Wilson called in his PR man and asked if this was true. When he said, "Yes," Wilson said, "Tell them they can have the checks back." So I'd won, and from then on I was *in*.

Q. How did you select your actors and work with them in their roles?

A. Most of the actors were collected around the police department, or around Northwestern University. The script called for types, very carefully worked out, and so I looked for types. I tend to cast from my belly. I look at a guy and if it clicks, he's in, because I realize that the audience is going to have exactly that same response. The only time I can get away from that is when I have a major character, when I have someone on the screen long enough to break the stereotype of immediate identification.

I very seldom talk with nonactors about motivation. I try my best not to show them the script, because then they start thinking in terms of ordinary acting. Many times I write out the dialogue fairly completely and then ask, "What would *you* say in a situation like this?" We talk it out, and often they finish up with almost exactly the words I have written but by that time it has come from them. For example, there is the case of the motorcycle cop who is contemplating suicide in the film. The cop didn't like me, and I knew he didn't like me. I weigh around 130 pounds, and I'm not particularly masculine as he sees it. I played into that. I admitted that I couldn't do all kinds of things he could do. I told him *I* wouldn't know what a man like this would do. "*You* would know. You tell me what the dialogue should be." You play into their ego structure.

My original script said something like "policeman sits on bed looking at his former trophies on the wall, and contemplates suicide. He is interrupted by his son." I don't think it said more than that. All the business about playing with the gun and the line, "Don't point it at anybody, you might get hurt," came out of the actor's own head as he talked with the boy. I had said to the fellow playing the part, "What would you do in a situation like this?" and he developed it from there. The more imput you give to a nonactor, the more chance he has to build a character. The times when the film gets weak and dramatically showy is when I am using people who have had some acting background and give them precise lines to work out and memorize. That's when I think the film shows up badly.

In most situations where you are doing dramatic films with nonactors, all the turmoil is happening beyond the camera; somebody fiddles with lights, somebody fiddles with microphones, and somebody else is fiddling with sets. Usually there is so much tension and argument behind the camera that you can forget what is happening in front of the camera.

When you have nonactors and there's that kind of turmoil behind the camera, it can so dominate your cast that they go to pieces. You have to build up the idea that the most important thing that is happening is what is taking place in front of the camera. The actor has to feel that he is the most important thing, not your lighting, not your sound, nothing. And everybody's ego feeds into that. You have to have an atmosphere where people can act and not feel self-conscious. Each of these people is living for one moment. You are getting the one characterization they can give. A good example is the homely lady, the cashier who slashes her wrists.

This was a very delicate thing. The character was written into the script together with every detail of what she did, such as turning the engagement ring to look like a wedding band. The lady who played the part was the wife of a friend. I had never met her until I went to Chicago. One look and I said, "She's it," and told her about the part. I told her why we were doing the film, and she agreed to be in it. I told her how much time I thought it would take, what she would get paid, and the things I wanted her to wear. I said I wanted her to have her hair done in the style of the twenties, but I didn't go into the whole business of "we'll make you ugly" or anything like that.

When she came on the set I said very little to her. I introduced her to the policeman and we kept jokes down to a minimum. I didn't attempt to get to know her so that when we were doing her highly emotional scenes, she was doing them with people with whom she had no reason to feel embarrassed. She knew this was almost the only time she would see them, and this was a thing she could do which was almost private. The crew was very quiet and nonintrusive. These are the things which are so important in handling nonactors.

Q. Did the police, who after all were going to use the film, attempt to change anything?

A. Most of the problems with the main sponsor had been solved in the first film in the series, which established a certain amount of confidence. There were, however, problems with the local sponsoring body, that is the Chicago Police Department, particularly in one scene where the police are cruel to the cashier who slashes her wrists. There was no problem with the policeman who did the scene. They knew that this had been approved by the chief, and they enjoyed

A CRY FOR HELP

Extract from treatment presented by George Stoney to the sponsor

. . . What is the average policeman's attitude toward suicide? We have made some effort to discover this. Fifteen police departments held round-table discussions on the matter, following a set of questions designed by Dr. Rowland, and taped the sessions for us. We have interviewed personally policemen in ten other departments. Our inquiries have gone far enough to suggest that attitudes on suicide *in the abstract* vary quite as widely among policemen as among laymen generally, being affected by such fundamental things as family background, religion, education, etc. However, the average policeman's attitude *toward the individuals* involved in such incidents has been made startlingly clear. . . .

In tape after tape one hears them talk about "sympathy bidders." In interview after interview they have made no effort to conceal their hilarity and disgust in telling us about the "repeaters" or "the nuts who call up."

Happily, we have found a good many policemen who have a great deal more understanding than this. Much of the material contained in the script has been developed with their help. In some situations it may be possible to assign only this kind of policeman to handle attempted suicides, working with properly trained medical personnel. In the vast majority of places, however, this is not a practical solution. The would-be suicide will be dealt with by the first policeman who can get to the spot. So it is to the average policeman that our film is directed.

Although the attached treatment will result in a film which we hope will be a single dramatic unit, it can be divided for purposes of subject matter analysis into four sections:

1. Ways of preventing suicide and suicide attempts in jail.
2. Emergency rescue procedures outside jails.
3. The role of the police in prevention.
4. The policeman's personal attitude toward people who attempt suicide—how this can hurt or help him in dealing with them.

throwing themselves into the role. But by the time we tested the scene the head of the academy, George O'Connor, had moved on. The new head of the Police Academy wasn't nearly so sure of himself. He was very worried about this scene and drew it to the attention of the PR man for the Chicago police. This man, who was scared of his shadow, said the scene had to be killed.

Fortunately, we had shown the film to lots and lots of other test audiences, and we knew from a teaching standpoint that the scene was realistic and was needed. In the end I had to make a personal appeal to the Chicago chief of police to save the scene. Fortunately, Chief Wilson understood what we were up against. He was convinced that the film would be used primarily for teaching and said, "Leave it in." But it was touch and go.

5. Understanding "the cry for help."

The film's first section deals with suicides and suicide attempts made by people who are in police custody. This is a problem almost every policeman will accept as part of his responsibility and here we can give him some fairly simple instructions.

The film's second section tackles a more difficult problem: suicides and suicide attempts made by people not in custody. The second section of the film undertakes these things:

1. To present suicide as a statistically important problem in the over-all well being of a community.
2. To stress the importance of responding to these cries for help as literally matters of life and death.

In part three the film begins to deal more directly with the policeman's role in preventing suicide. To help develop in our viewers an understanding of people who attempt suicide we sketch four case histories, moving from one to another as our analysis demands. One of the individuals happens to be a policeman. . . . His story is developed through section four, interspersed with more direct material. In this final section we carry this one case through to a conclusion. The police officer involved makes an attempt at suicide more flamboyant and troublesome to the police than any shown in our film. If our film has done its work, however, our audience by this time will not be sneering at his action as a "bid for sympathy." They will be appreciating it as "a cry for help."

q. What procedures do you use to test the efficacy of your films?

a. What you do is to try to agree with your sponsor on the main objectives and purposes of the film. You have to know precisely what you want the film to achieve in terms of altering or reinforcing attitudes. Then while the film is still in fine cut, you have a series of test screenings, ideally with the same kind of audiences for whom the film is ultimately intended. And they must see it in normal surroundings, rather than in a screening room. If the sponsoring committee is present its members should sit in the back of the room, not say anything, but see what the film does. This solves a great many problems. In the first place, you can say to the sponsor or committee, "Let's try it out; how do we know, we can always cut it out," and they can say the same thing to you. For example, on *Booked for Safe Keeping*, we had the mentally disturbed person using a lot of four-letter words. Now, the police specialist said that they should be cut. They were words policemen see and hear all the time, but the police specialists argued the other people present at the screenings would be embarrassed to hear them in a film. Yet when these "other people"—sociologists, nurses, and the like—didn't object in any of the test screenings, the police specialist said, "Okay, we'll forget it." So that was that. The test screening really helped.

15

The Future Came Yesterday

Antony Jay

Antony Jay's The Future Came Yesterday *is the best industrial film I have ever seen. Its message is very simply to show how a factory can be more logically organized through the use of a computer—if creative and executive personnel can understand each other's problems.*

One of the most instructive things in the film is the use made of a gently drawn characterization of the two or three main "stars." To this element one has to add wit, humor, and a very lucid and personalized commentary that makes the film informative and entertaining not only to those professionally concerned, but also to the average viewer.

At the age of forty Antony Jay is known as one of the top commentary and script writers in England. I first met him across the table at a BBC interview in 1963. He was then thirty-three years old, was head of talks features, and had a long string of television accomplishments behind him, including five years constructive work with the "Tonight" magazine program.

I met Jay for the second time in December 1969. At close quarters I was struck not only by his intelligence and verbal brilliance, but also by his tremendous charm, warmth, and desire to help in the interviews in any way possible.

In the intervening seven years Jay had left the BBC to act as freelance writer-director and had added yet another crop of successses to his name. These include two scripts for "The Great War" *series, and commentaries for* Fifty Years a Winner *(a profile of the physicist Sir Lawrence Bragg) and* Journey to a Legend *(a study of T. E. Lawrence before 1914.)*

Jay's talents range outside serious documentary to include a highly polished sense of comedy and satire. He wrote all the theme scripts for the first two English series of the "Frost Reports," featuring David Frost. He also contributed very frequently to "That Was The Week That Was" and "Not So Much a Programme . . . ," the two series most noted for putting British television satire on the map.

In 1967 Jay wrote To England with Love *with David Frost. In the same year he also published a slightly more serious book* Management and Machiavelli, *which eventually won the 1969 American Management Academy Award.*

Jay was educated at St. Paul's School and Magdalene College, Cambridge, where he took first class honors in classics and modern languages. Internationally he is best known for the script he wrote for Our World, *the first global telecast, and for the commentary he wrote for Richard Cawston's* Royal Family *(see p. 199).*

Q. You are chiefly known as a political or satirical documentary writer and director. How did you come to get involved in business films?

. A. International Computers Limited, asked me to work for them. At first I just came in to help produce and direct their presentations, for they had no idea how to use visual material. Then they moved on to film making and asked me to make this film, *The Future Came Yesterday,* which was to be about electronic numeric control, machine tools, and all that.

As I moved into the film, I made a discovery which has been extremely valuable to me ever since in dealing with commercial organizations and that is, if you can't deal with the top person, you must at least deal with a person who is a good and tough enough manager to know what he wants. He must be able to tell you what he wants, and be happy when he gets it. The trouble with industrial and business films is that the film makers don't dare go up high enough. They talk to the assistant public relations officer who, by definition, is terrified of what's going to happen on this film. He is therefore going to crib at anything and cancel anything that smacks of being new or original, or takes a risk with the audience. Suggest these things and he is going to jump on them and say, "Impossible! We can't possibly have that!" And then he'll want to cram in shop signs and products all over the place and will absolutely destroy the film and defeat the purpose it was made for, even though it's not the company's wish that he should do that. Like so many corporate employees, he's "plus royaliste que le roi."

If you deal with a high enough man and you can talk to him sensibly, you'll find you can make a very, very good film and he won't quarrel with you in the slightest. In fact, he'll back you up. And so long as everybody knows you're talking to him, you can turn to anybody who objects to your methods and just say, "Well, I'm sorry, but that's what I'm going to do, and you'll have to get the managing director to stop me if you don't like it."

Q. Would you say there was any one essential factor that differentiates an approach to industrial film from, say, making documentaries? Any vital clue or guide that must be kept in mind from the start?

A. I've seen a hell of a lot of commercial and industrial films that have been very badly done, and nearly all of them have gone wrong because the person doing the film never really understood what the people in the company wanted to say. I agree that part of the time, you've got to talk them out of saying things that aren't worth saying; but you have to remember that you're not making the film for the company, but for the people the company is going to show it to. So it's not enough just to make the company happy. Sometimes you have to make them unhappy so as to make their audience happy, and get the right idea across.

What you have to explain to the company is that you are not out to pat the managing director on the back or boost the ego of the chairman of the board. Your job, instead, is to capture and hold the attention of people who don't necessarily want to be sold to or preached to, and who want an entertaining half hour. If the film remains in the vaults and nobody ever asks to see it, it's not really a useful or worthwhile film for them.

Another factor of extreme importance is that you must come to grips with the subject intellectually. This is particularly true as things get more and more technical. You have to learn about numerical control, you have to learn about computers, about programming, about circuitry—not in order to become an expert but just enough to be aware of how things happen, what certain things do, and what produces certain effects. In other words you have to acquire the knowledge of an educated and intelligent layman.

Q. You've mentioned the necessity of going to the top person. Who filled that role in *The Future Came Yesterday?*

A. I had to deal with a tough engineer-manager named Douglas Hughes. He was marvelous to work with because he was willing to take total responsibility—in fact, it's quite significant that one of the reasons he wanted the film made was in order to show it to his own board. There were lots of other people he wanted to show the film to as well, but he felt he couldn't talk to his board—they didn't understand his words; his memos never got read. So he reckoned the only way he would ever get through to his board was to make a film. And he made it and they all looked at it; and he reckoned it had paid for itself when they'd seen it—more than paid for itself in the effect it had on the alterations of company policy.

Hughes had left school at fourteen. He'd had little systematic education but understood engineering in great flashes of insight, which he could communicate but not in any logical way. Because of his unsystematic mind it took me some nine or ten meetings before I began to see that there was a rounded and complete story in numerical control, how it worked, its place in an engineering factory, and so on.

Q. Did the company clearly outline to you the kind of film they wanted? Did they know their objectives?

A. Well, all too few people really know what they want; they just have a feeling they want to make a film. You have to start by asking if they really do want a film. An awful lot of the films go wrong because the people don't actually want a film at all. They want a whole series of live presentations, or they want a touring party going round with film strips. But if they do want a film, you have to find out exactly who they're aiming at, because this affects the level of knowledge that you can assume of the audience. If they're aiming at kids who have left school at the age of sixteen or seventeen you can't assume that they understand words like "production control"; whereas if you're aiming at people in the engineering business, you can assume that.

After that you have to find out exactly what the concept is that they want to get across. In fact, I always ask one question, "What is the single sentence you want to say to the person who has just seen this film? What's the single one-sentence idea you want left with him?" And if your sponsor doesn't know that, you can't make the film. If he does, then you can always come back to that idea at every stage in the making of the film.

In this particular film the sentence was, "I realize that the computer can enormously simplify production control; but first of all I've got to reorganize my factory, to prepare to use the computer." It was as simple as that.

Q. After you had grasped "the concept" what kind of film approach crossed your mind in this particular case?

A. It always seems to me you have to spend a certain amout of time in a public speech or anything of a communicative nature in harnessing the horse of your ideas to the wagon of your audiences' understanding. Otherwise, you can go hurtling off, riding your ideas away without realizing that the wagon isn't actually coming with you at all. You've got to show your audience that you're the sort of person that understands their problems. You have to tune into them, so that they can say, "Yes, he's a reasonable sort of fellow; yes, he's right about that anyway, and if he's right about what's wrong, maybe he's right about what ought to be done."

Here it seemed to me very clear that I had to start *The Future Came Yesterday* with a sequence satirizing an existing factory setup. So I deliberately said nothing in the beginning about new ideas. Instead I tried to make people agree that the old ones were ludicrous. All this eventually led into Doug's concept. What he wanted to do, in fact, was to show that engineering factories are organized the wrong way. They are organized by internal convenience. They are an organization of milling shops and turning shops, when they should be organized according to the products they actually turn out. This means dividing the workshops up into complete batches of machines that are self-contained little factories—not just lathes all in this area or milling machines all over there—and then adding the odd milling machine and drill to complete the whole operation. I'm sure Doug's idea was right, and as I said, I had a lot of talks with him before I finally saw what he wanted.

When I thought I was familiar with the factory and had grasped the basic idea, I looked through my notes and wrote up a complete commentary that would run about thirty of forty minutes. It seemed to me that the only way I could get it down was just to write down how I would say it. Of course, being a film producer and director I don't write things down unless I see pictures in my mind, but the concept was very much that of an illustrated talk. It was the logic of the explanation that had to dominate, not the logic of pictures. The pictures had to follow.

I wrote out the commentary and then started thinking about the quality and flavor of the narrator's voice. I'd never been happy with the idea of the familiar neutral voice of the commentator; it seemed to me that one could humanize the commentator and add a great deal more personal warmth if one stopped thinking of the commentator or journalist as just reading words, and instead considered the commentary as a dramatic monologue written in character, for a character actor. In this case my model was Douglas Hughes himself, who has a rich sarcastic cockney voice, and if you could get some of that kind of personality into the commentary you'd feel for once that a real person was talking to you. Eventually, I got Richard Pasco, whom I'd seen do a marvelous bit of cockney acting in *Look Back in*

Sound	*Vision*
Have you met Adrian, our design engineer? Clever chap. University degree. Has lunch in the staff dining room. Doesn't talk to the production people very much. Well, they haven't got much in common. Except that they're going to have to make what he designs. But that's their problem.	5. Dissolve to INTERIOR DESIGN OFFICE. MCU same sketch, now on drawing board with hand doing more detailed sketch. Cut or zoom out and up to MS of Adrian sketching. Occasionally looks dreamily out of window.
Look at that job he's drawing now. Every figure and line he puts down is full of implications for the production people. Costs. Size of machine. Precision of machine. Tooling. Labor skilled or unskilled?—and type of trade. Machine loading. Tremendous responsibility? No, bless you, Adrian doesn't worry about little things like that. He's not a computer. And anyway, no one ever tells him.	Adrian writes ".0005" against a point on the drawing.
Look at his last job. Really beautiful design, that was. Multiple camshaft. He used that kind of shaft because he knew there was a nice bit of bar that size in the lab. He put the cams on a keyway: they made a lovely model in the lab. Trouble was, those clots on the floor couldn't repeat it. Had to go back and design it again. Now it's got the cams and the shaft all in one piece. Real bull-at-a-gate job. Oh yes, it *works* all right. But there's no satisfaction in that sort of thing.	Pan over to drawing on floor. Hold then pan to first camshaft acting as paperweight on pile of drawings on nearby table.

6. Dissolve to FACTORY INTERIOR. Second camshaft being machined in final stages: pile ready for assembly. |
| Anyway, off this one goes. 500 a year, Adrian designed that for. As it happens, marketing already knows they're only going to want 100. But no one has bothered to tell Adrian. What's it got to do with him? | 7. INTERIOR, DESIGN OFFICE. Adrian into shot, quickly makes final adjustment to his sketch. Cut to CU sketch finished.

8. Dissolve to MCU DRAUGHTSMAN'S DESK with Adrian's sketch being copied by a hand (nearly finished). |

Anger as Jimmy Porter, and he caught the kind of whining, sarcastic tone—"Oh, marvelous; of course he don't care that someone else had changed it too"—that I'd heard from Doug. I managed to write this into my original treatment and it's surprising how close the final film stayed to that very first original draft.

Q. It seems to me there's always a danger in industrial films of getting involved in the sheer beauty of machinery and gadgets and things. Did you find this happening to you?

A. No. Everybody had agreed on the formulation of the ideas and then I thought, How do we convey all this in actual terms? And it seemed to me that since this was about people—people's mentalities—it had to be a "people film"; it couldn't be a "things film." It wasn't really about how you program a computer; it wasn't about APT or the other software they were using. It wasn't really about numerical machine control at all, although that produced very nice pictures. It was really about people's mentalities—the way people block things and are organized to clash with each other instead of to cooperate with each other in a factory.

Q. Had you considered using actors?

A. I wasn't keen on using actors, because actors can't handle machine tools. They can't operate lathes; they just don't look as if they belong in factories, unless you get absolutely brilliant actors, and then, of course, you pay a fortune and the gross overall cost of this film ran about £6,000. Anyway, I've worked with ordinary people and so I believed I could use the ordinary men working in the factory. Having worked in television, I knew I couldn't give them dialogue. The way I did it was I told the people in the factory exactly the sort of person I wanted—bright, intelligent, not shy—and then made it a rule never to ask my "actors" to do anything that they wouldn't normally do. In fact, we approached it the other way around. When we had the row, for example, between the time setter and the operator, I got the two together and said, "Alright, you're the rate fixer. What would you say to him?" I gave him the situation and we acted it out. The time setter would tell me something and I would say to the operator, "Would you stand for that?" and he would say, "No," and so on. They would build a sort of method scene between them based on stuff they'd done before.

They were always doing it—they knew the attitudes and the role playing; and when we shot it, it was highly convincing. It was a real worker in a factory, a real lathe operator, a real rate fixer; the scene was real. This went on all the way through. The designer really was a designer; if he stared into space, he stared into space, and if he wasn't that sort, he didn't. They'd read the script, and they picked the right designer. He really was like that; he really was slightly dreamy. We got these chaps all the way through and I thought they were marvelous. Once they saw what you wanted—once you stopped saying "do this" and changed it to "you tell me what I should ask you to do"—they would get into it splendidly and would say, "Ah well, I'll look over here, and then I'll probably do that." If that didn't seem enough to me, I'd help them along and say, "I don't quite follow what you're doing; would you do that a bit more slowly or do it twice." They contributed an enormous amount so that, finally, it was their film just as much as mine.

Q. Was there any opposition or resistance by the management to specific ideas within your film?

A. There's a point in the film where we cut from a factory with lots of men working to the same factory without a soul, where everything is running automatically. This sequence was deeply resisted by the public relations officer, who said, "That's terrible; people are going to think they're all going to be redundant." That's just the sort of thing public relations people worry about, and you just have to tell them to relax. The people in the factory were well aware of the potential of computers. All the labor force is perfectly clear about this and didn't seem to me to be the least bit worried; they had seen it coming before the management. I hadn't said anything they didn't know, and I kept the sequence in.

One major thing that happened was that halfway through the film I realized I had to change direction. Because of Doug Hughes's emphasis on engineering, I had unconsciously been stressing the work of numerically controlled machine tools. However, my sponsors were more interested in the role of the computer in all this. But it wasn't difficult to make a change; I just redrafted the ending, and instead of ending on the machine tools as in the original draft, I ended on the computer. It was the computer that made the new factories possible. It was the computer that made the organization feasible.

Q. I notice there are one or two hard ideas which you get across by the use of graphics. What is your thinking on this point?

A. There were one or two things that really weren't possible to get over by filming in the factory. I wanted to make a point about the commitment to tremendous, unknown costs going into the millions

245

before you knew what the break-even point was. It wasn't the sort of idea that commentary could handle very easily or clearly, but I thought the point could well be made by animation.

There's another thing; I have often found that there are times when you have to put over a concept, and it's difficult to put it over using a physical object. For example, I wanted to make a comparison between the private grocer and the supermarket organization. The factory was changing over from one to the other, and the analogy was quite reasonable. However, I couldn't lay out the factory as a self-service shop or as a family grocer, so I got an artist to draw some sketches of these things—a sort of concept of reorganization. It wasn't expensive. I think this kind of animation is underused; people think "I'm making a film, and therefore, I've got to be filming something," whereas a film maker has to be able to use every technique at his disposal.

Besides animation I also used quite a lot of music in *The Future Came Yesterday*, but the trouble with music is that it can make a film look like a feature film or a newsreel and can detract from reality. Therefore, you have to use it very sparingly in this kind of film. In the end I used music satirically—a kind of march music for people going up and down and through the factory and, in one case, to get a sort of urgency when we had a good visual sequence of the machine tool. Apart from that, it seems to me that this sort of film really needs natural effects, particularly when you've got a lot of commentary. The natural effects help a great deal, whereas music in a genuine factory film tends to make people stop believing in the truth of the whole experience.

Q. What was the time allotment for the film?

A. I was there on and off for about four months—this included discussions, meetings, and drafting sessions. When I finished the script, we did a plotting session to see what we were going to shoot and where, and to break it all down into days and firm and specific locations. The actual shooting time was about two or three weeks, and of course we absolutely disrupted the factory. But they were fairly happy about it and keen to get it done.

What we did was invent a mythical company, Universal International. Then we had some things stamped and printed and some letterheads made, which was all very cheap.

I used to come along in the morning and while the cameraman was setting up and lighting, I would be talking to the men, who would be enacting the scenes and showing me how they would behave so that the shooting could really be quite quick. Indeed, you didn't want to give them too long to worry about it; you didn't want them to go home in the evening, and start acting in front of their mirrors and telling their wives how they were going to do it. You wanted them to tell you what they were going to do, and then do it quickly while it was still fresh and natural before it had time to become studied, stilted, and unreal. I was very precise about all the shooting of people, and I directed nearly all of that myself, while my associate director directed the shots of machines.

Q. Did you take general shots of machines with the intention of fitting them in afterwards, or was your shooting more planned?

A. Everything was taken with the precise knowledge of where it was going to go in the film and what it had to say. I didn't use general shots of factories and machines and say, "We'll find a place for them." That's not my way of film making.

As I see it, you don't turn a single foot of film without knowing exactly what weight it has to carry, what point it's making, what it precedes and what it follows in the film. Everything has an exact place. I may have dropped it later, but I always knew exactly why I wanted a particular shot and where it was going to fit. In fact, as soon as my original draft of the commentary had been agreed on, I wrote in every shot and every sequence I wanted alongside the commentary. I didn't specify whether it was mid or top shot, but I knew exactly what should be shot. The combination of commentary and shot list was then typed up in the second draft.

Q. Where you faced with many lighting problems?

A. My own feeling, quite honestly, is that there is no such thing as a lighting problem, because I don't write them. If a thing cannot be done, then we don't do it; we do something else. In any film that I write, there's always a way round it. It seems a kind of incompetent kind of writing for the whole film to hinge on lighting the whole of Albert Hall so that you can see every detail of decoration. My way is to say: Let's assume this is a simple unit, with ordinary lighting. Now how far will the lights stretch? And the further the better. But if they can't stretch, if the maximum we can shoot is about two machines at a time, then we can always put the lights onto a dolly, and do a tracking shot down the aisles to give the thing a sense of space. If that won't work, we can cover the situation with quick cuts or pans or something like that.

I think it's a great advantage being a producer and a director as well as being a writer, because I write thinking of the technical problems. I don't write anything that's going to be technically difficult, or if I do, I make sure it can be done before I write it. However, I do try to give people scope to do technically ingenious things like craning up and down, if they've got a crane. You want to give them scope to do that.

The other thing is that being a producer, I am also budget conscious; I don't write anything that's going to be particularly expensive or which I suspect will be very expensive. I try to write a cheap film, the cheapest that can do what has to be done. It may still cost a great deal of money, but it will be the cheapest and the most economical way that money can be spent. The budget in this film was about £6,500, which included my own fee of £2,500.

I think it was one of the happiest films I've ever worked on, partly because the man I was making it for was so clear and partly because I was very excited about putting over a new idea to a lot of people who needed it; in fact the reception was quite extraordinary. Normally, the sponsors reckon to make four prints of this sort of film; but they've had to make 128 prints of this one and have calculated that it has been seen by about one and a half million people in two years. I'm also told that it has had a profound effect on many people's attitudes to the computer and engineering. A number of production engineers have seen it and then asked for copies to show to all their colleagues and associates. And then there have been the letters. The thing that I most like about the letters are the many ones that said, "It was so painfully close to the current condition in our factory that it hurt," and that sort of thing. It obviously had a quite extraordinary effect.

Candid Camera

16

What Do You Say to a Naked Lady?

Allen Funt

Allen Funt is a super-American cultural manifestation. Since the late forties he has turned the invasion of privacy into big business by catching people in off-guard moments and has then, with vulgarity and vigor, purveyed the moment back to them as television comedy.

Funt's uniqueness lies in his being one of the first people to realize the curiosity value of ordinary behavior. His first radio experiments began with a candid microphone in 1947, and "Candid Camera" itself went on the air two years later. "Candid Camera" was and is purely commercial, and operates with scant regard to artistic considerations. The show sets out to give the masses what Funt thinks they want, which is humor, relaxation, and escape. And the measure of Funt's success can be gauged from the fact that between 1960 and 1964 the show rated among the top ten television programs in the United States.

In the heyday of "Candid Camera" one could observe three formulas for Funt's sketches: (1) straight observation of ordinary actions taken in private moments, such as a girl admiring herself as she combs her hair, with the action being shot through a one way mirror; (2) exposés of the tricks used by traders to swindle oustomers; and (3) illustrations of people's reactions when faced with petty crises or unusual situations engineered by Funt.

Although Funt has often been criticized for his peeping Tom approach, he has an undeniable filmic sense for an interesting situation. He can also occasionally produce a sketch where candid exploration suddenly reveals a moment of truth not generally provided for in ordinary television till recently.

One can also say that, in a limited sense, "Candid Camera" has been genuinely innovative. In the early fifties, for example, it was one of the first shows to take cameras into the streets and present a certain realism as opposed to reenacted documentary.

Funt himself is certainly not modest on this question of pioneering. Thus, in an interview with Harrison Engle he remarked, "I am vain enough to think that not only camera vérité, but all the realism in television commercials stems from our work."* The claim strikes

* *Film Comment* (fall 1965).

one as rather preposterous, but this is not to dismiss the fact that Funt found a popular "slant" for realistic documentary material where none existed before.

What Do You Say to a Naked Lady? (1970) *is Funt's first feature and is a candid camera examination of nudity and sex. A nude girl walks out of an elevator before various men who don't know how to deal with such a phenomenon. A girl in the shortest of miniskirts asks different men to hold her shaky step ladder while she climbs it to look for her cat; some of the men enjoy the view, while others red-facedly contemplate every place but the top of the ladder. A sex instructress walks into a class stark naked, and in yet another episode the fig leaves on a nude statue begin to revolve in front of some elderly women. And once more the reactions of the "innocent victims" of Funt's contrived situations provoke good-humored laughter on the part of the audience rather than embarrassment.*

Besides these obvious elements, Funt also conducts a number of sex surveys, such as an exploration of high school morality and a quiz on the sexual hunger of basketball players deprived of women. There is also a rather bizarre scene in which a voluntary prostitute tells Funt quite openly about her own strong sexual needs and the various expectations of her clients.

While a few of the incidents in the film are a little unfunny or slightly tasteless, the film as a whole is remarkably fresh and good natured in its exploration. Altogether it seems to achieve a much more honest examination of sex than most of the scores of television programs that have researched the subject to death.

Q. What was the background of the "Candid Camera" series?

A. I started making motion pictures in 1947. The first thing I did was a series of shorts based on a radio program called "The Candid Microphone." These shorts were the forerunners of "Candid Camera." A newsreel company had wanted to cover the origination of a program in which we had microphones; in order to do it without getting in our way, they used hidden cameras. Their sample was the basis for selling the whole series of shorts.

In 1947, I did forty ten-minute shorts for Columbia Pictures and soon afterwards began what turned out to be a twenty-one year weekly series of television shows for the various networks. The series started on ABC, then moved eventually to CBS. During the same period of time I did approximately forty industrial motion pictures, all with a hidden camera. However, my eagerness to make a full-length picture predated the actuality by many, many years; and it wasn't till the television series ended in 1968 that I tried to sell the feature idea. A little while later United Artists said they'd go along with me.

Q. What kind of treatment did you have to give United Artists?

A. In this particular case, I gave them only about three sentences; but you have to remember that I was bringing to this man, the United Artists representative, a twenty-one year history of experience and productivity in this field. I said, "I want to do a hidden camera, feature-length comedy, episodic, about sex." He said, "How much?" I really wasn't prepared and just reached for a price and said, "About half-a-million dollars"; and he said, "Go ahead and do it." That was truly the only arrangement and the only meeting about price that we ever had.

Q. Were the studios wary as to your material or taste or things like that?

A. No, not really. You see, maybe if my transition from one medium to another had been reversed, if I had come from the permissiveness of motion pictures to television, they might have had some wariness; but since I had come from the very refined, very puritanical world of television into motion pictures, they weren't afraid I was going to be too liberated, but that I wouldn't be liberated enough. There was no question of taste, because they had a double protection in that respect. In the first place, they would see the film from time to time—it was episodic, and was correctable—and also they knew that I knew the ground rules.

Strangely enough, after I sold United Artists, I had a hard time selling myself on the notion that I had a marketable idea, because I was terribly concerned about the transition from a medium where people would see a regular show for nothing, to one where they had to pay $2.50 to see something. I was also very much concerned with the idea of an episodic feature film. I had been talking about its desirability for a long time; but now, finally, when somebody said, "Go ahead and do it," I was afraid that it just wouldn't stick together without the benefit of a story, or without some device that would really frame it.

I also had a great struggle with myself about my own standards. You see, I had a little too much freedom. Coming from the confines of television into the freedom of motion pictures, I did for three months some of the most awkward and tasteless things in the world; but fortunately, very few people were with me at the time or had to see it. I could only be likened to a young man who comes into the army and finds that he can say almost anything he wants to, and finds that his vocabulary is reduced to about three or four four-letter words. I was free, and I was so uninhibited that I became very tasteless. I'll give you an example of what I mean.

One of the things that I remember trying in the early days had to do with a brothel. A young man was to be brought to an apartment which was arranged to look like a brothel, and we had assembled for that particular purpose a dozen of the most atrocious-looking women we could find in the entire city. They were presented to him one at a time for his selection and were presented in the order of ugliness—that is, each time he passed one, the next one to appear was even more hideous than the first. Our procedure was that if he should find no woman to suit him, at some time or other, the madam would tell him that they were closing the shop and he would have to come back tomorrow. If he should finally find somebody whom he liked, we were prepared to have this lady tell him that she didn't like him. That was about the basis of what we were doing.

The whole thing was done about two or three times; but it was the essence of all the wrong things, all of the mistakes that you can make in candid camera. The worst mistake is to show people at such an enormous disadvantage, at such an embarrassing point of decision or point in their lives, that one simply starts laughing at them with total sympathy and exhibits a total antipathy toward the people who are perpetrating the hoax. But originally the idea sounded funny; and if you were crude, the brothel scene was just hysterical; but the minute you felt this poor guy's predicament you turned against the film maker.

There were also a few scenes in which there was too much nudity. We had a very strange problem about nudity; we had wrong notions at the time about the rules with regard to frontal nudity and complete male nudity. The film business had a number of unwritten precepts. The easiest thing to get by was a female bosom; the second was a female derriere; the third was a female frontal nude. The man's frontal nude was the hardest and the most objectionable. When we tried in our earliest experiments to have a brief amount of clothing, so that there was no frontal nudity, it was absolutely abominable. The girls really looked salacious and obscene. Eventually, we changed that; but in the finished film, we did run into some problems about total nudity and received some undeserved criticism about covering up.

A number of people said that, seeing the finished film they noticed that the girl would wear a briefcase or a handbag in front, whereas otherwise she was totally nude. Wasn't this inconsistent on our part? In fact the handbag or briefcase was used only when there was no other place to hide the microphone. The girl was carrying a portable, transistorized microphone. These were some of the problems—where to draw the line, how much nudity—but eventually we found a level; we found it not by any genius or any insight, but by the most wonderful device of all, which was to screen the material over and over and over again. As always the good pieces got better, and the bad pieces got worse.

Q. You mentioned the brothel scene. Can you remember other scenes which you dropped because of taste, or which just wouldn't work?

A. Well, the concepts were rather limited in the beginning. The idea of the confrontation of a man or woman with a nude person, out of the normal context, was only to be one small part of the film; the total film had to do with other elements of sex and sex morality, and so on. But the nude confrontation always proved to be the most exciting, the most fun, the most stimulating, and the most novel; so we did too many of those in the beginning.

One of those we eventually dropped was where this girl, fully clothed, stands on a street with her dress caught in an automobile door; the door is locked and the car is locked, and she complains to a passerby that the keys are in the car and she needs help in extricating herself. As he tries to tug with her—she is wearing a break-away dress—she sudenly becomes totally nude, and the man is left with her dress in his hand. The funny part of it was that, over and over again, people would have this nude woman to their rear, sort of over their left shoulder, and they would never turn around. It was obvious that she was totally disrobed because her dress was in his hand, but there again it was really an illustration of politeness, of consideration by the men for a girl in an awkward predicament. The men weren't averting their faces because of a wrong timidity; they were generally embarrassed for the girl, and according to their light it seemed more polite not to turn around. Anyhow, we kept those films for quite a while, but we dropped them gradually.

There was another episode that didn't work for different reasons. We had heard of a group of nudists in Miami who performed a military drill. They were nudists, but they were also neo-Nazis. So, with an incredible amount of contrivance we managed to tell this group that someone had sold a story to *Playboy* magazine, the theme of which was that you can't make war in the raw; and they were supposed to be training, and they were to illustrate the story. We got a drill sergeant to work with these people; we sent down guns, helmets, army shoes, nothing else, and the drill sergeant gave his orders in double-talk. After he really got them worked up, he gave them the most confusing kind of orders; and it was hysterical to see their confusion. We then wrote a song called, "You can't make war in the raw." In the course of doing this film, we had an infinite number of screenings which were photographed for our own use; and we noticed that when you had on the screen material of tremendous embarrassment or pungency, the audience would often look away from the screen to see who else was looking or how they were reacting. In other words you could clearly see when the audience was getting uncomfortable. Now when you saw this row of male figures in double-time drill, totally disrobed, there was virtually no place on the screen that your eyes could go for escape, and there was an overpowering sense of inundation in this shocking kind of visual thing. So we took it out.

Q. We've talked of whole sequences that you abandoned. Were there certain types of individual confrontations that you avoided?

A. The kind of things we took out almost always followed a more or less predictable pattern. First of all, there are always a number of black people who are not used because they don't look sufficiently presentable. We think that the black people are part of our population and deserve to be treated with total equality—the ones that make fun of them are always the white people. But we lean over backwards not to use a weak or poor sample of a black person. In other words there's a tendency to overcompensate, and so if a guy looked as if he was too rough, or too ignorant, or too Uncle Tom, I left him out of the picture.

I also tried not to show people who are totally unable to contend with a situation. Strangely enough, the most difficult confrontations were women with other women. A man, somehow or other, nearly always seems to feel equal to the task he is confronted with. He may not know exactly what to say, or he may do the rather unexpected thing of treating a nude lady like she was totally dressed; but he isn't thrown by it. A woman can be totally unnerved. Some of my psychologist friends tell me that a woman feels a threat when she sees another nude girl; in a remote way she somehow feels this may be the vogue of the future or some other thing like that. And she feels uneasy.

Q. Let's go back to your actresses in the film. You have one sequence where you interview an actress, but can you tell me a little more about the reactions of the girls when you told them the idea of the film, that they'd have to appear in the nude?

A. I would like to say, first of all, that in the two-and-a-half-year time span between starting and completing the picture, the whole world—particularly the motion picture world—had changed its standards and its tastes enormously. In the early days, we wouldn't get any actresses to do disrobed scenes; we used models from modeling agencies, dancers, anything but motion picture actresses. But in the two-and-a-half years, it became commonplace; and by the time it ended, there was no problem at all.

One of the strange things about our kind of material was that we were looking for non-Hollywood types. We didn't want the pulchritude to be artificial, and we wanted the whole thing to seem as if the person was somebody's neighbor or somebody's friend taking part. But we found, much to our dismay, that if we weren't careful, we got the look of a stag movie, because there is such a small difference between an "non-Hollywood type" and a "stag-movie type." We had to get girls who came somewhere in the middle. In the end the girl who comes out of the elevator in the opening scene of the movie proved to be our sort of standard type. She was reasonably young, reasonably attractive, reasonably pleasant to look at, and from there on we knew what we wanted; but until that point we wavered and had problems in finding the right girl.

Q. Did you do any basic psychological research or did you construct your episodes purely intuitively?

A. Every single episode except two has a psychological or sociological framework. It is either a group pressure experiment, or a nude male to female confrontation, or evidence of, say, prejudice in the terms of the sound of a word—for example, where somebody prejudges a word that he doesn't really understand and assumes that it is dirty. Then there is a constant emphasis on the notion that each man sees the same thing, only differently, and that's woven around about three or four episodes.

Q. You have several rather serious episodes. One of them is the confrontation between people in the cinema watching the film and discussing it afterwards. At what stage did you decide to put that in?

A. When we began searching for a device to hold the material together. Early in the making of the film, we got the notion that maybe the whole episodic structure of the picture could be linked and

257

strengthened by showing an audience *in the film* watching the material and interrupting and commenting from time to time. That idea came to us about a third of the way through. It happened because we were screening a piece of material for a parent to get clearance, and we got the notion that it might be interesting to photograph the response. We wavered about using that device almost to the last minute; we were never sure whether it was effective or not. It seems to me that it worked because it held the film together.

Q. Do you always require clearances?

A. Of recent date, there have been two major thoughts about clearances in documentary-type motion pictures. Haskell Wexler in *Medium Cool* takes the position that anybody photographed in a public event that is not brought upon him, and in which he willingly participates, is not required to be given a release. Recently a lot of people have taken that position. So in *Woodstock* there were 400,000 people and no releases.

Because of my background in television, however, I take an entirely different view. I know that it isn't worth my while not to get the release. In most of my cases I am filming people in some sort of contrived situation and I don't believe the fact that they are in a public place is sufficient permission for me to use their likenesses for commercial profit. Therefore, I try to get every single recognizable person covered by a release, for which I usually have to pay. And if a person refuses to give me a release, I don't even bother to get the film developed.

Q. You mentioned parents seeing their children. There was one interesting episode where two or three girls and one or two fellows talk about their sexual experiences. Were those episodes seen by the parents?

A. Only afterwards, only in the session where you saw them watching it. In other words, the first filming sessions were with some thirty or forty youngsters who were expressing themselves about their own sexual tastes and experiences. We then selected the most interesting episodes out of the forty and had a screening for the parents, and in that screening we filmed the responses.

Q. How did you get these high school children to open up?

A. I said to their schoolmaster that I wanted them to think I was doing a study of a psychological phenomenon called the "Blink Rate," and it was going to be great. I told him that we were making photographic studies of people under stress, and I needed to photograph the rate of their eye blinks on the premise that one could obtain a sort of cardiograph of emotional response, if you charted the eye-blink rate. So I needed these kids in a place where they would think we were going to photograph them—but for an entirely different purpose, and then I needed to precondition them for some shocking kind of questions.

Now in the initial try, I made a bad mistake. I did this thing with them alone in a room, and I found that kids of that age are so anxious to talk about sex to a stranger that they simply went out of bounds. They were like dammed up people dying to talk about things way beyond the scope of my inquiry. But when you brought a few in, then their own ego pressure and the social pressure changed, and they started to talk in a way I wanted.

Q. You have one episode where a woman talks about her experiences with men, and how she prostitutes herself for nothing. Can you tell me something about the background of that episode? Was it an episode that you planned for a long time, or was it the result of a lucky chance?

A. Our movie, and most of our work, is a series of "misses" and lucky accidents for which we sometimes get credit. As it happened, the episode you mention was shot while I was in northern Michigan doing an entirely different film and had a half day with a full crew. Suddenly in the motel where we were staying I saw something I had been looking for for a long time. In the interior of the room was a woman in a swimming pool, and outside was a snow blizzard; people were at the window of this room. Because of the whiteness of the snow there was a beautiful silhouette, and I figured if I could get something in the silhouetted light, even without a release, I could use it because the face was virtually undistinguishable. While I was thinking about the best ways of using the silhouette effect I suddenly remembered I had promised this guy over at United Artists to include a section about a prostitute, and I was still anxious to get it. When the silhouette effect hit me it was nine o'clock in the morning, and we had until half past eleven to get a plane. So I rushed over to the motel guy and said, "I must have a prostitute right away." Obviously this guy thought I was nuts; but with the help of a local sheriff, he got a prostitute, who was told that I was a writer, doing a piece about the lighter side of a hustler's life. She came in, had a drink and we talked, and that's the way it happened. But it took all of those things. Every other episode in the movie is photographed with ratios as high as 200 to 1; this particular scene was one try, one take, and finish!

Q. Can you explain your hidden camera technique?

A. The concealment in our work is less important than the distraction. In almost every sense, it isn't important to hide any piece of equipment. It's much more important to make the subject totally unaware. Our difficulties are neither the camera nor the microphone, but the lights. We shoot in color; and even with the fastest new 35mm color film, it's hard. So the most obvious thing we do is to overlight decoy areas. In other words, you want to shoot in position *A* so you make positions *B* and *C* more suspicious, so that people come out of the light of the decoy areas into the light where we want them.

The same thing applies to a microphone. For years we used to try to get a smaller and smaller and smaller mike; but we would lose quality, lose sleep, lose everything, till we discovered that, if you took the largest microphone ever made, people were so unaware that it could ever be a microphone that there was no problem.

Concealment of the camera is simply a mechanical thing. We have fifteen different devices, and they are extremely ingenious. We are very good at that. We used to use two-way mirrors, but they became very unsophisticated and cut out some light. Now we use a method of reflection; it's an oblique piece of glass which carries a reflected light from below and can reflect a sign or a pattern in this oblique light. From one side it's totally transparent and from the other it's totally opaque. Again, the basic principle of hiding a camera or a microphone is not to spend so much time hiding it. Instead you construct a very engrossing happening; and secondly, you rely on the engaging quality of a man who doesn't let the subject get away from him. When I talk to somebody, I mustn't allow them the liberty of searching the area and becoming suspicious.

Q. When you were filming outside, did you run into any trouble with local authorities, passersby, anything like that?

A. You remember the brief scene about the nude hitchhiker; that was done right outside of London. The curious thing about it was that we tried sixteen other countries, but only staid old England let us do it. In other places we were considerably hampered before we stopped bothering them. The major problem was that we didn't want the kind of publicity that was attendant to arrests and police inquiries. We avoided this by careful preanalyses of the kind of thing that would get us into trouble with the local authorities.

Q. Outside North America I expect there will be considerable censorship.

A. In Canada, so far no problems. In America, there has been one case in which a drive-in movie was prohibited from showing the picture temporarily because, of all things, a neighbor not in the theatre complained that her children could see the nudes on the screen with binoculars; but so far the censorship has been rather indirect. It was given an X rating; and as a study about documentary techniques, I think you have to know the strange quirk in the rating system. Dr. Stern, who is the head of the Motion Picture Association and who does the rating, holds with his group that the documentary technique itself makes a thing more likely to be given an X rating because a fictional piece has less impact, according to him, than a documentary or a reality piece. That's the main reason why our piece is an X.

Q. One of the best things in the film is the combination of music and words. Were the songs prewritten, or were these written afterwards?

A. They were done both ways. The young man who wrote the music and the lyrics, and who did most of the singing himself, had no background in motion pictures; he had done only television commercials, and I was very much impressed with his things. However, the lyrics have given rise to quite a lot of criticism. The young people despise the lyrics in our film because they find them too specific. They wish we had been more general and less specific, but we knew that this was a problem almost from the start because Steve Karmen, the composer-lyricist, felt that I was being too specific; but I felt you could never do any moralizing in any other part of the film, and I felt that the younger audiences were accepting a certain kind of message in lieu of this, so we did write in those things.

I'll give you an illustration. In a thing like "The Keyhole," the song was written after the film was completed. In another case Steve had written a terribly cute song about "Rape is not as easy as it looks" and we just put a lot of pieces together, so it worked both ways. However, we used the music as a pace element in the picture. We knew that all the things that worried us about the episodic form required us to keep the film buoyant and together, so that you never had more than two dialogue episodes without some musical piece to keep it going.

Q. Can you recall any situation where you had to act very quickly to save the day?

A. When you work with actuality, you work with your wits because you are being constantly confronted with the unexpected and the unpredictable and the uncontrollable. In the film there's a little episode where we sent kids into a drug store to buy contraceptives. This is the classic scene that every reasonably mature man knows: you go into a drug store to buy a contraceptive and you can't find a male clerk, and it's terribly embarrassing, or traditionally it is, to tell a young lady that you want contraceptives. Now in order to do this, we had engaged about a dozen part-time young men who, in an office in a hotel, were busy mimeographing and so on. Then one at a time somebody would tap a kid on the shoulder and say, "Go down to the drug store—the boss has an account here—and get him a dozen condoms." Now, if you are twenty-one or twenty-two in this society, you don't know what a condom is because you probably rely on your girl friend to use the pill. And even if you do, you are generally that easy about it that you don't mind telling it to a young lady.

So here we have eleven kids, and the day's cost is $7,000, and one after another they come in and tell our girl, who is the only clerk in the store, exactly what they want. No embarrassment! Nothing! Now, what do you say to that? How do you protect your investment? Finally, however, the last kid that went in was told to get the smallest size they had. Well, he wouldn't be caught dead telling that to a girl, and actually in the film you see him leaning over and whispering it into her ear, and he also says, "Of course, it's not for me!" I simply mean, it's the twist, the last-minute bright idea that impels people into action and saves an otherwise useless day.

Q. What percentage of people refused to appear?

A. It is extremely small, probably less than 3 percent of all the people who were ever asked; but the reasons people have for not giving us a release are never what you expect. First of all, there were several cases of photographing somebody with the wrong person at the wrong time; but the oddest release problem that we had in this picture was in regard to one of the high school kids talking about her experience. Among all the girls we talked to, there was one girl who said she was a virgin, and her parents refused to allow her to be used on the grounds that they didn't want their daughter to be held up as the single example of nonconforming behavior. Eventually, we persuaded the parents. In this particular case, we did use some persuasion and said we needed one virgin to complete our film. There was one guy who said he had had ninety affairs a year at the age of sixteen, and his parents were quite willing to let him be in the film; but the virgin's parents objected. You can never tell!

Q. What have been the most criticized areas of the film?

A. A lot of people blamed us for a concentration of semitic types like the Brooklyn Jewish women commenting about what's going on on the screen. At some point, I had to make this agonizing appraisal—this wasn't a survey. I wasn't anxious to try to have a cross section of anything. These people were outspoken, and I just hated the idea that I was so self-conscious about the fact that they were Jewish. As a Jew, I was supersensitive about that. There was a time when I was tempted to go out and supplement these studio scenes with other kinds of people, but then I said, "To hell with it, these are simply people" and that's why I kept it that way. A lot of people have said that they were too special.

Besides the scene with the women, there were two other areas which were heavily criticized. Many people have said that the attempt to go from pure farce comedy to almost clinical, serious, in-depth interview is just impossible and a contradiction, and the film falls apart on that level. Strange how this came about, but I was so anxious to keep the pace and the content of the material varied that I wanted to be able to call on every facet and every level of it. When we first put one of two serious pieces in it, they were most unhappy with the fact that they stood out, and strangely enough, we found that they blended a little bit better when we added a few more, so that it wasn't just two serious ones.

Another major criticism is one that has followed us for twenty-five years. There will always be a large segment of the public that is uncomfortable about the whole idea of hidden cameras and microphones and will interpret it in fifty different prejudices and points of view. It all comes generally under the heading of embarrassment to them. If you are a certain kind of person, the predicament in which you see someone else makes you uncomfortable and you will never like it.

Q. You spent two-and-a-half years on the film. Is there anything you would have changed, or any one incident you would like to have added?

A. I think that one or two pieces don't stand up in terms of quality; I think that would be a minor thing. But I think the major thing I did wrong, believe it or not, was to present the film as a hidden camera movie. It would have been infinitely more acceptable, more appreciated, if it were just a piece of screen craft.

I also eliminated a lot of references to hidden camera during the making of the picture, but as we came to the end, some people from United Artists and other sources said, "My goodness, you've got this whole big thing going for you, why turn your back on it completely." On the other hand, if we had gotten people as naturally as we did with the hidden camera but had never said how we got them, they would have said, "If he directed it, he's a great director." That's how it goes.

Optical Transformations

17

Neighbours
and
Pas de Deux
Norman McLaren

Norman McLaren is a rather gentle and shy man who has played the role of teacher, film maker, and poet in a career spanning three decades with the Canadian National Film Board. He was born in Scotland in 1914, and studied at the Glasgow School of Art where he made his first film Seven Till Five. *Soon after, another film of McLaren's caught the eye of John Grierson at an amateur film festival, resulting in an invitation to McLaren to join the General Post Office film unit, which was about the only bright spark on the rather dull English film scene of the day.*

McLaren made four films for the GPO including Love on the Wing, *before emigrating to America.* Love *was a short advertising film made on the occasion of the establishment of a new British airmail service, and achieved its effects by drawing directly on film. McLaren existed as a free-lancer in New York till 1941 when Grierson asked him to join the Canadian National Film Board, where he has remained ever since.*

In his early period in Canada, McLaren spent considerable time developing the animation department of the board and in creating a group of first-class animators. Among his pupils are numbered James McKay of Toronto and George Dunning who designed the animation for the Beatles' film Yellow Submarine.

The teaching element has also been linked to a profound social conscience, revealing a more or less unknown side of McLaren. Thus, he taught the making of simple animation and visual aids in China in 1950, and a few years later he was sent on a similar mission to India by UNESCO. However, McLaren's chief claim to fame rests on his work as an innovator, and his genius in this direction can be seen most clearly in Neighbours *and* Pas de Deux.

McLaren made Neighbours *in 1952, and was given an Academy Award for it a year later. In the film two neighbors read peacefully in their respective gardens till a flower grows up on their common bor-*

der. *Both covet the flower, and the desire for exclusive possession leads to a bitter fight culminating in the death of both.*

What was most interesting about Neighbours *was the elaboration on the various possibilities of animating human beings by single frame shooting (or "pixilation" as it is sometimes called), which enabled the "stars" of the film to seemingly ice skate over grass and float in circles in the air. This style has since been widely copied by other film makers and has been extended into surrealist directions by the Polish animators Jan Lenica and Walerian Borowczyk.*

Pas de Deux *(1967) shows the infinite possibilities arising out of multiple image techniques. A girl dances and suddenly meets her twin. They dance alone, together, and sometimes as mirror images of each other. A male dancer appears and woos each girl in turn. Finally, one girl disappears, and the remaining couple dance and intertwine as lovers.*

The story is merely a thread to illustrate the potential of the technique. What one is really being treated to is an amazingly graceful study of movements of light and form, with the screen being continuously filled with complex and dense images of tremendous beauty, reminding one of the elegance of Swedish wire and light sculptures.

McLaren's innovative work in so many styles has been widely recognized, but he has also been rebuked for a number of deficiencies. Many critics have questioned the harshness of his colors and the too often repeated simplicity of his forms. They feel he lacks a certain sophistication, and is altogether too much of a primitive for them.

Other critics, like Ralph Stephenson, have commented on a certain lack of passion and fire in McLaren's output. They admit the exquisitely delicate level of his work but also ask of him a large-scale emotional commitment which he seems unable or unwilling to provide. There is, I think, some truth in the first comment, but believe the second is ill-directed. McLaren is certainly a worker on the small scale, but as is shown in Pas de Deux *his work is that of an artist and poet who has selected his form and brought it to perfection. What more can one demand of anyone?*

Q. What did you do during your early years at the Canadian National Film Board, and how much were you left to your own devices?

A. During my first few years at the board, I didn't make very many films because I had been given the job of building up an animation department and training young artists. Towards the end of the war, however, I switched entirely to making my own films. I was free enough, although it all depends on how free you mean. For instance, someone had recorded a number of French Canadian folk songs, and we were asked to make films illustrating them. In that group of films, I was not "free"; the theme was set for me. But apart from those, I've been free ever since—and I mean real freedom. I don't have to submit a script or a treatment before starting a film, but I do have to make a budget estimate and give a two- or three-line description of what the film will be about.

Q. How much do you plan your films in advance? Do you make preliminary sketches?

A. I never write a script although I usually have a skeleton of an idea in my mind. Occasionally I make films just by starting with a kind of hunch about something or having images in my mind of a few shots, or perhaps even a few sequences, and a feeling that I could expand these and build them up into a film; but that is a risky way of going about things. I find the most satisfactory way is to have a skeleton worked out, but not worked out too much, as I am a great believer in improvisation during the process of filming. I should add that for me a film begins not so much with a theme as with a curiosity about some special technical aspect of filming which I feel hasn't been adequately explored. This excites me. For instance, *Neighbours* began with my curiosity about what could happen when you shot people frame by frame at very low camera speeds.

Q. But this had been done before *Neighbours*?

A. Only occasionally. Méliès had used the technique; but as I hadn't seen it done systematically before, Grant Munro and I set out to make a series of technical tests and for two or three days shot any subject that came into our heads which involved animating people frame by frame. When we looked at the rushes we saw one shot, about twenty seconds long, of two men fighting. This fight, done one frame at a time, was terrific, and I immediately felt this sequence contained the germ of a film. The following morning I woke up with the idea of *Neighbours* in my head, and in a matter of four or five days I'd thought out the general layout of the film though I had nothing written down on paper.

When we started shooting I had Wolf Koenig for my cameraman, and Grant Munro and J. P. Ladoucer, who are both animators, to play the neighbours. We knew that the two guys were going to begin as good friends and a flower was going to grow up between them, and they were going to enjoy it. Then one would begin to get covetous, the other would begin to get covetous, and they would start arguing and finish up fighting. Most of my films are shot in natural sequence, so we began shooting *Neighbours* at the beginning. Each day the four of us would spend about an hour discussing how to advance the action and what we should shoot that day. When that was decided, we would go ahead and start filming, and little by little the film evolved in this way.

Q. You've mentioned that the genesis of *Neighbours* lay in the possibilities of pixilation, or single-frame shooting. How did you handle the technique?

A. Many of the sequences had to be shot frame by frame; where you see people sliding on the grass or flying in the air, or the fence was rippling into place, we had to stop the camera quite a long time, rush in, change the position and rush out before taking the next frame. But this was very tiresome, so wherever it was possible to avoid single framing we did. We also never shot at normal camera speed. The shots that look normal-speed were probably shot half-speed, or even one-third-speed; if we wished the actors to appear normal or almost normal in the final footage, we would get them to move at half-speed or one-third-speed.

Q. What was the object of this speed alteration?

A. To gain control over the action. Both of the actors, for instance, had to be synchronized to arrive at the flower at exactly the same moment, so if we were shooting slow, and they were moving slow we could get this synchronization to work out very precisely. This idea of a flexible camera speed and a flexible acting speed was very useful and allowed many variations. In quite a lot of action in *Neighbours*, we clicked the camera's single-frame button quite rapidly and counted— the cameraman shouting out loud each frame as he exposed it—"One, two, three, four, five." The actors would move slowly, knowing that, possibly on the count of twelve, the fist of one of them had to hit the face of the other. It was all worked out in metrical lengths so that the job of fitting music to it would be that much easier.

Q. There is one scene in *Neighbours* where one of the protagonists moves around in a circle in the air, with his feet completely off the ground. It looks a very tricky job of pixilation, or was it in fact another technique?

A. That was achieved by having the actor jump up and having the cameraman click a single frame at the maximum height of the jump. The actor then jumped again, but from a slightly different position, and again one frame of film was exposed. So this went on with the actor's position being modulated with every jump. Of course, the shooting of the actor at the correct height was a matter of the cameraman's alertness. Koenig had to wait and press the button just at the peak of the jump. Everything was done that way, in the camera. There was no subsequent optical work or selection of frames.

Q. As the neighbours fight each other towards the end, their faces get streaked with war paint. Whose idea was that?

A. I don't remember. We thought of painting it on frame by frame, or by a series of mixes, and then we thought of having the actor drop out of the bottom of the frame, at which point we stopped the camera, changed the paint and had him rise up again into the frame—a much simpler solution.

Q. How long did *Neighbours* take to shoot?

A. About six months. We were held up because of cloudy weather much of the time. If we had had good weather, it could have been done in three months.

Q. Were there any sections which you finally cut out of *Neighbours*?

A. Yes. The disadvantages of working without a script show up particularly in editing, and when we made the first assembly cut we realized that certain parts of the film were out of balance with each other. For instance, we had much too much of the fight—we had just gotten carried away with filming all kinds of violence—so a lot of that had to be cut out. Also, halfway through, we had thought of two possible ways of developing the action, and since we could not make up our minds we shot both up to a point where we could link them on again to a subsequent shot.

Q. I understand that it was an incident in *Neighbours* which sparked off *Chairy Tale*?

A. Yes. There are two deck chairs in the opening scene of *Neighbours*. One day while we were getting ready, one of the actors had trouble with one of the chairs. It opened out the wrong way and he got caught in it, and he tried it this way and that to get free. I remember looking back on the scene and thinking that the struggle between a man and a chair might be a good basis for a film, but I could not think of an ending for it until a couple of years later.

Q. How far did you go along with pixilation and variable camera speeds in *Chairy Tale*?

A. We used the same flexible camera speed, but it was handy for another reason. We started out trying to animate the chair frame by frame but it was very slow; and while we were changing the position of the chair, the actor had to hold his pose for so long that he tended to lose his psychological momentum. So instead of pixilation we strung the chair with three, four, or six strings of black nylon fishing line. The chair was then manipulated by two or three people holding the nylon lines and synchronizing their actions to get the chair to do all the kinds of things you see in the film.

Q. So there was not much pixilation in *Chairy Tale*?

A. No, except for one or two shots in the middle where the action is very fast. Throughout most of the film we shot at twelve frames per second; it gave us additional control over the movements of the chair, and at that speed an actor can still move and maintain his psychological momentum.

Q. Most people think of you as one of the pioneers of painting and drawing directly on film. Could we cover these techniques in some detail?

A. When working directly on film without a camera, I use two main methods. One is to work with clear film on which you apply india ink and transparent dyes with pens, brushes, sponges, or sprays. The other way is to start with black opaque film and engrave on it by scratching off the emulsion. Sometimes I used to scratch away an image, then paint it with color, and that would become the master positive from which a negative would be made; but you could work the other way—you could call that a negative and get the opposite results. In working with grey film, for example, you would be free to use both scratching and drawing.

Q. In your earlier films you appear to have respected the individual frame a great deal. What method did you use to maintain correspondence between the frames?

A. Basically I worked over ground glass with a light behind, and used an identical grid behind each frame for reference and registration. Later I designed a machine which projected the image of one frame onto the next frame—the frame I had just drawn on to the frame I was going to draw.

The method of engraving on black film to create moving images posed a real problem. With clear film you have a method of registering the image from frame to frame either by using a grid behind the film or the optical reflecting device; but with black film there is no way of registering your image from frame to frame. So, when making *Blinkity Blank* I thought, "Why is it necessary to draw an image on *every* frame?" I realized that this is a concept that comes from an actuality camera, and animated films have generally followed this concept. I therefore experimented to find out how long a gap or blank I could leave between one image and another.

Subsequent to this I experimented with small "frame clusters" where I had a section of blank, followed possibly by four frames with a different image on each, followed in their turn by another blank. Some interesting and unexpected optical effects or illusions arose out of these experiments. For instance, I found that if you have a cluster of four frames, each with a different image, the last will be the most dominant if they all have the same degree of contrast. The first image is the next most dominant, and the middle two are the least dominant of all and likely to be lost, or almost lost.

Q. Many of your films like *Begone Dull Care* use Len Lye's technique of disregarding the frame and painting along the whole length of film. How does one prepare this kind of film. Do you do preliminary color sketches? Do you work back from the music?

A. Let's take *Begone Dull Care* as an example. It started with the music of Oscar Peterson. I had heard Peterson's first 78-rpm disk, which was a very fast boogie, found it very exciting, and asked Peterson whether I could use it for an abstract film. After Peterson agreed, we spent four days working on the music and shaping it, and these were very important days for the film. I had told Peterson certain basic requirements: I wanted a three-part form—medium tempo, very slow, and very fast—with some additional material for titles at the beginning and the end. After letting me choose some themes, Peterson then started developing variations. Sometimes, when he would play a particular variation, I would instantly see certain colors and movements. Sometimes I would dictate what I specifically wanted. For example, after some very fast, intricate music I might say to him, "Now I want about fifteen seconds of very slow, thin music with an empty sort of feeling in it," because I knew that at that point the eye would tire from too much fast imagery. The whole thing was shaped bit by bit as we worked our way through. Since Peterson seldom wrote down notes but carried everything in his head, I suggested we make a recording the following day, but he said he would like to have a couple of weeks to polish up everything.

Two weeks later I returned to Montreal and set up a studio recording session. However, Peterson's first run-through was almost unrecognizable. What had happened was that, because he always improvised, the whole thing had gradually shifted with each rehearsal. We therefore had to spend a hectic hour getting the music back into its original shape. Where we thought the variants were an improvement we incorporated them into the old score.

Once the music was recorded we were able to start on the visual material. Here I was joined by Eve Lambart. We would paint long strips; as soon as we would get about ten or fifteen feet which we thought suited a particular section, we would run the section on a Moviola together with the music. In other words the music set the mood. We would paint maybe five or six variants for a particular section of music, and then select what seemed the best. Later, when we had about a dozen ten- or fifteen-second pieces joined together, we would view them on the Moviola and maybe decide that some pieces, in the context of all the other pieces, weren't right (although alone they may have been) and would go back and redo them. So it was a piecemeal building of a film.

Q. How did your partnership with Lambart work?

A. We divided the work, each doing some of the painting with transparent acetate dyes—spraying them on, rubbing them on, brushing them on, rubbing, and sprinkling dust on the wet paint. Occasionally one of us would do one whole section and the other another, but generally we both worked on the same section. Sometimes we would each do our own *version* of a section and then choose the best one.

Q. In *Begone Dull Care* you use one painting-on-film method. In *Canon* it seems you used a greater variety of techniques, including the aid of the optical camera.

A. In *Canon* we set out to make a visual illustration of a musical canon. The principle of a canon is that a melody starts and then after several beats or bars, the identical melody enters again, and this can occur a number of times. The melodies can also be inverted, or reversed or stretched, or condensed in time. It can be extremely complimated or as simple as "Three Blind Mice."

While we did not start out with any preconceived ideas about techniques, we soon thought of three different possibilities. We took the well-known "Frère Jacques," and illustrated it by moving children's blocks on a checkerboard by means of single-frame animation. The problem was to work out a path for the first block to follow so that when the second block followed the same path two or three seconds later, it would by its movement fit around the first block, and so on for the third and fourth blocks—interlocking motion and meshing as an appropriate four-part canon should.

The second technique involved using paper cutouts. We animated a small man doing a little dance, and then we worked out the dance in such a way that, when the sequence of frames was superimposed optically (and delayed by several seconds), the two images of the little man would fit together to form an integrated dance. All this was shot in black and white, with the colors added by filter in an optical printer.

In the third sequence, we used a live man, Grant Munro, and thought out a path of action which was such that, when the shot was opticalled and staggered—not just twice but many times—the superimpositions would all fit together and would not overlap.

Q. What about the background on that section?

A. We had to be very careful to shoot against black since we were filming in color and had planned as many as eight superimpositions. Any light on the background would add up, in the many superimpositions, to a gray which would render the figures semitransparent. Actually, even with a completely black background, we ended up finally with a sort of dull blue-gray tone.

Q. I would like to hear something about the way you plan your superimpositions.

A. Every frame is accounted for on a dope sheet, which is a great mass of numbers and is, in effect, a set of instructions to the operator of the optical camera. We lay it out so that he follows automatically what we have written down—running his camera continuously forward or backward, freezing the frame, double-printing frames, skipping frames, and so on.

Q. When did you start taking advantage of the optical camera and its possibilities?

A. I didn't use it at all in most of my early films. Then I started using it for coloring black-and-white films. The simplest method is to take the negative and positive of the black and white, and print them successively onto the same color negative, each with a different filter. This gives a colored figure on a colored ground. More recently, I have tended to use the optical camera more and more intricately, as in *Canon* and *Pas de Deux*.

Q. I remember seeing an old painting of yours in which the spirit of a ballerina appears to rise out of her body. It would seem that the idea behind *Pas de Deux* has been with you for some time?

A. It certainly goes back over twenty years. I was in France in the late forties or early fifties and saw a ten-second commercial advertising women's corsets. The commercial consisted of a woman running in slow motion across the screen from left to right against a plain background. There were six images of the woman, each staggered and delayed a little bit—and that was all. It immediately occurred to me that there were all sorts of possibilities in the technique; and as so often in the past, I tucked it in the back of my mind knowing it was the seed for a new idea. Years later, around 1961, I got excited about the possibility of this kind of "stroboscopic" effect in film. I had no idea of a theme but many ideas of a technical nature, and so started shooting experimental takes of Grant Munro and myself walking, running, and playing leapfrog.

I also had another technical idea that I thought would make it very easy to convert the material into a stroboscopic effect and, in fact, I think this was why I got excited about the whole project. If you print from a negative to a positive on a standard laboratory printer and both of them are in loop form, and if the negative loop is a few frames shorter than the positive loop, then each time they come around the image will be delayed or "staggered." We tried it in the lab and the results were wonderful. We now had these running, walking, and leapfrog shots considerably multiplied, while in some cases the image repeated itself thirty-four times giving a fantastic visual flow, which was very exciting. The running shots looked like a river of human motion because they filled the screen solidly from left to right. The leapfrog shot was also marvelous because the person who leapt, suddenly shot out from a single image into thirty-four images, landed on the ground, and all the thirty-four images then proceeded to collapse into a single image. This was immediately followed by the second person leaping and expanding into thirty-four images.

It seemed clear that I could use acrobatics or some kind of sport or dance for this technique; but since I didn't have a theme, I did nothing about it at that time. Three or four years later I felt I would like to try it with ballet movement, so I approached the directress and choreographer of a Montreal ballet company and showed these running and leapfrog tests. I told her that I wanted to investigate a number of fairly standard ballet movements to see what they looked like. Following our talk she worked out some material, of which we shot about twenty minutes as a test, and then had it multiplied in the manner I have described. Some of it worked very well.

Q. You must obviously have had to carry out numerous tests with lighting.

A. Yes. Before we did the running and leapfrog tests, I multiplied some stock shots of a man walking through a kitchen. It was all utterly confused, because the background cluttered up the action, and I realized it was best to do without background in shots intended for multiplication. I also noticed from the kitchen scene that normal front lighting creates confusion when the images overlap, and that what was needed was mere edge lighting, either on one edge of the figure or on both edges. We therefore used this edge lighting in the running and walking tests. In the subsequent ballet tests we became even more refined and used thinner edge lighting which worked even better.

Despite the success of these tests, I still didn't have an overall theme and delayed going further with the project. A couple of years later, however, I began to see how the basic idea of the beauty of motion could be pinned onto the very simple theme of two ballerinas and the man in the middle. I then contacted the choreographer, Ludmilla Chiriaeff, once again and explained my theme to her. She worked it out in ballet terms, and we rehearsed it with two of her dancers. This first version was shot without special lighting, and I went through it very carefully on the Moviola to figure out if it would lend itself to "stroboscopic," or multiplied, treatment.

Q. How did you do this?

A. If, for example, I wanted to stagger the image by three frames, I would draw the outline of the figure with a grease pencil on the ground glass on the Moviola. I would then move the film on three frames and draw another outline, move it on again three frames, and so on, until I had a series of traced outlines which gave me a picture of the ultimate density or separation of the multiplied effect. By shooting more tests we discovered that you could stagger the images by anything from one frame (which gave a solid dense effect) to twenty frames or more (when the images were very wide apart, as in the final sections of *Pas de Deux*).

Q. Did you use the loop-printing method you described earlier?

A. No. We discovered this wasn't satisfactory for several reasons. The unexposed stock had to be spliced into a loop in complete darkness, and was very difficult to keep in frame. Also large loops tended to get dirty, since they were handled and strung out in the printing room. Moreover, the laboratory printer did not eliminate a slight (and undesirable) "weaving," as between one superimposition and another, so we switched to an optical camera which gave us precise image registration.

In a typical shot of the film where there would be, say, nine different superimposed images, the dope sheet for the optical work would also have nine columns. In the first column the shot would start at zero and run to frame 250. The optical cameraman would then photograph these 250 frames onto the negative. After that he would have to wind back the exposed negative and the high-contrast positive (which carried the series of images to be multiplied) and start again by exposing the same negative, but staggering the high-contrast positive by five frames. He would subsequently have to wind back the negative and positive and repeat the process, each time staggering the positive by five frames, and so on until he had built up nine different superimpositions on the negative, each staggered by five frames.

Q. At one point in *Pas de Deux* you have a mirror image of the dancer. That was again done on the optical camera?

A. The negative and high-contrast positive were shot once through and wound back to the start; the positive was then flipped over from left to right. This took the dancer out of her correct relationship to the unflipped image on the exposed negative. The optical camera or the projector in the printer then had to be adjusted by horizontal panning to give the correct relationship. Sometimes we would have to run through the whole shot, and keep looking in the viewer of the printer to see that the two images maintained the correct relative position to each other as they moved.

Q. How long did all this take?

A. It's difficult to calculate but, taking into account our tests about ten years ago and the ballet tests about six years ago and the final shooting, I would say about a year and a half.

Q. How did you handle the music for *Pas de Deux*, since you were working very elastically with time?

A. As you've noted, it would have been impossible for the dancers to dance to music of any kind which could have been used in the final film, because although the initial shooting was straightforward, the multiplied images extended the length of almost every action by varying amounts. Thus, we only had precise timing and measurements when we had finished making the visual part of the film.

Then came the problem of sound. I had some idea of music for male and female voices without actually using words, and I asked Eldon Rathburn to compose something along these lines. I also showed the film to several people at the board to get their suggestions for music. Eventually, Maurice Blackburn saw the film and proposed using a particular recording of Roumanian panpipes which he had in his private collection. When we tried the disc the tempo was right and the mood very appropriate, but it was only two or three minutes long while our film ran for fourteen minutes. Maurice, however, had a solution. He recorded the disc a number of other times, fragmented it, and reedited it to fit the picture. In the original recording there is a sustained orchestral drone in one key behind the melody which continues throughout. What Maurice did was record additional material of the same chord played on a harp in the low, middle, and high registers. He then cut the recorded tape into a number of different loops each of slightly different lengths. The first three or four minutes of the film has nothing but this chord changing its texture, color, and register. Then one gets fragments of the panpipe melody from the original disc, and gradually these fragments become more complete until the entire melody is played at the end.

Q. Although you use panpipes in *Pas de Deux*, you are very widely known for your use of "synthetic" sound and have now got this down to a very elaborate technique.

A. I call it "animated" or "graphic" sound. There are two ways of doing this: one with a camera, the other without a camera. In the latter, you either take clear film and make small marks on the edge in the sound track area with pen and india ink; or you take black film and scratch small marks on it in the sound track area. I've used both. In *Rythmetic* and *Mosaic* I used the scratching method.

Q. How does one method compare with the other?

A. In my early films like *Dots* and *Loops* the sound was made by pen and ink on clear film, but I don't use that method now. Later I used the engraving or scratching method because black film is much easier to keep clean than clear film. Both painting and engraving could be called the "direct" method, which is excellent for producing short, percussive sounds but is quite unsuited for sustained tones. It is just too much labor to keep drawing the same unvaried shape over and over again, scores of times—which needs to be done in order to produce a sustained tone.

Q. Did you set up experiments to establish your high pitch and low pitch?

A. I found that out by trial and error. By doing different kinds of marks on a small loop and running it in a Moviola, I soon discovered that marks close together created a high pitch and marks further apart a lower pitch.

But for very precise pitch and continuous tone, I use an animation camera which takes a frame at a time and has a full aperture gate (in other words, the lens takes in the sound track area). I also have a precise position on the animation table marked out to correspond to the sound-track area on the film in the camera. Nearby, I have a box of cards, each about a foot long by two inches wide, each card bearing black and white marks representing sound waves. The marks are simple stripes which give "square waves," and there is a card for each semitone in the chromatic scale covering six octaves.

When I'm shooting I pull out of the box the particular pitch I want—say, a C sharp—and place it on the table top in the "sound-track" position. I then control the volume by using a "shutter" above the card which can close down (or open up) the width of the sound track. So for pianissimo I use a very narrow opening, and for fortissimo a maximum opening. Once that's set, I expose one frame for a note lasting a twenty-fourth of a second, two for a twelfth of a second, and so on. This method was used for the music of *Neighbours* and on some other films like *Canon*, where it was combined with piano, and *A Phantasy*, where it was combined with saxophones.